CONFIGURING A COMPANY IMPORT TEMPLATE USING DYNAMICS AX 2012

Second Edition

Murray Fife

ISBN-13: 978-1518898549

ISBN-10: 1518898548

Preface

What You Need For This Guide

All the examples shown in this blueprint were done with the Microsoft Dynamics AX 2012 virtual machine image that was downloaded from the Microsoft CustomerSource or PartnerSource site. If you don't have your own installation of Microsoft Dynamics AX 2012, you can also use the images found on the Microsoft Learning Download Center or deployed through Lifecycle Services. The following list of software from the virtual image was leveraged within this guide:

>   Microsoft Dynamics AX 2012 R3 CU9

Even though all the preceding software was used during the development and testing of the recipes in this book, they may also work on earlier versions of the software with minor tweaks and adjustments, and should also work on later versions without any changes.

Errata

Although we have taken every care to ensure the accuracy of our content, mistakes do happen. If you find a mistake in one of our books—maybe a mistake in the text or the code—we would be grateful if you would report this to us. By doing so, you can save other readers from frustration and help us improve subsequent versions of this book. If you find any errata, please report them by emailing editor@blindsquirrelpublishing.com.

Piracy

Piracy of copyright material on the Internet is an ongoing problem across all media. If you come across any illegal copies of our works, in any form, on the Internet, please provide us with the location address or website name immediately so that we can pursue a remedy.

Please contact us at legal@blindsquirrelpublishing.com with a link to the suspected pirated material.

We appreciate your help in protecting our authors, and our ability to bring you valuable content.

Questions

You can contact us at help@blindsquirrelpublishing.com if you are having a problem with any aspect of the book, and we will do our best to address it.

Table of Contents

daxc

www.dynamicsaxcompanions.com
Dynamics AX Companions

- iii -

www.blindsquirrelpublishing.com
© 2015 Blind Squirrel Publishing, LLC, All Rights Reserved

INTRODUCTION

Have you ever struggled with importing or updating lots to data within Dynamics AX?

Wouldn't it be nice if there was a tool out there that would allow you to just feed in an Excel Spreadsheet and have everything magically update in the blink of an eye?

Have you ever had to ask a developer to create an import or update script that would allow you to update data and by the time you did get the script you had forgotten why you needed the script in the first place?

Wouldn't it be nice if you could create custom imports without having to write a single line of code?

Have you ever set up data within one company within of Dynamics AX wanted to move all of it over to a new company only to have to make the changes by hand?

Wouldn't it be nice if you could just tell the system to move the data for you?

Have you ever tried to create a new Dynamics AX environment (like a training system) and populate it with sample data and spent days loading the base data?

Wouldn't it be nice if you could create one data template and have the system populate all of the core data in minutes?

Don't fret any more, help is on the way. The Data Import Export Framework within Dynamics AX, is the answer to all of your needs and in this guide we will show you how you can do all this and more.

 www.dynamicsaxcompanions.com
Dynamics AX Companions

- 5 -

www.blindsquirrelpublishing.com
© 2015 Blind Squirrel Publishing, LLC, All Rights Reserved

BLIND SQUIRREL
PUBLISHING

CONFIGURING THE DATA IMPORT EXPORT CONTROLS

Before we start importing data into Dynamics AX using the Data Import Export Framework, there is just a little bit of configuration that we need to do. We need to make sure that a few of the parameters are configured and also create definitions for how we want to import in the data.

daxc
www.dynamicsaxcompanions.com
Dynamics AX Companions

- 7 -

www.blindsquirrelpublishing.com
© 2015 Blind Squirrel Publishing, LLC, All Rights Reserved

BLIND SQUIRREL
PUBLISHING

Configuring the Data Import Export Parameters

To start off we will do a little bit of configuration to the Data Import Export Framework Parameters in order to make sure that everything runs smoothly.

daxc
www.dynamicsaxcompanions.com
Dynamics AX Companions
- 9 -
www.blindsquirrelpublishing.com
© 2015 Blind Squirrel Publishing, LLC, All Rights Reserved
BLIND SQUIRREL
PUBLISHING

Step By Step Walkthrough

Configuring the Data Import Export Parameters

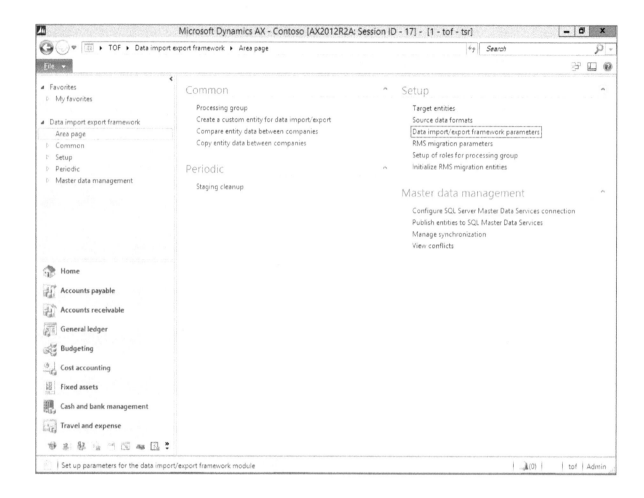

Before we start though there is a little bit of configuration that we need to do in order to make sure that everything runs smoothly. So to start off, click on the **Data Import Export Framework Parameters** menu item within the **Setup** group of the **Data Import Export Framework** area page.

Step By Step Walkthrough

Configuring the Data Import Export Parameters

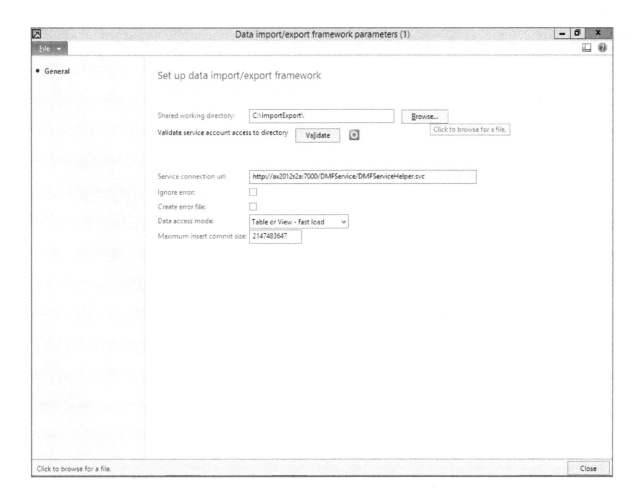

When the **Data Import Export Framework Parameters** maintenance form is displayed, make sure that you have a valid **Shared Working Directory** defined.

Step By Step Walkthrough

Configuring the Data Import Export Parameters

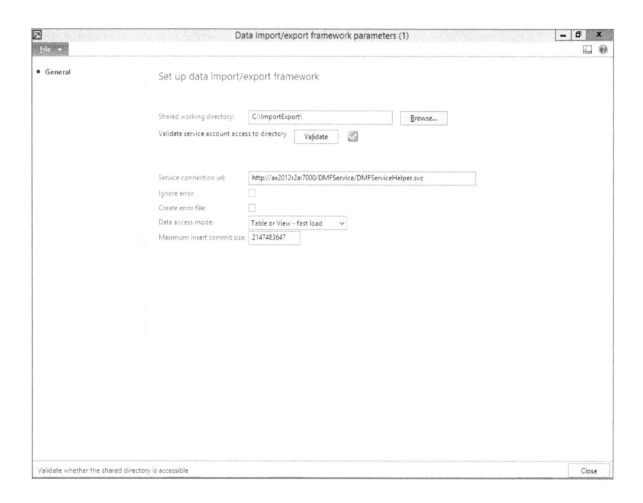

If you have not validated the directory, click on the **Validate** button, and you should get a green checkmark beside the button.

 www.dynamicsaxcompanions.com
Dynamics AX Companions

- 12 -

www.blindsquirrelpublishing.com
© 2015 Blind Squirrel Publishing, LLC, All Rights Reserved

 BLIND SQUIRREL
PUBLISHING

Step By Step Walkthrough

Configuring the Data Import Export Parameters

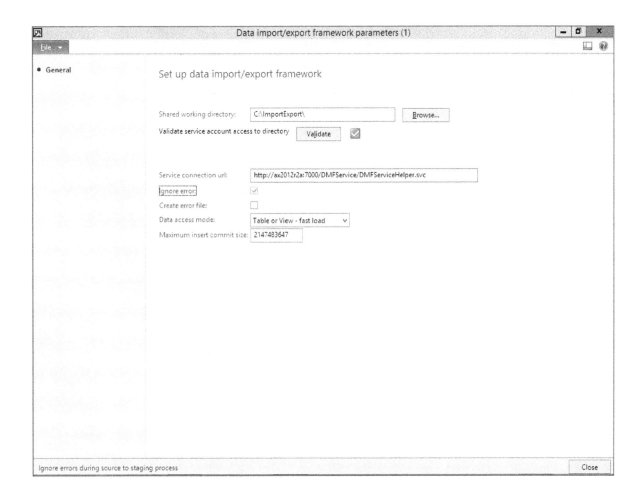

Tip: you may also want to check the **Ignore Error** flag. In the production system you probably don't want to do this, but for the learning process, this helps a little because you don't have to debug small errors during the import.

Once you have done that, just click on the **Close** button to exit out of the form.

Configuring a CSV Source Data Formats

Next we will need to configure the import formats that we will use for the data. The first one that we will configure is a **Comma Separated Value** format for some of the simple imports that we will be loading in.

Step By Step Walkthrough

Configuring a CSV Source Data Formats

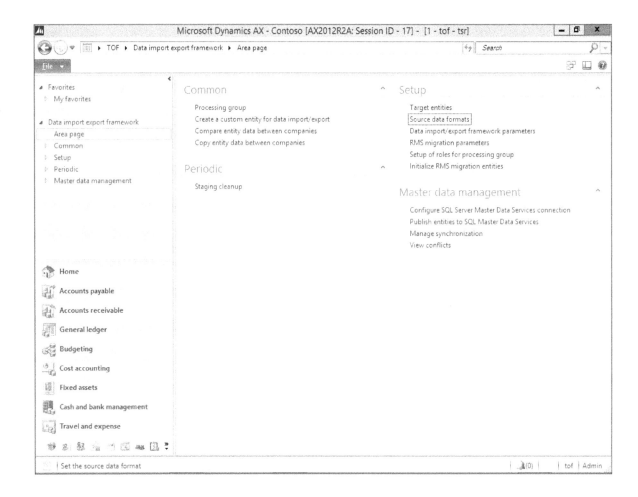

To do this, click on the **Source Data Formats** menu item within the **Setup** group of the **Data Import Export Framework** area page.

Step By Step Walkthrough

Configuring a CSV Source Data Formats

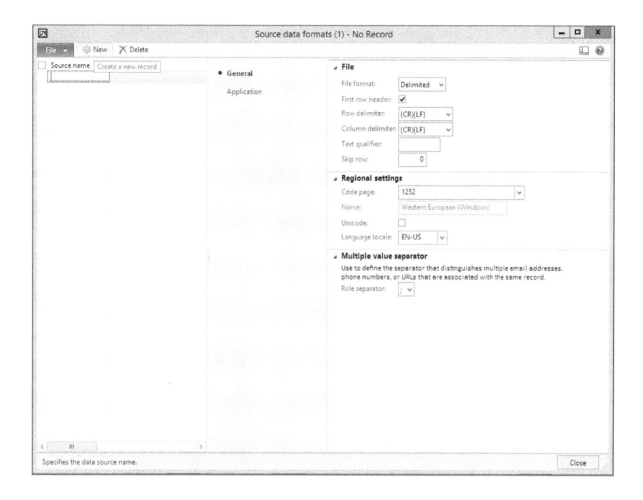

When the **Source Data Formats** maintenance form is displayed, click on the **New** button in the menu bar to create a new record.

Step By Step Walkthrough

Configuring a CSV Source Data Formats

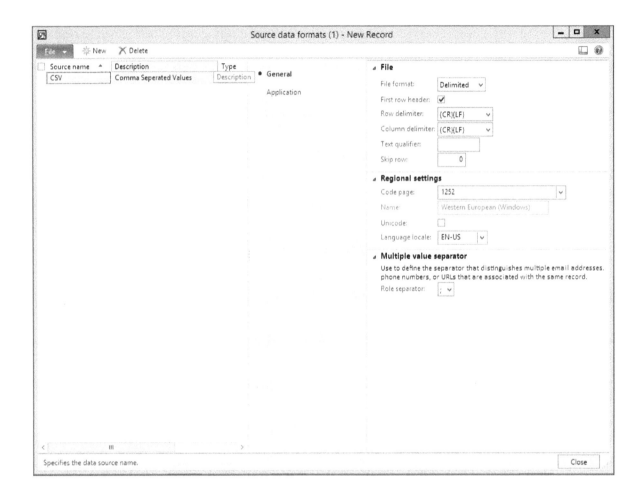

Set the Source Name to CSV and a Description to Comma Separated Value.

BARE BONES CONFIGURATION GUIDE
CONFIGURING A COMPANY IMPORT TEMPLATE USING DYNAMICS AX 2012   CONFIGURING THE DATA IMPORT EXPORT CONTROLS

Step By Step Walkthrough

Configuring a CSV Source Data Formats

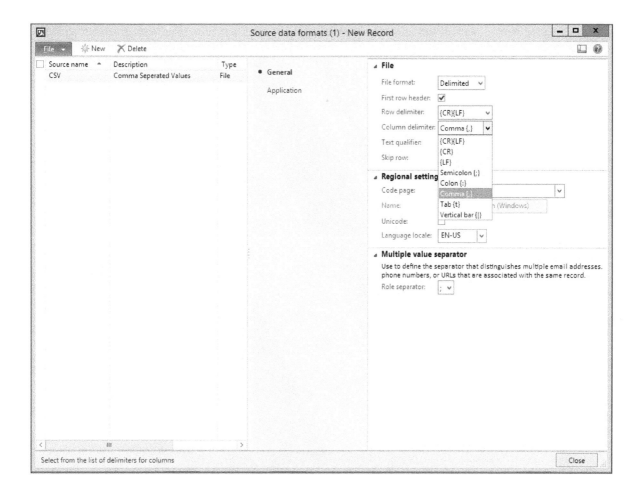

By default, the format will be a **Delimited** type, and all you have to do is select the **Column Delimiter** which will be a comma for this example.

www.dynamicsaxcompanions.com
Dynamics AX Companions

- 19 -

www.blindsquirrelpublishing.com
© 2015 Blind Squirrel Publishing, LLC, All Rights Reserved

BLIND SQUIRREL
PUBLISHING

Step By Step Walkthrough

Configuring a CSV Source Data Formats

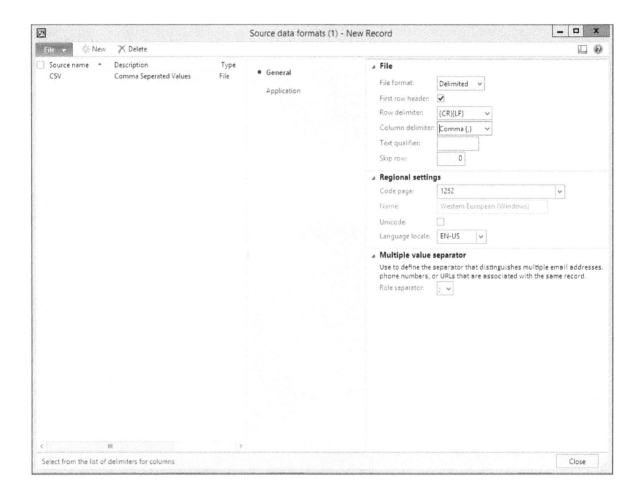

When you are done, you can click on the **Close** button to exit from the form.

Configuring an Excel Source Data Format

Sometimes importing data through CSV files doesn't quite cut it through. The CSV files tend to have the numbers changed when you view them in Excel and also all of the quotes around the data can be a little cumbersome. So we will also set up a more advanced format that allows you to import your data directly from Excel workbooks. This makes sure that your data remains in the format that you paste it into the worksheet in, and also has an added benefit that you can have multiple sets of data stored within one worksheet.

 www.dynamicsaxcompanions.com
Dynamics AX Companions

- 21 -

www.blindsquirrelpublishing.com
© 2015 Blind Squirrel Publishing, LLC, All Rights Reserved

BLIND SQUIRREL
PUBLISHING

Step By Step Walkthrough

Configuring an Excel Source Data Format

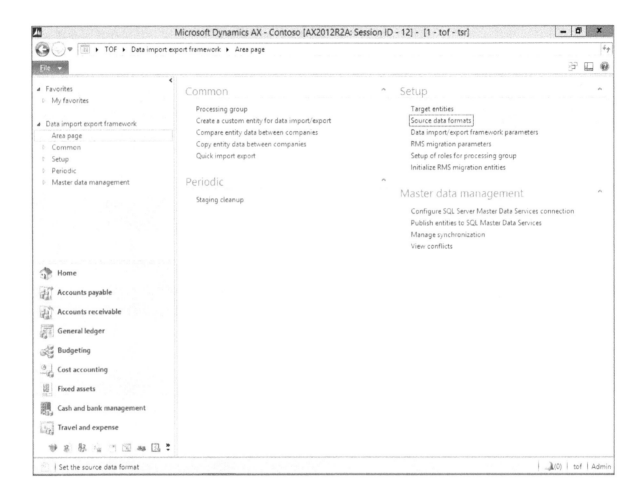

To do this, click on the **Source Data Formats** menu item within the **Setup** group of the **Data Import Export Framework** area page.

Step By Step Walkthrough

Configuring an Excel Source Data Format

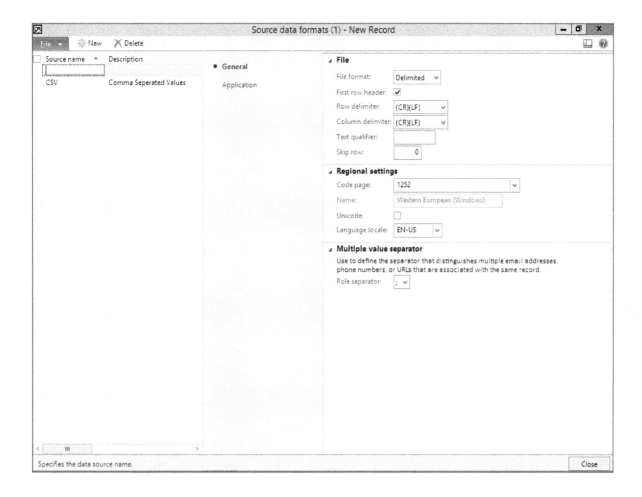

When the **Source Data Formats** maintenance form is displayed, click on the **New** button in the menu bar to create a new record.

Step By Step Walkthrough

Configuring an Excel Source Data Format

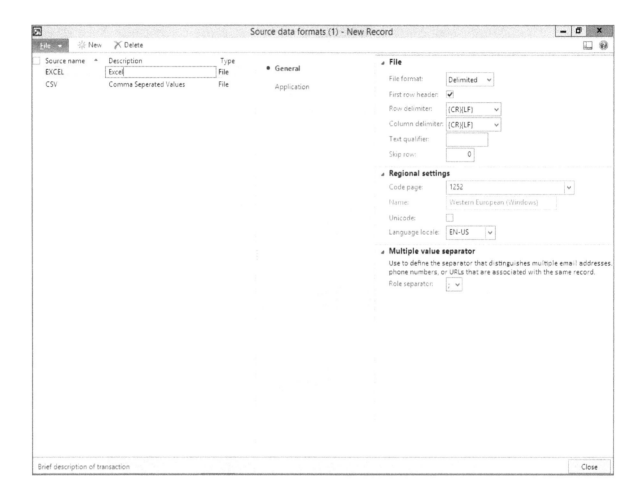

For this record, set the **Source Name** to EXCEL and the **Description** to **Excel**.

Step By Step Walkthrough

Configuring an Excel Source Data Format

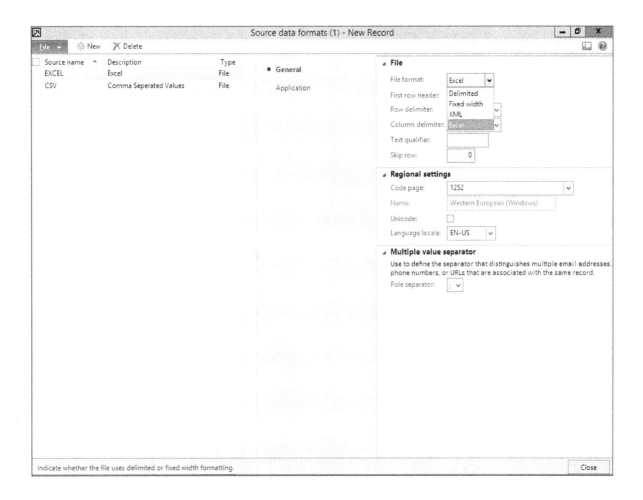

Now click on the **File Format** dropdown list and select the **Excel** option to indicate that you want to use Excel Workbooks to store the sample data in.

Step By Step Walkthrough

Configuring an Excel Source Data Format

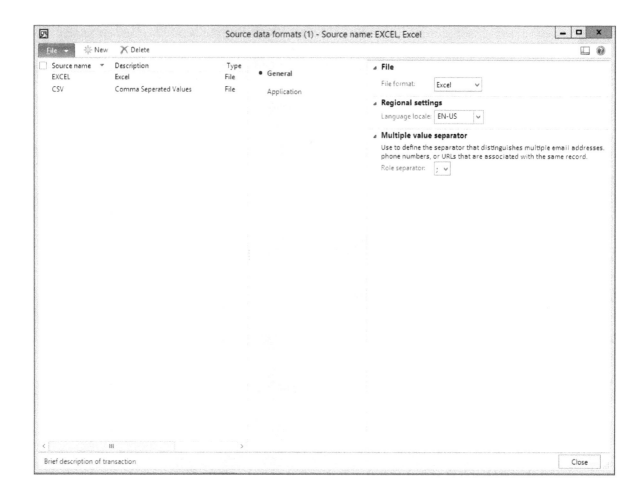

After you have done that, just click on the **Close** button to exit from the form.

Summary

That's pretty much all you need to do in order to set up the Data Import Export Framework so that you can start using it. The next step is to start building some templates for your data.

CREATING A MASTER COMPANY IMPORT TEMPLATE

When you are creating a new company from the ground up there is a lot of base data that you will want to load in. You can do this the hard way by loading the data by hand, or you could take advantage of the Data Import Export Framework, create a company template that has all of the core data that you can possibly think of for your company and then let the importing framework do all of the heavy lifting for you.

To make this even easier, rather than creating a separate import template for each of the entities like the **Customer**, **Vendors**, **Chart Of Accounts**, **Products** etc. you can create one master template that you can then populate all at once and then just import all of the data in one fell swoop, saving you even more time because you don't need to run each of the imports individually.

In this chapter we will step you through the creation of a Master Company import template showing you the key fields that you need in the templates and also how to organize them so that importing your base data is a breeze.

Creating a Master Data Processing Group

The first step in this process is to create a new **Processing Group** within the **Data Import Export Framework** module that will allow you to group all of the import entities together.

Step By Step Walkthrough

Creating a Master Data Processing Group

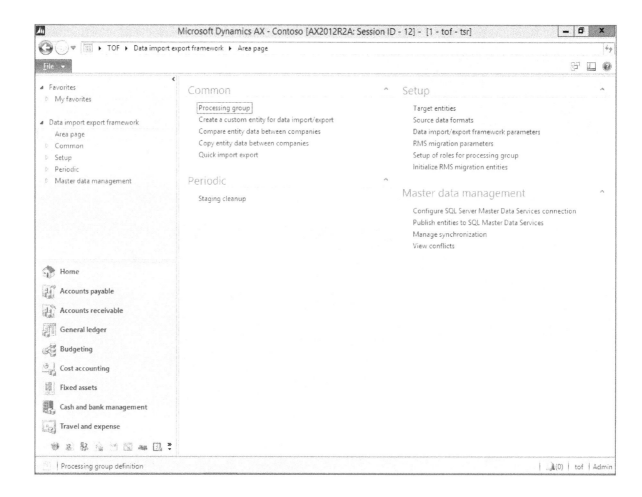

To do this, click on the **Processing Groups** menu item within the **Common** group of the **Data Import Export Framework** area page.

Step By Step Walkthrough

Creating a Master Data Processing Group

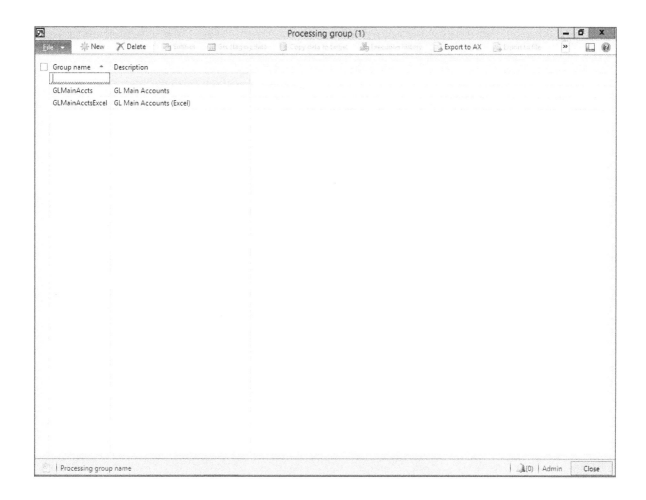

When the **Processing Group** list page is displayed, click on the **New** button in the menu bar to create a new **Processing Group** record.

Step By Step Walkthrough

Creating a Master Data Processing Group

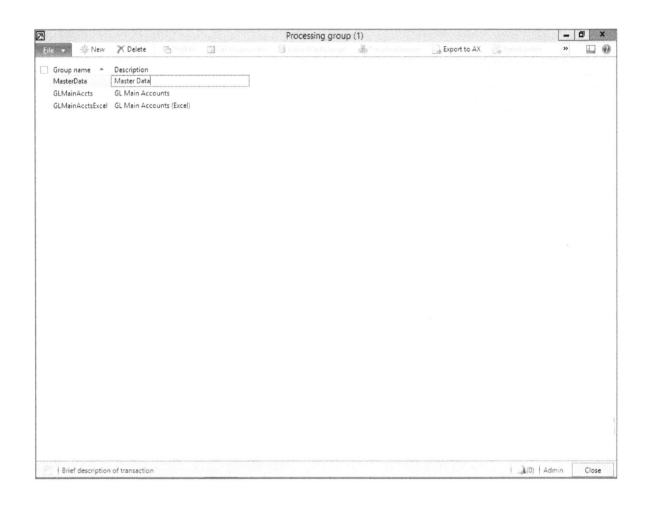

Set the **Group Name** to **MasterData** and the **Description** to **Master Data**.

Creating a User Account Import Entity

Once you have a processing group created you can start creating the Entity mappings. These are the links back to the Dynamics AX data that you then tell the system what data you want to populate with. We will create a number of these to get all of the base data loaded into Dynamics AX, and we will start with the **User Accounts**.

Step By Step Walkthrough

Creating a User Account Import Entity

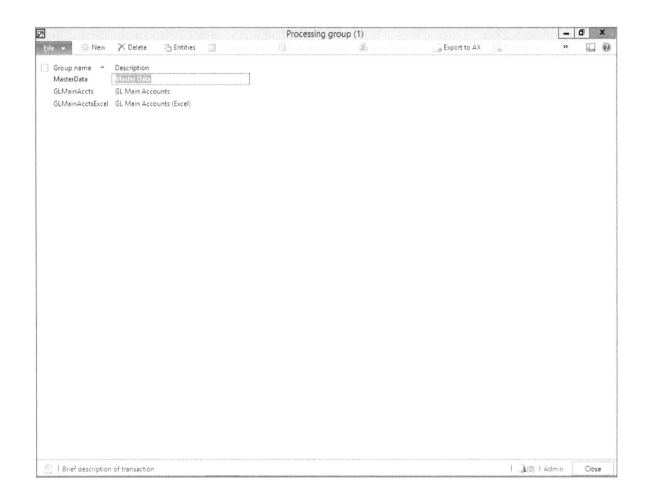

To do this, select the **MasterData** processing group and then click on the **Entities** button in the menu bar.

Step By Step Walkthrough

Creating a User Account Import Entity

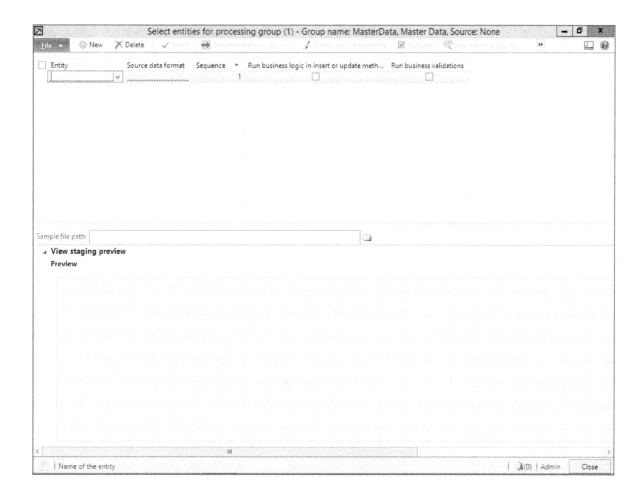

This will open up the **Processing Group Entities** maintenance form. Click on the **New** button within the menu bar to create a new record.

Step By Step Walkthrough

Creating a User Account Import Entity

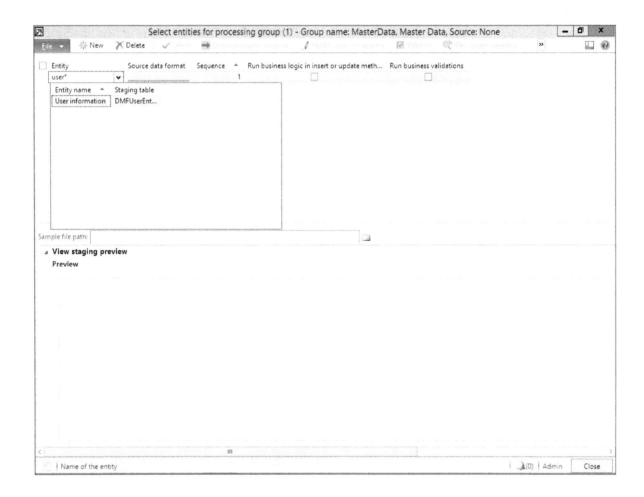

Then click on the **Entity** dropdown list and find the **User Information** entity which is used to map all of the user names into Dynamics AX.

Tip: If you want to cheat a little, just type in **user*** and it will narrow down the search for you a little bit.

Step By Step Walkthrough

Creating a User Account Import Entity

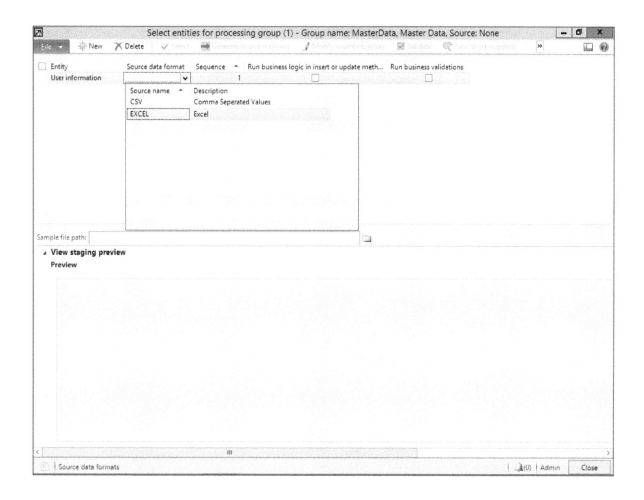

Now click on the **Source Data Format** dropdown list and select the **EXCEL** format that you created earlier on.

daxc   www.dynamicsaxcompanions.com
Dynamics AX Companions

- 39 -

www.blindsquirrelpublishing.com
© 2015 Blind Squirrel Publishing, LLC, All Rights Reserved

BLIND SQUIRREL
PUBLISHING

Step By Step Walkthrough

Creating a User Account Import Entity

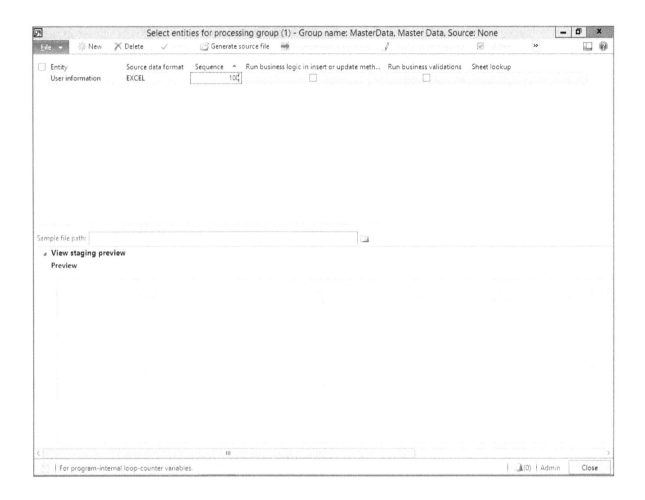

Then set the **Sequence** to **100**.

Note: This is going to tell the system what order we want to run all of the imports and since some are dependent on others then we want to make sure that we have large enough numbers and also large enough gaps just in case we need to slip another entity between other ones.

Step By Step Walkthrough

Creating a User Account Import Entity

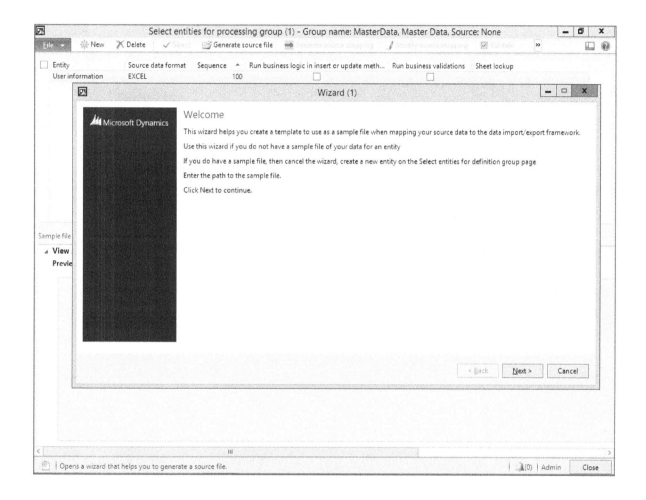

Now we want to create the mapping that we will be using to import in all of the data. To do this click on the **Generate Source File** button in the menu bar and when the **Wizard** appears, click on the **Next** button to start setting things up.

Step By Step Walkthrough

Creating a User Account Import Entity

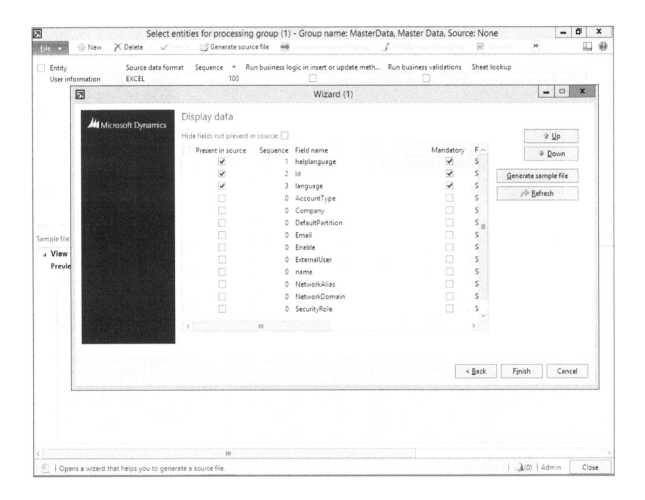

Then the **Display Data** page is shown you will be able to see all of the fields that you can possibly map, and also some of the fields will already be selected for you. These fields are the key index fields so you want to keep them in the import.

www.dynamicsaxcompanions.com
Dynamics AX Companions

- 42 -

www.blindsquirrelpublishing.com
© 2015 Blind Squirrel Publishing, LLC, All Rights Reserved

BLIND SQUIRREL
PUBLISHING

Sample Data

Creating a User Account Import Entity

Here are the fields that you will want to have within your import definition if you want to use the sample company import template that we provide.

Sometimes the key index fields don't show up in the most intuitive order so we have reordered them as well to make the template a little easier to manage.

Present in source	Sequence	Field name	Mandatory	Field type	Field size
Yes	1	Id	Yes	String	8
Yes	2	helplanguage	Yes	String	7
Yes	3	language	Yes	String	7
Yes	4	name	No	String	50
Yes	5	NetworkDomain	No	String	255
Yes	6	NetworkAlias	No	String	80
Yes	7	SecurityRole	No	String	1000

www.dynamicsaxcompanions.com
Dynamics AX Companions

- 43 -

www.blindsquirrelpublishing.com
© 2015 Blind Squirrel Publishing, LLC , All Rights Reserved

BLIND SQUIRREL
PUBLISHING

Step By Step Walkthrough

Creating a User Account Import Entity

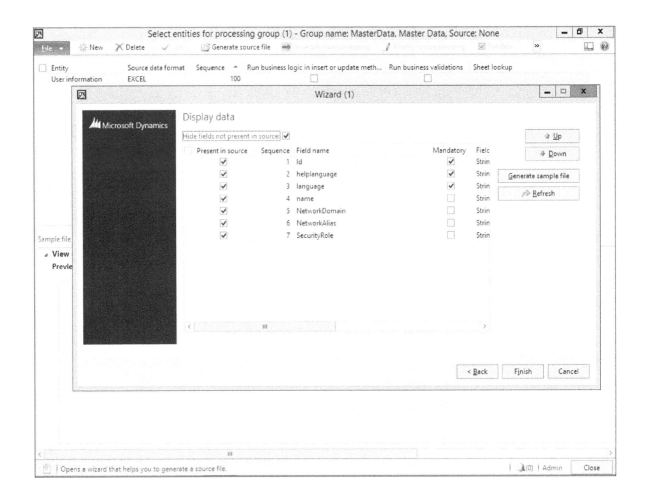

All you need to do is find each of the fields in the template and then just click on the **Present In Source** checkbox, which will enable to field to be used within the template. If you need to re-order any of the fields then select the field and then click on the **Up** or **Down** buttons to rearrange them.

Once you have all of the fields selected and you have them in the right order then click on the **Generate Sample File** button.

Step By Step Walkthrough

Creating a User Account Import Entity

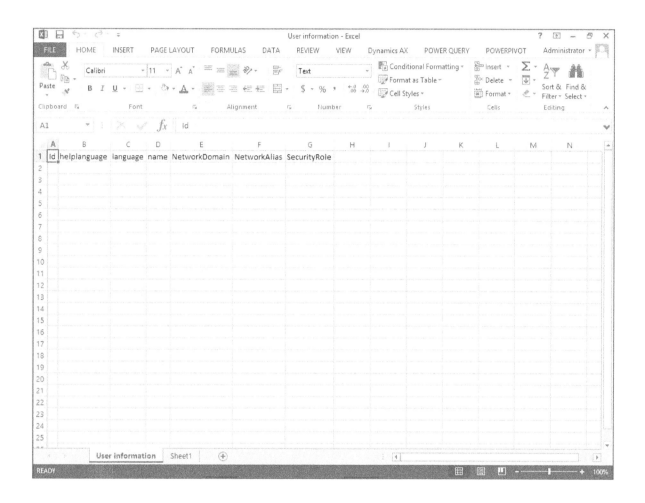

This will create a blank Excel Workbook for you and the first Sheet will already be set up with the fields that you need for the import.

Step By Step Walkthrough

Creating a User Account Import Entity

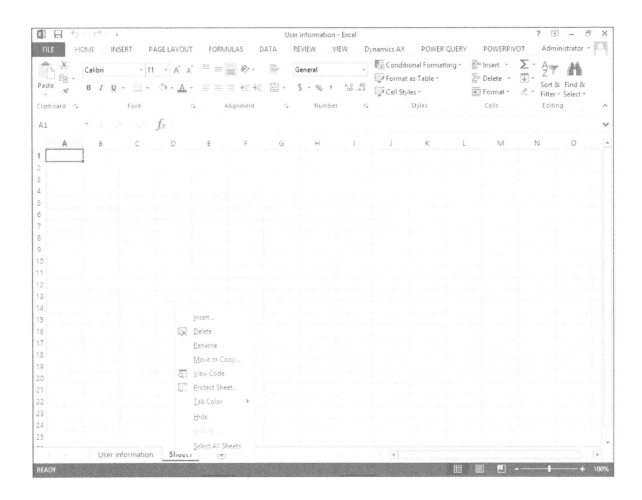

We are going to use this spreadsheet as the basis for our Master spreadsheet that will have all of the import templates within it, so let's tidy it up a little. Start off by right-mouse-clicking on the extra **Sheet1** worksheet and select the **Delete** option.

Step By Step Walkthrough

Creating a User Account Import Entity

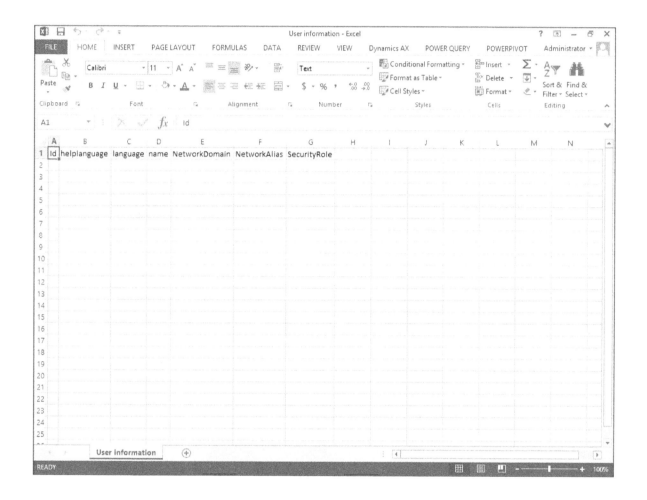

Now you should have a workbook with just one Worksheet.

Step By Step Walkthrough

Creating a User Account Import Entity

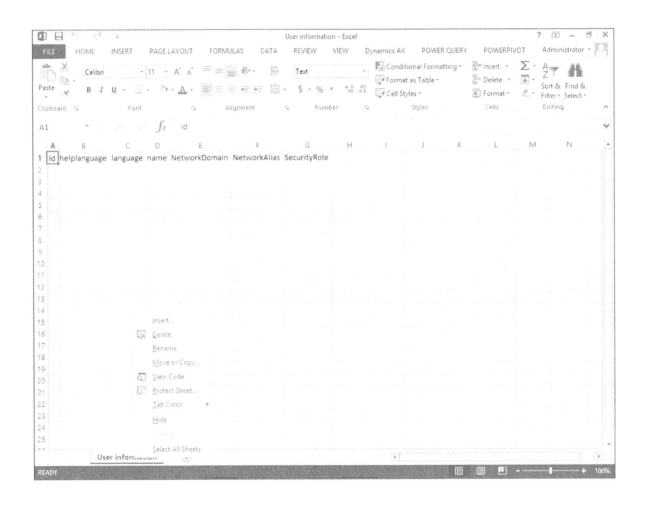

We will make one more change, and that is to rename the default label for the **User Information** worksheet. To do this Right-Mouse-Click on the **User Information** worksheet tab and select the **Rename** option.

Step By Step Walkthrough

Creating a User Account Import Entity

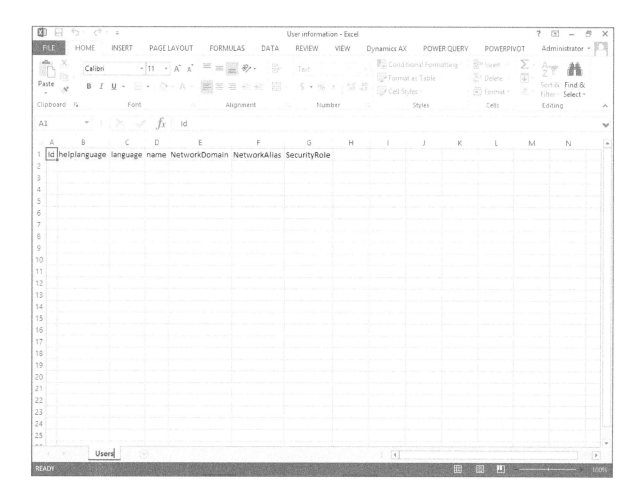

Then change the name on the sheet to **Users**.

Step By Step Walkthrough

Creating a User Account Import Entity

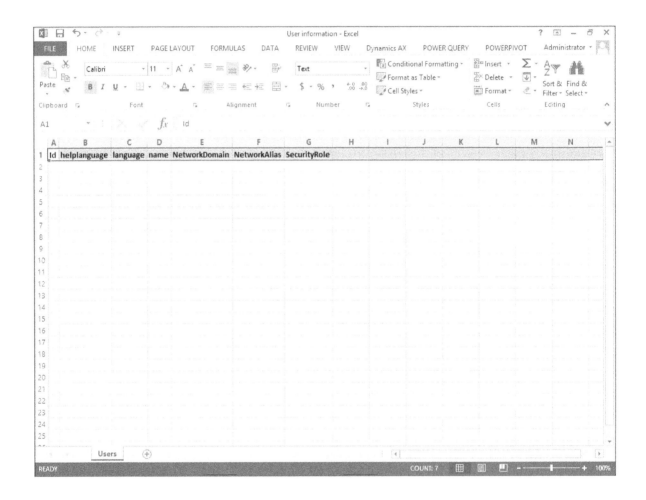

If you are like me, you may also want to make things even more tidy, you may want to resize all of the columns so that they match the headings. Or you could leave them as they are – we won't judge... much...

www.dynamicsaxcompanions.com
Dynamics AX Companions

- 50 -

www.blindsquirrelpublishing.com
© 2015 Blind Squirrel Publishing, LLC, All Rights Reserved

BLIND SQUIRREL
PUBLISHING

Step By Step Walkthrough

Creating a User Account Import Entity

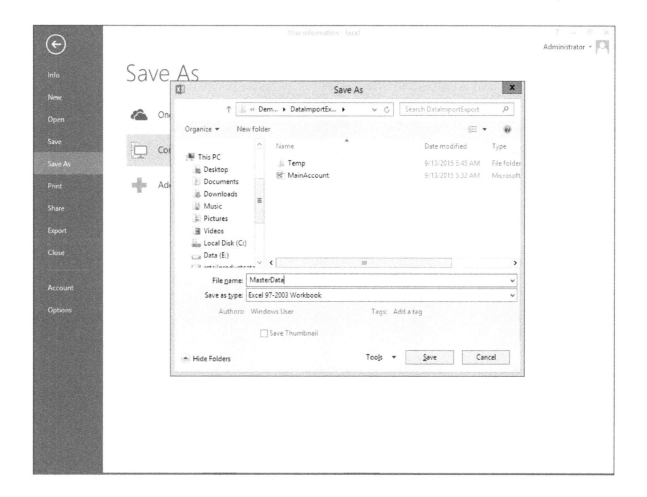

Now save away the Excel Workbook into a safe location so that you can reference it later on. In our example we have set up a directory called **DataImportExport** where all of the templates are stored.

Step By Step Walkthrough

Creating a User Account Import Entity

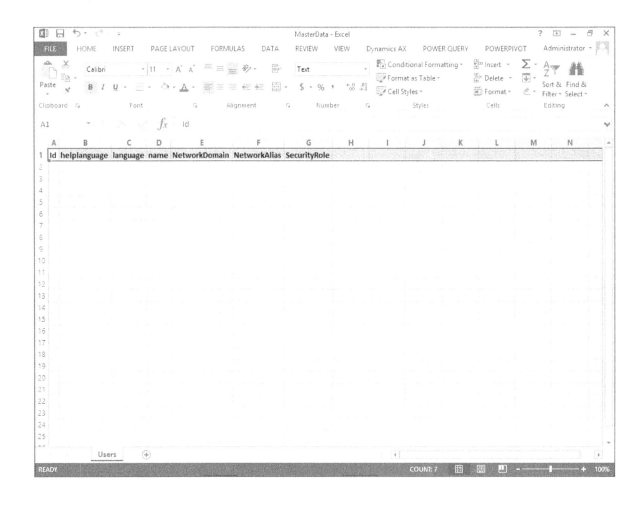

After you have done that you can close the Worksheet.

Step By Step Walkthrough

Creating a User Account Import Entity

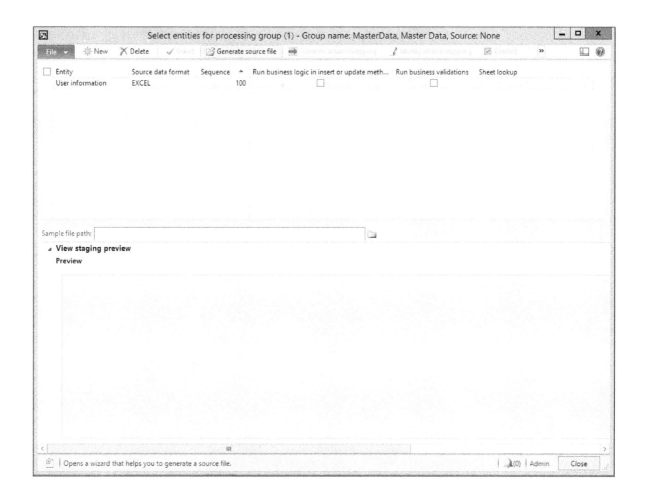

Now that we have the template built we will need to link it to the **Entity** that we just created. To do this click on the **Folder** icon to the right of the **Sample File Path** field.

Step By Step Walkthrough

Creating a User Account Import Entity

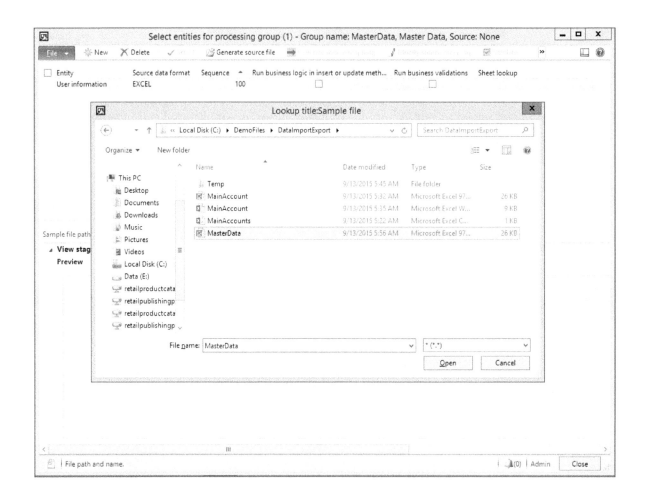

This will open up a file explorer and you can navigate to where you saved your **MasterData** worksheet that you just created, and then click on the **Open** button.

Step By Step Walkthrough

Creating a User Account Import Entity

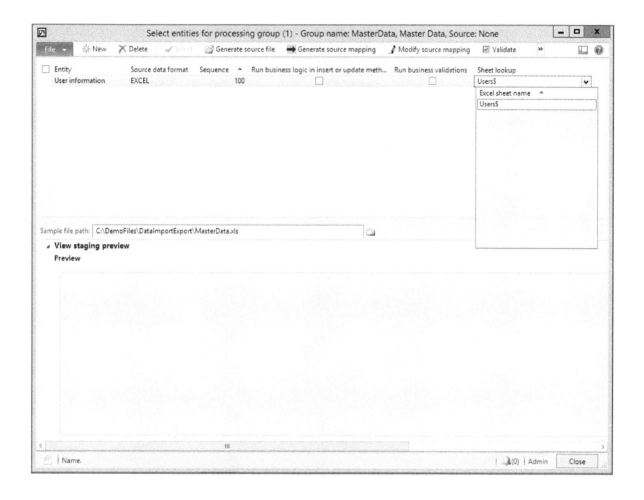

Once you have done that you will notice that you can now click on the **Sheet Lookup** dropdown list and you will see the worksheet that you just renamed to **Users**. It has a **$** at the end of it because that's how Excel indicates that it's a worksheet. If the **Users$** sheet is not selected then just click on the dropdown list and select it.

Step By Step Walkthrough

Creating a User Account Import Entity

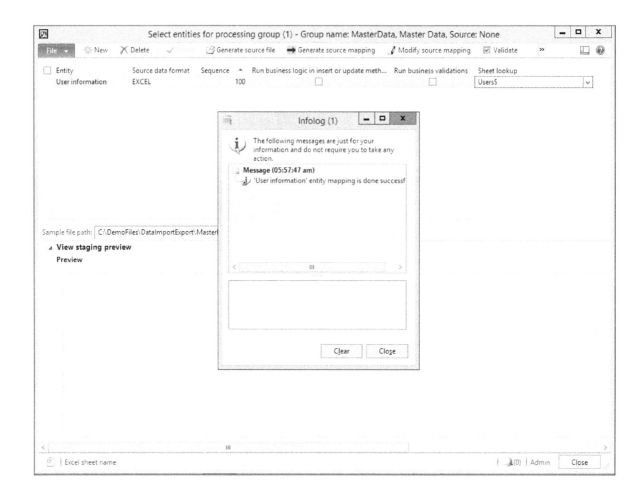

The final step in the process is to tie up all of the loose ends for the import entity and that just involves clicking on the **Generate Source Mapping** button within the menu bar. If everything is linked up correctly and you have all of the key fields within your map, then you will get a quick message saying that the entity mapping was completed.

All you need to do is click on the **Close** button and you are done.

Creating an Ethnic Origins Import Entity

Next let's load in some of the base Human Resources codes into Dynamics AX. If we are going to the trouble of loading in all of the employees later on we might as well have some of the demographics loaded as well.

Step By Step Walkthrough

Creating an Ethnic Origins Import Entity

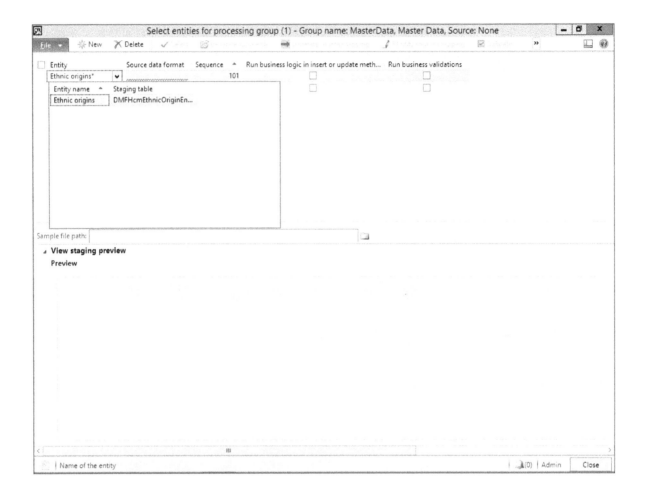

Return to the **Processing Group Entities** maintenance form and click on the **New** button within the menu bar to create a new record. Then click on the **Entity** dropdown list and find the **Ethnic Origins** Entity type.

Now click on the **Source Data Format** dropdown list and select the **EXCEL** format that you created earlier on.

Step By Step Walkthrough

Creating an Ethnic Origins Import Entity

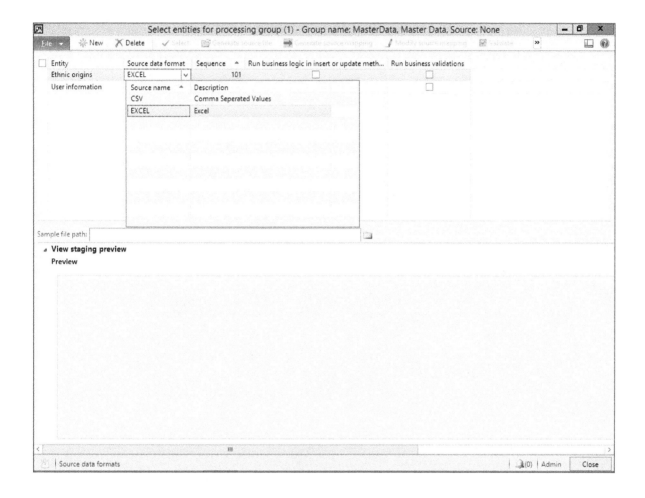

Now click on the **Source Data Format** dropdown list and select the **EXCEL** format that you created earlier on.

Step By Step Walkthrough

Creating an Ethnic Origins Import Entity

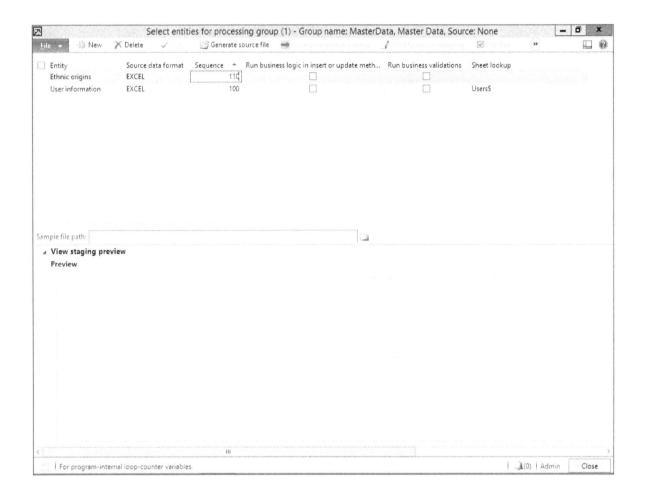

Then set the **Sequence** to **110**.

Note: Since we want this to be processed after the **User Information** we increased the Sequence from the default of **101** to **110**. We kept the gap so that we could put in extra entities if we needed to, stealing the numbering format from old school BASIC.

Step By Step Walkthrough

Creating an Ethnic Origins Import Entity

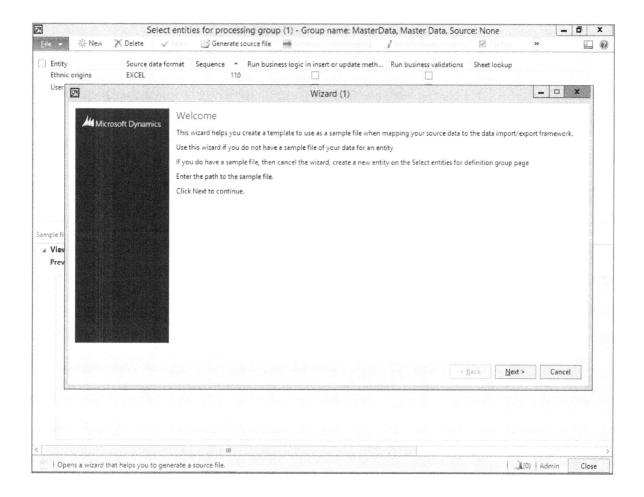

Now we want to create the mapping that we will be using to import in all of the data. To do this click on the **Generate Source File** button in the menu bar and when the **Wizard** appears, click on the **Next** button to start setting things up.

Step By Step Walkthrough

Creating an Ethnic Origins Import Entity

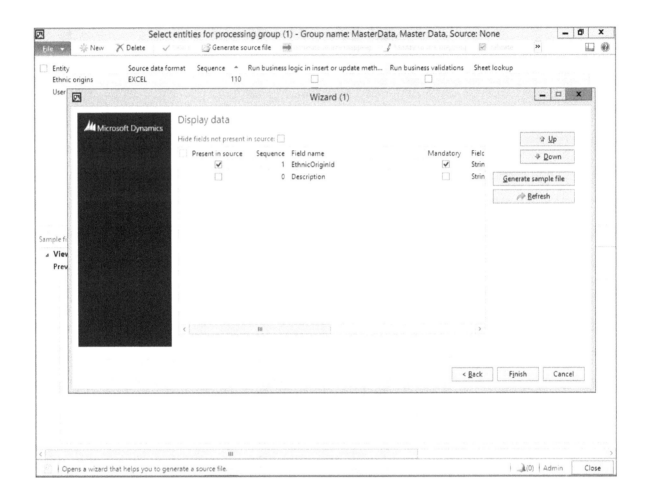

When the **Display Data** page is shown you will be able to see all of the default fields in the entity map.

Sample Data

Creating an Ethnic Origins Import Entity

Here are the fields that you will want to have within your **Ethnic Origins** import definition if you want to use the sample company import template that we provide.

Present in source	Sequence	Field name	Mandatory	Field type	Field size
Yes	1	EthnicOriginId	Yes	String	15
Yes	2	Description	No	String	60

daxc

www.dynamicsaxcompanions.com
Dynamics AX Companions

- 63 -

www.blindsquirrelpublishing.com
© 2015 Blind Squirrel Publishing, LLC, All Rights Reserved

BLIND SQUIRREL
PUBLISHING

Step By Step Walkthrough

Creating an Ethnic Origins Import Entity

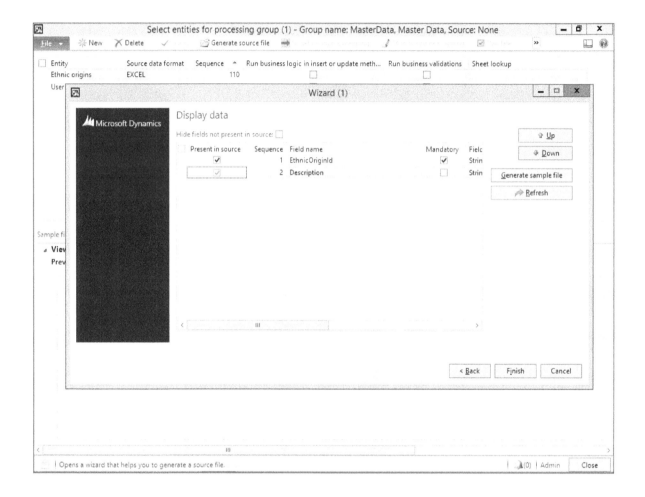

All you need to do is find each of the fields in the template and then just click on the **Present In Source** checkbox, which will enable to field to be used within the template. If you need to re-order any of the fields then select the field and then click on the **Up** or **Down** buttons to rearrange them.

Once you have all of the fields selected and you have them in the right order then click on the **Generate Sample File** button.

Step By Step Walkthrough

Creating an Ethnic Origins Import Entity

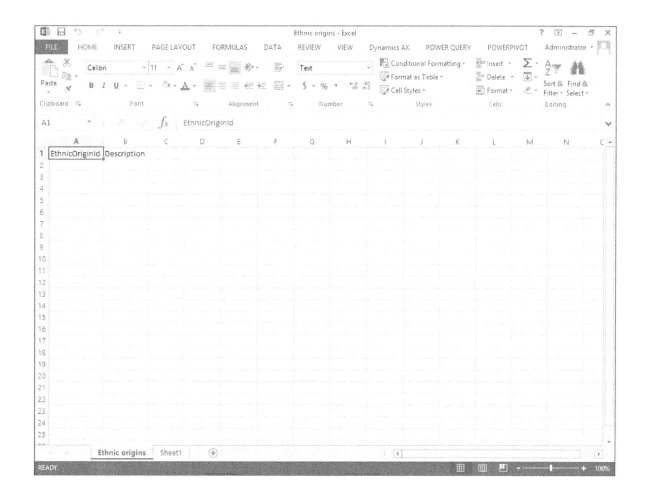

This will create new a blank Excel Workbook for you just like before and the first Sheet will already be set up with the fields that you need for the import.

Step By Step Walkthrough

Creating an Ethnic Origins Import Entity

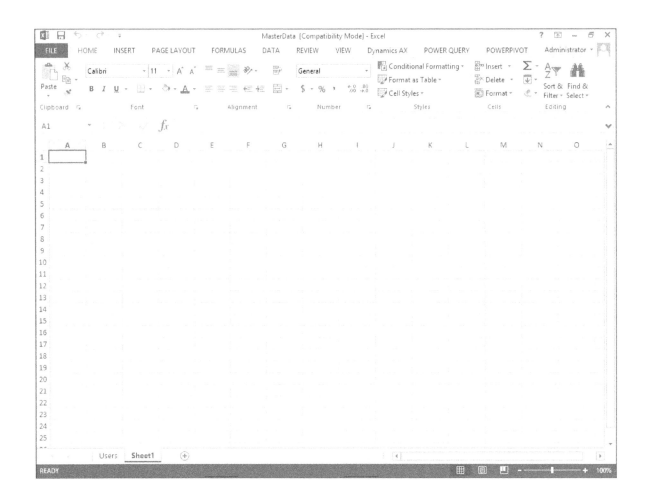

Open up the **MasterData** template that you created in the previous step and add a new Worksheet to the workbook by clicking on the + button to the right of the **Users** tab.

Step By Step Walkthrough

Creating an Ethnic Origins Import Entity

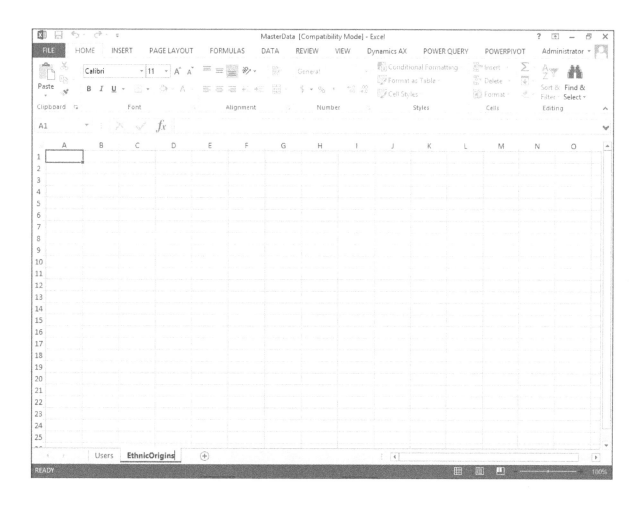

Double click on the **Sheet1** tab and rename it to **Ethnic Origins.**

www.dynamicsaxcompanions.com
Dynamics AX Companions

- 67 -

www.blindsquirrelpublishing.com
© 2015 Blind Squirrel Publishing, LLC , All Rights Reserved

BLIND SQUIRREL
PUBLISHING

Step By Step Walkthrough

Creating an Ethnic Origins Import Entity

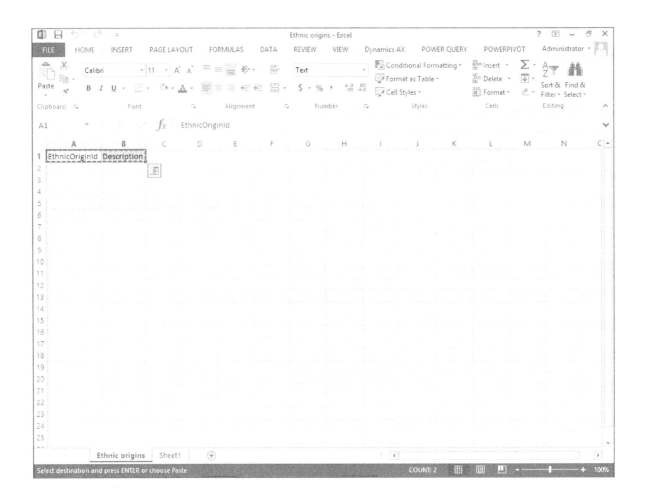

Now return to the workbook that was automatically generated by the wizard and select the auto-generated columns and copy them (**CTRL+C**).

Step By Step Walkthrough

Creating an Ethnic Origins Import Entity

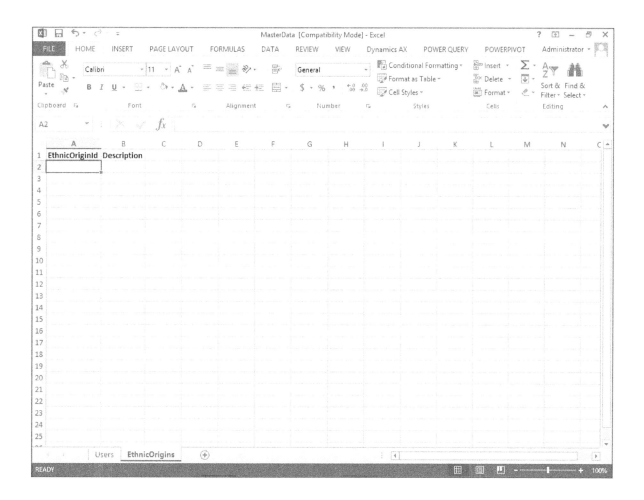

Now return to the **MasterData** workbook and paste (**CTRL+V**) them into the **EthnicOrigins** worksheet and format the columns to make it look tidy.

When you have done that, close out of the **MasterData** workbook.

Step By Step Walkthrough

Creating an Ethnic Origins Import Entity

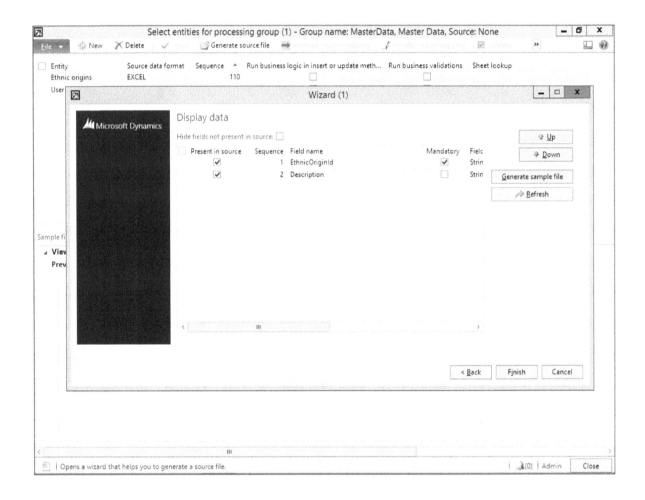

When you return back to the wizard, just click on the **Finish** button to exit from the form.

Step By Step Walkthrough

Creating an Ethnic Origins Import Entity

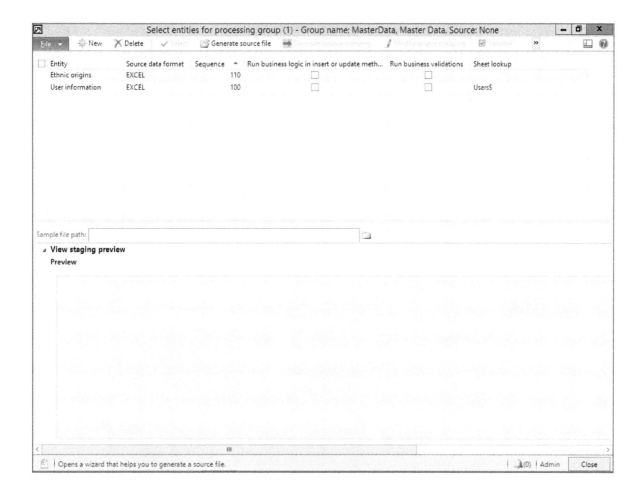

Now that we have updated the master template we will need to link it to the new **Entity** that we just created. To do this click on the **Folder** icon to the right of the **Sample File Path** field.

Step By Step Walkthrough

Creating an Ethnic Origins Import Entity

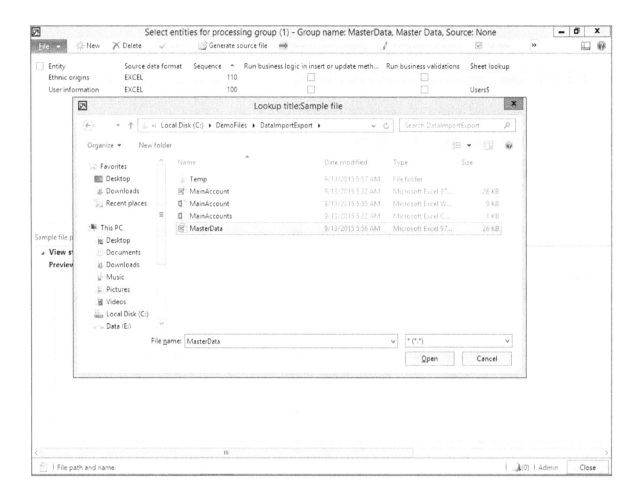

This will open up a file explorer and you can navigate to where you saved your **MasterData** worksheet that you just created, and then click on the **Open** button.

Step By Step Walkthrough

Creating an Ethnic Origins Import Entity

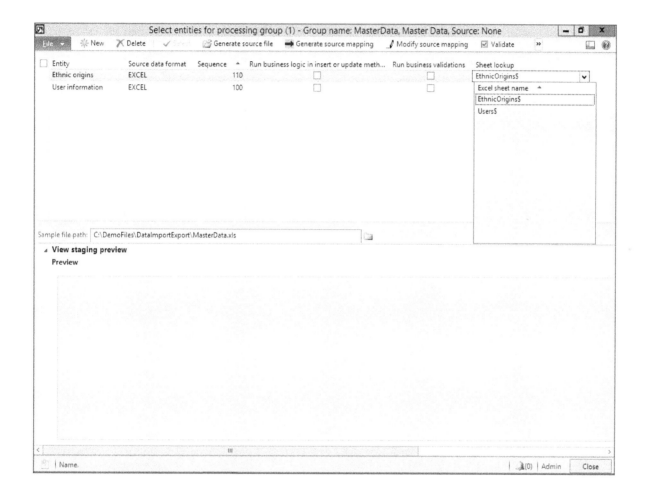

Now you can now click on the **Sheet Lookup** dropdown list and you will see the new **EthnicOrigins** worksheet that you just added. Select the **EthnicOrigins$** record.

Step By Step Walkthrough

Creating an Ethnic Origins Import Entity

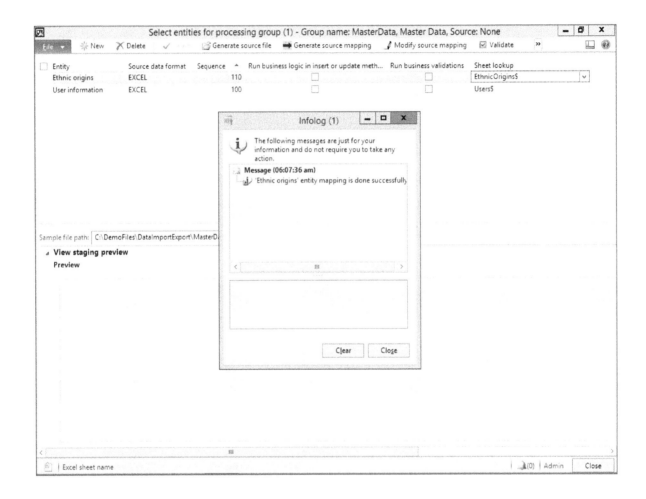

The final step in the process is to tie up all of the loose ends for the import entity and that just involves clicking on the **Generate Source Mapping** button within the menu bar. If everything is linked up correctly and you have all of the key fields within your map, then you will get a quick message saying that the entity mapping was completed.

All you need to do is click on the **Close** button and you are done.

Example Data

Creating an Ethnic Origins Import Entity

Now that you have the worksheet created you can start populating the worksheet with your own set of **Ethnic Origins**. Here is an example of how the data should look.

EthnicOriginId	Alaska Natives
Description	A person having origins as Alaska Natives

Sample Data

Creating an Ethnic Origins Import Entity

If you are looking for some sample **Ethnic Origins** data to load, then here is a snapshot of the data that we use in the sample template.

EthnicOriginId	Description
Alaska Natives	A person having origins as Alaska Natives
Albanian	A person having origins as Albanian
Algerians	A person having origins as Algerians
American Indian	A person having origins American Indian or Alaska Native
American Jews	A person having origins as American Jews
Angolan	A person having origins as Angolan
Appalachian	A person having origins as Appalachian
Arab	A person having origins as Arab
Armenian	A person having origins as Armenian
Ashkenazi Jews	A person having origins as Ashkenazi Jews
Asian	A person having origins in the Far East, Southeast Asia...
Asian Pacific	A person having origins as Asian Pacific
Assyrians	A person having origins as Assyrians
Bangladeshi	A person having origins as Bangladeshi
Black Dutch	A person having origins as Black Dutch
Black/African	A person having origins in ... Africa
Brazilian	A person having origins as Brazilian
British	A person having origins as British
Cambodian	A person having origins as Cambodian
Canadian	A person having origins as Canadian
Chilean	A person having origins as Chilean
Chinese	A person having origins as Chinese
Cuban	A person having origins as Cuban
Egyptian	A person having origins as Egyptian
European	A person having origins as European
French	A person having origins as French
Frisian	A person having origins as Frisian
German	A person having origins as German
Greek	A person having origins as Greek
Haitian	A person having origins as Haitian
Han Chinese	A person having origins as Han Chinese
Hispanic/Latino	A person of Cuban, Mexican, Puerto Rican, South or Central..
Indonesian	A person having origins as Indonesian
Iranian	A person having origins as Iranian
Iraqi	A person having origins as Iraqi
Irish	A person having origins as Irish
Italian	A person having origins as Italian
Jordanian	A person having origins as Jordanian
Mexican	A person having origins as Mexican
Native Hawaiian	A person of native Hawaiian or other Pacific Islander
Pakistani	A person having origins as Pakistani
Palestinian	A person having origins as Palestinian
Portuguese	A person having origins as Portuguese
Romanian	A person having origins as Romanian
Russian	A person having origins as Russian
Two or More	Two or More Races

BLIND SQUIRREL
PUBLISHING

EthnicOriginId	Description
White	A person having origins Europe, Middle East, or North Africa

www.dynamicsaxcompanions.com
Dynamics AX Companions

- 77 -

www.blindsquirrelpublishing.com
© 2015 Blind Squirrel Publishing, LLC, All Rights Reserved

BLIND SQUIRREL
PUBLISHING

Creating an Employee Import Entity

Now let's create an import entity for the **Employees** so that we don't have to load them all in by hand.

daxc
www.dynamicsaxcompanions.com
Dynamics AX Companions

- 79 -

www.blindsquirrelpublishing.com
© 2015 Blind Squirrel Publishing, LLC, All Rights Reserved

BLIND SQUIRREL
PUBLISHING

Step By Step Walkthrough

Creating an Employee Import Entity

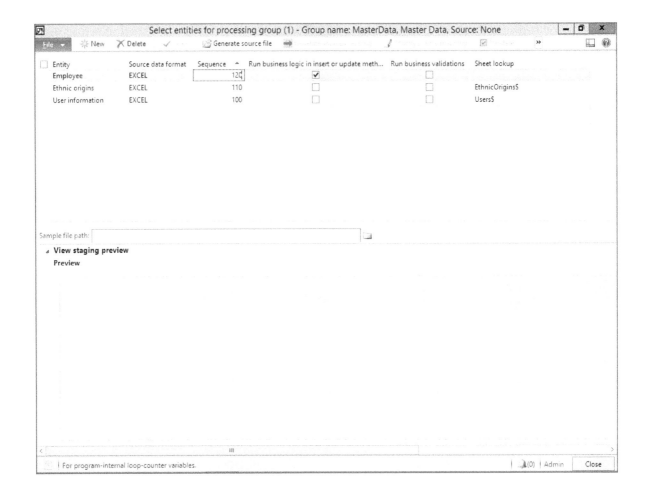

Return to the **Processing Group Entities** maintenance form and click on the **New** button within the menu bar to create a new record. Then click on the **Entity** dropdown list and find the **Ethnic Origins** Entity type.

Click on the **Source Data Format** dropdown list and select the **EXCEL** format, and then set the **Sequence** number to **120**.

Now we want to create the mapping that we will be using to import in all of the data. To do this click on the **Generate Source File** button in the menu bar and when the **Wizard** appears, click on the **Next** button to start setting things up.

When the **Display Data** page is shown you will be able to see all of the default fields in the entity map.

Sample Data

Creating an Employee Import Entity

Here are the fields that you will want to have within your **Employees** import definition if you want to use the sample company import template that we provide.

Present in source	Sequence		Field name	Mandatory	Field type	Field size
Yes		1	PersonnelNumber	Yes	String	25
Yes		2	FirstName	No	String	25
Yes		3	LastName	No	String	25
Yes		4	Gender	No	String	7
Yes		5	LegalEntity	No	String	10
Yes		6	EmploymentType	No	String	10

Step By Step Walkthrough

Creating an Employee Import Entity

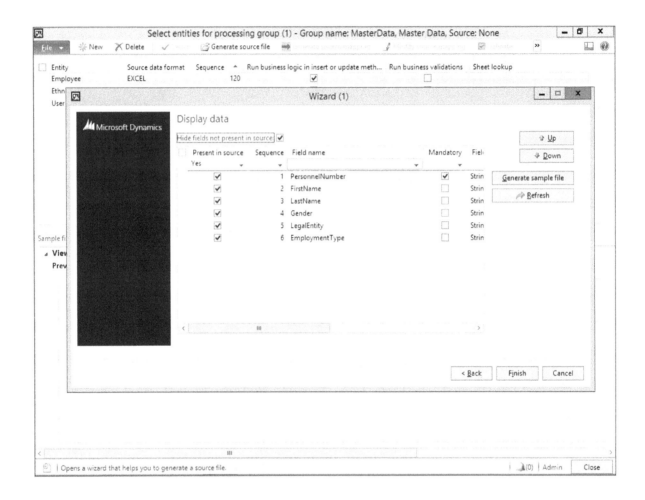

Find each of the fields in the template and then just click on the **Present In Source** checkbox, which will enable to field to be used within the template. If you need to re-order any of the fields, then select the field and then click on the **Up** or **Down** buttons to rearrange them.

Once you have all of the fields selected and you have them in the right order then click on the **Generate Sample File** button.

Step By Step Walkthrough

Creating an Employee Import Entity

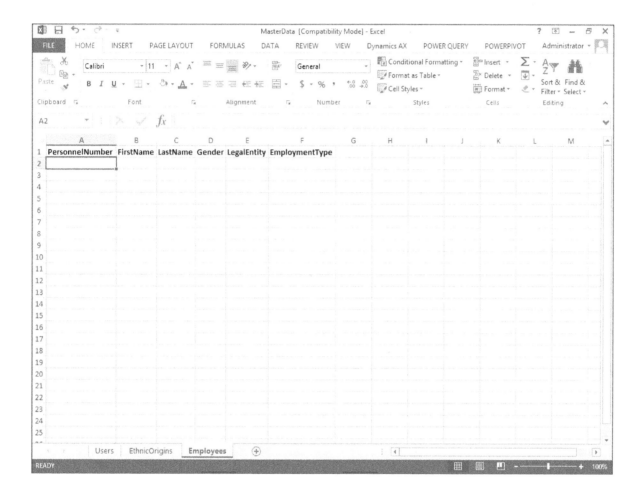

This will create another Excel Workbook for you just like before and the first sheet will already be set up with the fields that you need for the **Employee** import.

Open up the **MasterData** template that you created in the previous step and add a new Worksheet to the workbook by clicking on the **+** button and rename it to **Employees.**

Now return to the workbook that was automatically generated by the wizard and select the auto-generated columns and copy them (**CTRL+C**) and paste (**CTRL+V**) them into the **Employees** worksheet within the **MasterData** workbook. You may also want to format the columns to make it look tidy.

When you have done that, close out of the **MasterData** workbook.

Step By Step Walkthrough

Creating an Employee Import Entity

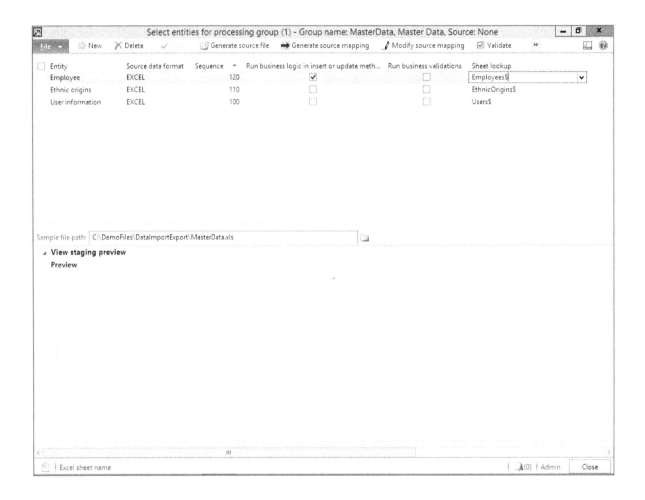

When you return back to the wizard, just click on the **Finish** button to exit from the form which will return you to the **Processing** Groups maintenance form. Click on the **Folder** icon to the right of the **Sample File Path** field.

When the file explorer opens navigate to where you saved your **MasterData** worksheet that you just created, and then click on the **Open** button.

Click on the **Sheet Lookup** dropdown list and select the **Employees$** record.

Finish off the process by clicking on the **Generate Source Mapping** button within the menu bar. If everything is linked up correctly and you have all of the key fields within your map, then you will get a quick message saying that the entity mapping was completed and you can click on the **Close** button.

Example Data

Creating an Employee Import Entity

Now that you have the worksheet created you can start populating the worksheet with your own set of **Employees**. Here is an example of how the data should look.

PersonnelNumber	100001
FirstName	Michael
LastName	Vaughn
Gender	Male
LegalEntity	TOF
EmploymentType	Employee

Sample Data

Creating an Employee Import Entity

If you are looking for some sample **Employee** data to load, then here is a snapshot of the data that we use in the sample template.

PersonnelNumber	FirstName	LastName	Gender	LegalEntity	EmploymentType
100001	Michael	Vaughn	Male	TOF	Employee
100002	Jack	Bristow	Male	TOF	Employee
100003	Arvin	Sloane	Male	TOF	Employee
100004	Marcus	Dixon	Male	TOF	Employee
100005	Marshall	Flinkman	Male	TOF	Employee
100006	Eric	Weiss	Male	TOF	Employee
100007	Julian	Sark	Male	TOF	Employee
100008	Will	Tippin	Male	TOF	Employee
100009	Francie	Calfo	Male	TOF	Employee
100010	Irina	Derevko	Female	TOF	Employee
100011	Lauren	Reed	Female	TOF	Employee
100012	Nadia	Santos	Female	TOF	Employee
100013	Renée	Rienne	Female	TOF	Employee
100014	Rachel	Gibson	Female	TOF	Employee
100015	Thomas	Grace	Male	TOF	Employee
100016	Kelly	Peyton	Female	TOF	Employee
100017	Anna	Espinosa	Female	TOF	Employee
100018	Katya	Derevko	Female	TOF	Employee
100019	Elena	Derevko	Female	TOF	Employee
100020	Judy	Barnett	Female	TOF	Employee
100021	Emily	Sloane	Female	TOF	Employee
100022	Carrie	Bowman	Female	TOF	Employee
100023	Arthur	Devlin	Male	TOF	Employee
100024	Charlie	Bernard	Male	TOF	Employee

Creating a Job Tasks Import Entity

Now let's configure the entities for the Jobs and Positions within the Data Import Export Framework so that we can import in all of the Employee data. The first entity that we need to configure is the **Job Tasks** entity which will be used within the **Jobs** later on.

daxc
www.dynamicsaxcompanions.com
Dynamics AX Companions

- 87 -

www.blindsquirrelpublishing.com
© 2015 Blind Squirrel Publishing, LLC, All Rights Reserved

BLIND SQUIRREL
PUBLISHING

Step By Step Walkthrough

Creating a Job Tasks Import Entity

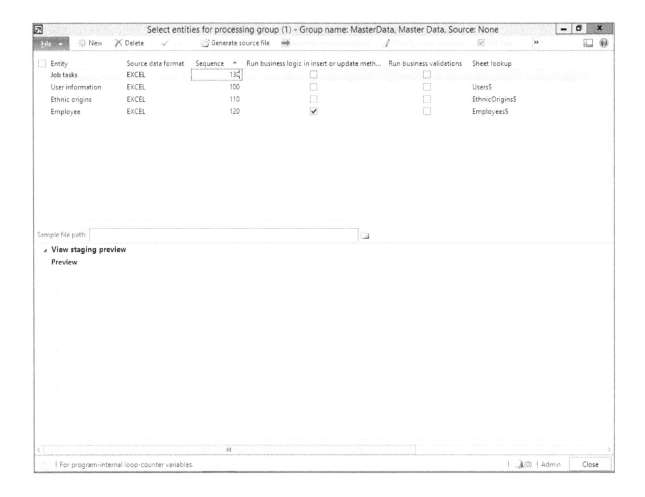

To do this, return to the **Processing Group Entities** maintenance form and click on the **New** button within the menu bar to create a new record. Then click on the **Entity** dropdown list and find the **Job Tasks** Entity type.

Click on the **Source Data Format** dropdown list and select the **EXCEL** format, and then set the **Sequence** number to **130**.

Now we want to create the mapping that we will be using to import in all of the data. To do this click on the **Generate Source File** button in the menu bar and when the **Wizard** appears, click on the **Next** button to start setting things up.

When the **Display Data** page is shown you will be able to see all of the default fields in the entity map.

Sample Data

Creating a Job Tasks Import Entity

Here are the fields that you will want to have within your **Job Tasks** import definition if you want to use the sample company import template that we provide.

Present in source	Sequence	Field name	Mandatory	Field type	Field size
Yes	1	Description	Yes	String	60
Yes	2	JobTaskId	Yes	String	15

Step By Step Walkthrough

Creating a Job Tasks Import Entity

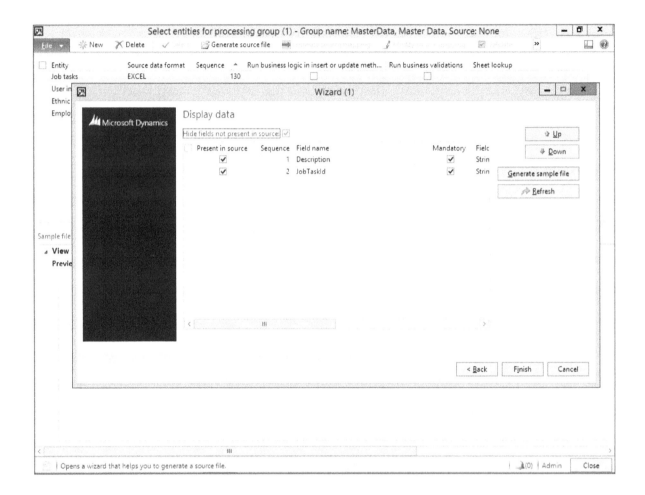

Find each of the fields in the template and then just click on the **Present In Source** checkbox, which will enable to field to be used within the template. If you need to re-order any of the fields then select the field and then click on the **Up** or **Down** buttons to rearrange them.

Once you have all of the fields selected and you have them in the right order then click on the **Generate Sample File** button.

Step By Step Walkthrough

Creating a Job Tasks Import Entity

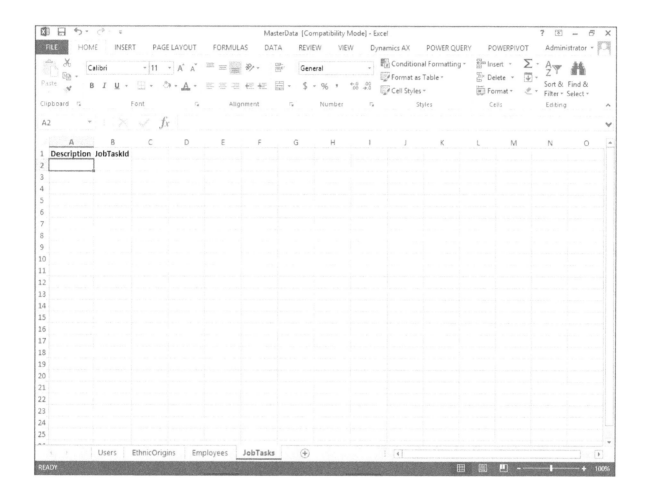

This will create another Excel Workbook for you just like before and the first sheet will already be set up with the fields that you need for the **Job Tasks** import.

Open up the **MasterData** template that you created in the previous step and add a new Worksheet to the workbook by clicking on the **+** button and rename it to **JobTasks.**

Now return to the workbook that was automatically generated by the wizard and select the auto-generated columns and copy them (**CTRL+C**) and paste (**CTRL+V**) them into the **JobTasks** worksheet within the **MasterData** workbook. You may also want to format the columns to make it look tidy.

When you have done that, close out of the **MasterData** workbook.

Step By Step Walkthrough

Creating a Job Tasks Import Entity

When you return back to the wizard, just click on the **Finish** button to exit from the form which will return you to the **Processing** Groups maintenance form. Click on the **Folder** icon to the right of the **Sample File Path** field.

When the file explorer opens navigate to where you saved your **MasterData** worksheet that you just created, and then click on the **Open** button.

Click on the **Sheet Lookup** dropdown list and select the **JobTasks$** record.

Finish off the process by clicking on the **Generate Source Mapping** button within the menu bar. If everything is linked up correctly and you have all of the key fields within your map, then you will get a quick message saying that the entity mapping was completed and you can click on the **Close** button.

Example Data

Creating a Job Tasks Import Entity

Now that you have the worksheet created you can start populating the worksheet with your own set of **Job Tasks**. Here is an example of how the data should look.

Description	ACCOUNTING
JobTaskId	Financials/Accounting

 www.dynamicsaxcompanions.com
Dynamics AX Companions

- 93 -

www.blindsquirrelpublishing.com
© 2015 Blind Squirrel Publishing, LLC , All Rights Reserved

BLIND SQUIRREL
PUBLISHING

Sample Data

Creating a Job Tasks Import Entity

If you are looking for some sample **Job Task** data to load then here is a snapshot of the data that we use in the sample template.

Description	JobTaskId
ACCOUNTING	Financials/Accounting
COMPENSATION	Comp and benefits
CUSTOMER CALLS	Customer calls
FINANCE	Finance
FIXED ASSETS	Fixed Assets
LOGISTICS	Manage Logistics
MANUFACTURING	Manufacturing
PROJECT	Project management
PURCHASING	Purchasing
RECRUITING	Recruiting
SAFETY	Safety
SALES	Sales calls
STRATEGY	Strategy
SUPPORT	Customer support
SYSTEMS	Internal systems

 www.dynamicsaxcompanions.com
Dynamics AX Companions
- 94 -
 www.blindsquirrelpublishing.com
© 2015 Blind Squirrel Publishing, LLC , All Rights Reserved
BLIND SQUIRREL
PUBLISHING

Creating a Jobs Import Entity

Now that we have the **Job Tasks** entity configured we will build out the **Jobs** entity so that we can import all of the default jobs within the organization.

daxc
www.dynamicsaxcompanions.com
Dynamics AX Companions

- 95 -

www.blindsquirrelpublishing.com
© 2015 Blind Squirrel Publishing, LLC, All Rights Reserved

BLIND SQUIRREL
PUBLISHING

Step By Step Walkthrough

Creating a Jobs Import Entity

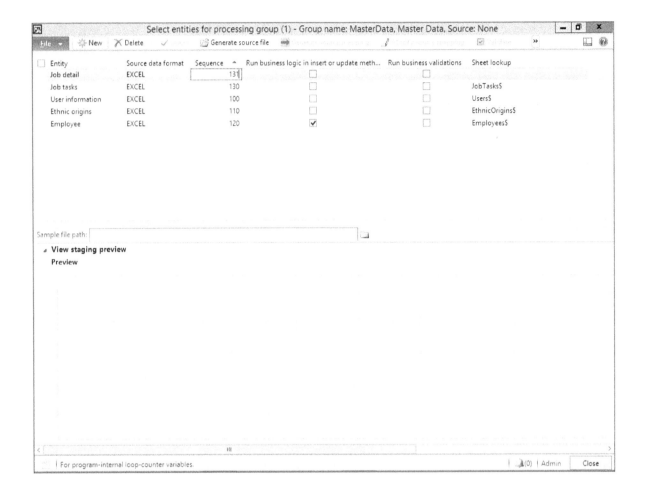

To do this go to the **Processing Group Entities** maintenance form and click on the **New** button within the menu bar to create a new record. Then click on the **Entity** dropdown list and find the **Job Detail** Entity type.

Click on the **Source Data Format** dropdown list and select the **EXCEL** format, and then set the **Sequence** number to **131**.

Now we want to create the mapping that we will be using to import in all of the data. To do this click on the **Generate Source File** button in the menu bar and when the **Wizard** appears, click on the **Next** button to start setting things up.

When the **Display Data** page is shown you will be able to see all of the default fields in the entity map.

www.dynamicsaxcompanions.com
Dynamics AX Companions
- 96 -
www.blindsquirrelpublishing.com
© 2015 Blind Squirrel Publishing, LLC, All Rights Reserved

BLIND SQUIRREL
PUBLISHING

Sample Data

Creating a Jobs Import Entity

Here are the fields that you will want to have within your **Jobs** import definition if you want to use the sample company import template that we provide.

Present in source	Sequence	Field name	Mandatory	Field type	Field size
Yes	1	HcmJobTask_JobTaskId	Yes	String	15
Yes	2	JobId	Yes	String	25
Yes	3	RatingLevelId	Yes	String	10

daxc   www.dynamicsaxcompanions.com
Dynamics AX Companions

- 97 -

www.blindsquirrelpublishing.com
© 2015 Blind Squirrel Publishing, LLC, All Rights Reserved

BLIND SQUIRREL
PUBLISHING

Step By Step Walkthrough

Creating a Jobs Import Entity

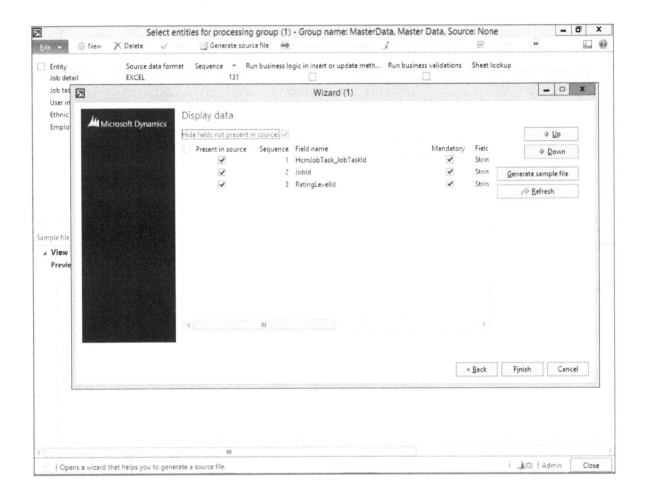

Find each of the fields in the template and then just click on the **Present In Source** checkbox, which will enable to field to be used within the template. If you need to re-order any of the fields then select the field and then click on the **Up** or **Down** buttons to rearrange them.

Once you have all of the fields selected and you have them in the right order then click on the **Generate Sample File** button.

Step By Step Walkthrough

Creating a Jobs Import Entity

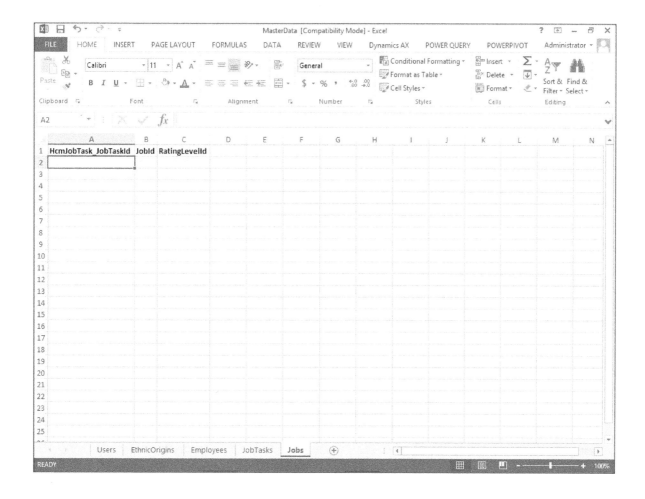

This will create another Excel Workbook for you just like before and the first sheet will already be set up with the fields that you need for the **Jobs** import.

Open up the **MasterData** template that you created in the previous step and add a new Worksheet to the workbook by clicking on the **+** button and rename it to **Jobs.**

Now return to the workbook that was automatically generated by the wizard and select the auto-generated columns and copy them (**CTRL+C**) and paste (**CTRL+V**) them into the **Jobs** worksheet within the **MasterData** workbook. You may also want to format the columns to make it look tidy.

When you have done that, close out of the **MasterData** workbook.

Step By Step Walkthrough

Creating a Jobs Import Entity

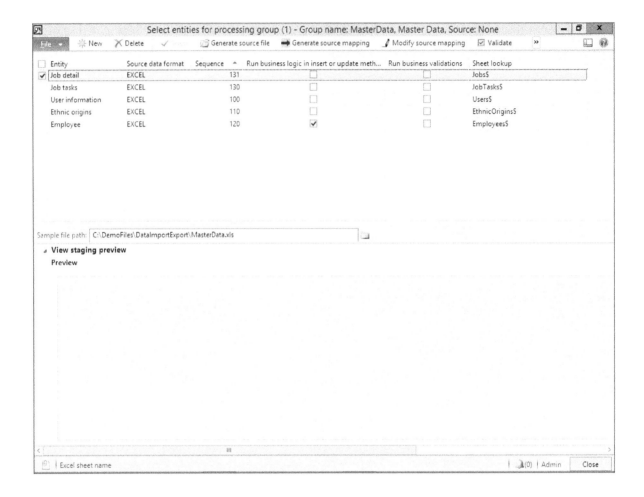

When you return back to the wizard, just click on the **Finish** button to exit from the form which will return you to the **Processing** Groups maintenance form. Click on the **Folder** icon to the right of the **Sample File Path** field.

When the file explorer opens navigate to where you saved your **MasterData** worksheet that you just created, and then click on the **Open** button.

Click on the **Sheet Lookup** dropdown list and select the **Jobs$** record.

Finish off the process by clicking on the **Generate Source Mapping** button within the menu bar. If everything is linked up correctly and you have all of the key fields within your map, then you will get a quick message saying that the entity mapping was completed and you can click on the **Close** button.

Example Data

Creating a Jobs Import Entity

Now that you have the worksheet created you can start populating the worksheet with your own set of **Jobs**. Here is an example of how the data should look.

HcmJobTask_JobTaskId	ACCOUNTING
JobId	Account Manager
RatingLevelId	B1

www.dynamicsaxcompanions.com
Dynamics AX Companions
- 101 -
www.blindsquirrelpublishing.com
© 2015 Blind Squirrel Publishing, LLC, All Rights Reserved
BLIND SQUIRREL
PUBLISHING

Sample Data

Creating a Jobs Import Entity

If you are looking for some sample **Job** data to load then here is a snapshot of the data that we use in the sample templates.

HcmJobTask_JobTaskId	JobId	RatingLevelId
ACCOUNTING	Account Manager	B1
ACCOUNTING	Accountant	B1
ACCOUNTING	Accounting Manager	B1
ACCOUNTING	Allocation Specialist	B1
ACCOUNTING	AP Coordinator	B1
ACCOUNTING	Application Developer	B1
ACCOUNTING	AR Administrator	B1
ACCOUNTING	AR Coordinator	B1
ACCOUNTING	Attorney	B1
ACCOUNTING	Budget Manager	B1
ACCOUNTING	Business Manager	B1
ACCOUNTING	Business System Dev	B1
ACCOUNTING	Catalog Manager	B1
ACCOUNTING	Category Manager	B1
ACCOUNTING	CFO	B1
ACCOUNTING	Client Services Mgr	B1
ACCOUNTING	Comp & Ben Specialist	B1
ACCOUNTING	Consultant	B1
ACCOUNTING	Contract consultant	B1
ACCOUNTING	Controller	B1
ACCOUNTING	Credit & Collections Mgr	B1
ACCOUNTING	Customer Service Mgr	B1
ACCOUNTING	Customer Service Rep	B1
ACCOUNTING	Dedicated Sales Rep	B1

 www.dynamicsaxcompanions.com
Dynamics AX Companions

- 102 -

www.blindsquirrelpublishing.com
© 2015 Blind Squirrel Publishing, LLC , All Rights Reserved

 BLIND SQUIRREL
PUBLISHING

Creating a Position Types Import Entity

Once the **Jobs** have been configured we can start working on the entities that will track the **Positions** within the company and also the reporting structure. The first entity that we need to configure here will be the **Position Types** which will be referenced in the **Positions** entity later on.

 www.blindsquirrelpublishing.com   BLIND SQUIRREL
© 2015 Blind Squirrel Publishing, LLC, All Rights Reserved   PUBLISHING

Step By Step Walkthrough

Creating a Position Types Import Entity

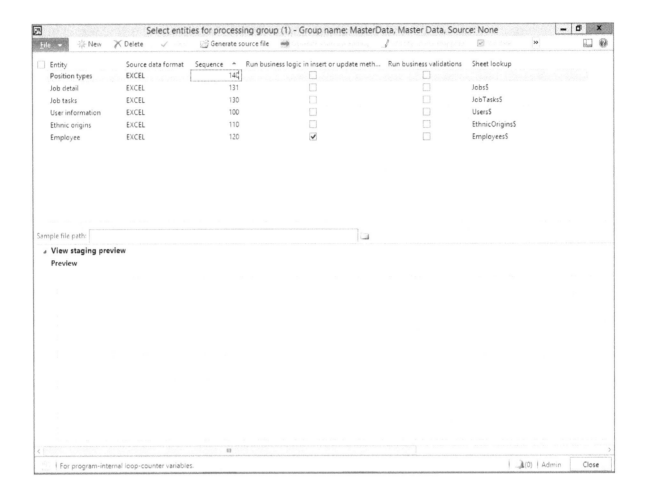

To do this, open the **Processing Group Entities** maintenance form and click on the **New** button within the menu bar to create a new record. Then click on the **Entity** dropdown list and find the **Position Types** Entity type.

Click on the **Source Data Format** dropdown list and select the **EXCEL** format, and then set the **Sequence** number to **140**.

Now we want to create the mapping that we will be using to import in all of the data. To do this click on the **Generate Source File** button in the menu bar and when the **Wizard** appears, click on the **Next** button to start setting things up.

When the **Display Data** page is shown you will be able to see all of the default fields in the entity map.

Sample Data

Creating a Position Types Import Entity

Here are the fields that you will want to have within your **Position Types** import definition if you want to use the sample company import template that we provide.

Present in source	Sequence	Field name	Mandatory	Field type	Field size
Yes	1	TypeId	Yes	String	20
Yes	2	Description	No	String	60
Yes	3	HcmEmploymentStatus	No	String	9

da×c

www.dynamicsaxcompanions.com
Dynamics AX Companions

- 105 -

www.blindsquirrelpublishing.com
© 2015 Blind Squirrel Publishing, LLC, All Rights Reserved

BLIND SQUIRREL
PUBLISHING

Step By Step Walkthrough

Creating a Position Types Import Entity

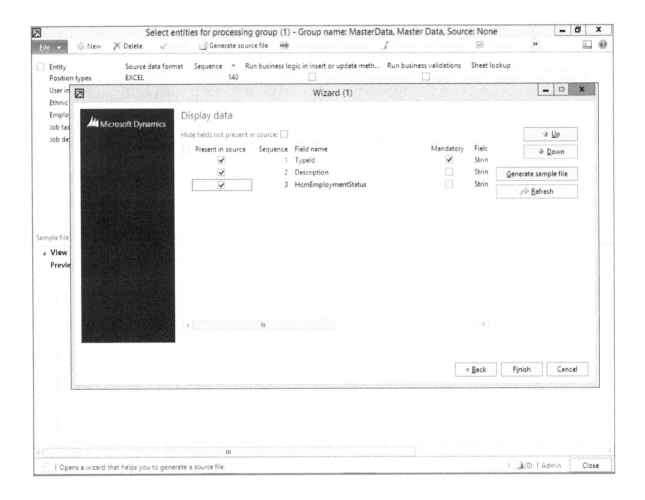

Find each of the fields in the template and then just click on the **Present In Source** checkbox, which will enable to field to be used within the template. If you need to re-order any of the fields then select the field and then click on the **Up** or **Down** buttons to rearrange them.

Once you have all of the fields selected and you have them in the right order then click on the **Generate Sample File** button.

Step By Step Walkthrough

Creating a Position Types Import Entity

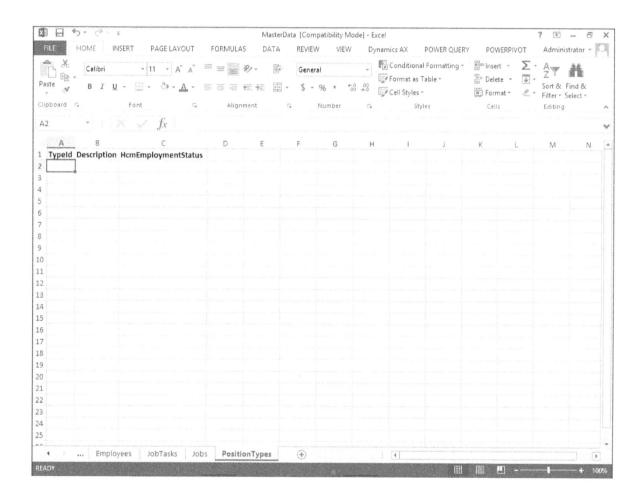

This will create another Excel Workbook for you just like before and the first sheet will already be set up with the fields that you need for the **Position Types** import.

Open up the **MasterData** template that you created in the previous step and add a new Worksheet to the workbook by clicking on the **+** button and rename it to **PositionTypes.**

Now return to the workbook that was automatically generated by the wizard and select the auto-generated columns and copy them (**CTRL+C**) and paste (**CTRL+V**) them into the **PositionTypes** worksheet within the **MasterData** workbook. You may also want to format the columns to make it look tidy.

When you have done that, close out of the **MasterData** workbook.

Step By Step Walkthrough

Creating a Position Types Import Entity

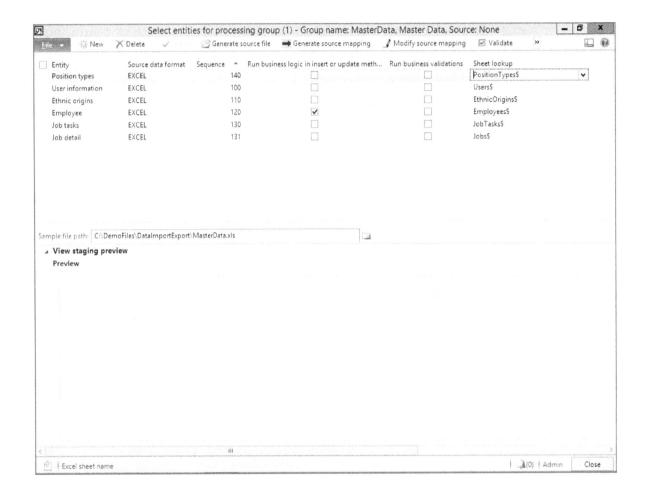

When you return back to the wizard, just click on the **Finish** button to exit from the form which will return you to the **Processing** Groups maintenance form. Click on the **Folder** icon to the right of the **Sample File Path** field.

When the file explorer opens navigate to where you saved your **MasterData** worksheet that you just created, and then click on the **Open** button.

Click on the **Sheet Lookup** dropdown list and select the **PositionTypes$** record.

Finish off the process by clicking on the **Generate Source Mapping** button within the menu bar. If everything is linked up correctly and you have all of the key fields within your map, then you will get a quick message saying that the entity mapping was completed and you can click on the **Close** button.

Example Data

Creating a Position Types Import Entity

Now that you have the worksheet created you can start populating the worksheet with your own set of **Position Types**. Here is an example of how the data should look.

TypeId	Full-time
Description	Full-time employee
HcmEmploymentStatus	Full-time

Sample Data

Creating a Position Types Import Entity

If you are looking for some sample **Position Type** data to load then here is a snapshot of the data that we use in the sample template.

TypeId	Description	HcmEmploymentStatus
Full-time	Full-time employee	Full-time
Part-time	Part-time employee	Part-time

Creating a Positions Import Entity

Now we will create the import entity for the **Positions** which are also linked back to the **Jobs** entity.

Step By Step Walkthrough

Creating a Positions Import Entity

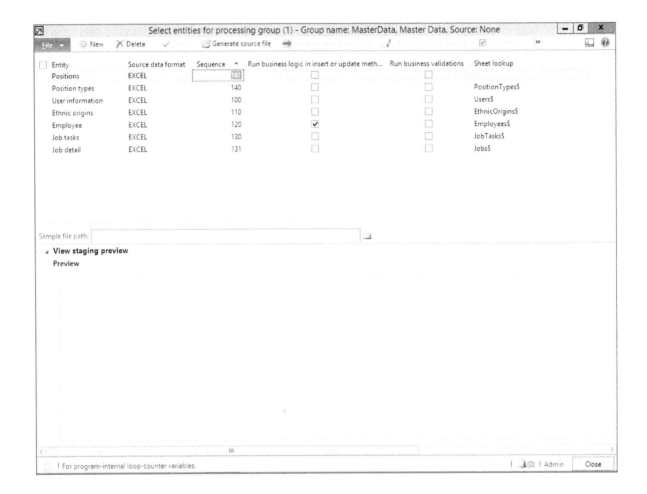

To do this return to the **Processing Group Entities** maintenance form and click on the **New** button within the menu bar to create a new record. Then click on the **Entity** dropdown list and find the **Positions** Entity type.

Click on the **Source Data Format** dropdown list and select the **EXCEL** format, and then set the **Sequence** number to **141**.

Now we want to create the mapping that we will be using to import in all of the data. To do this click on the **Generate Source File** button in the menu bar and when the **Wizard** appears, click on the **Next** button to start setting things up.

When the **Display Data** page is shown you will be able to see all of the default fields in the entity map.

Sample Data

Creating a Positions Import Entity

Here are the fields that you will want to have within your **Positions** import definition if you want to use the sample company import template that we provide.

Present in source	Sequence	Field name	Mandatory	Field type	Field size
Yes	1	PositionId	Yes	String	25
Yes	2	Description	No	String	60
Yes	3	HcmJob_JobId	No	String	25
Yes	4	HcmTitle_TitleId	No	String	30
Yes	5	HcmPositionType_TypeId	No	String	20
Yes	6	HcmPositionDuration_ValidFrom	No	DateTime	30
Yes	7	HcmPositionDuration_ValidTo	No	DateTime	30
Yes	8	HcmPositionHierarchy_ParentPositionId	No	String	25
Yes	9	HcmPositionHierarchyType_Name	No	String	60

Step By Step Walkthrough

Creating a Positions Import Entity

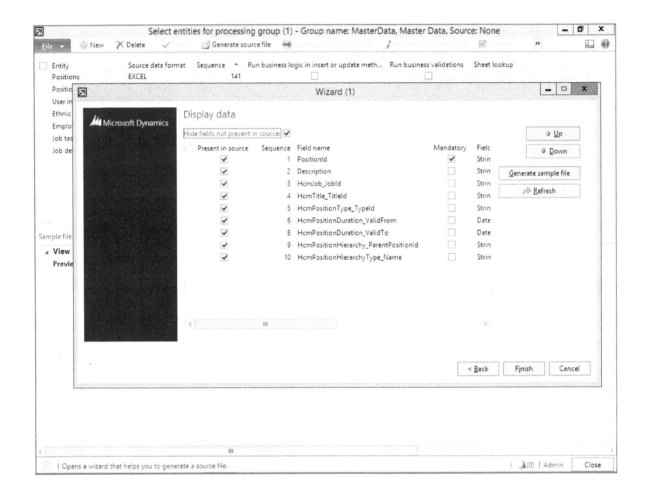

Find each of the fields in the template and then just click on the **Present In Source** checkbox, which will enable to field to be used within the template. If you need to re-order any of the fields then select the field and then click on the **Up** or **Down** buttons to rearrange them.

Once you have all of the fields selected and you have them in the right order then click on the **Generate Sample File** button.

daxc   www.dynamicsaxcompanions.com
        Dynamics AX Companions

- 114 -

www.blindsquirrelpublishing.com
© 2015 Blind Squirrel Publishing, LLC , All Rights Reserved

BLIND SQUIRREL
PUBLISHING

Step By Step Walkthrough

Creating a Positions Import Entity

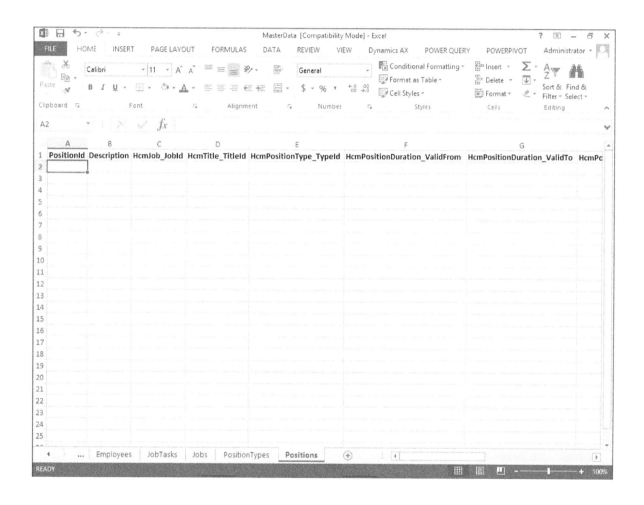

This will create another Excel Workbook for you just like before and the first sheet will already be set up with the fields that you need for the **Positions** import.

Open up the **MasterData** template that you created in the previous step and add a new Worksheet to the workbook by clicking on the **+** button and rename it to **Positions.**

Now return to the workbook that was automatically generated by the wizard and select the auto-generated columns and copy them (**CTRL+C**) and paste (**CTRL+V**) them into the **Positions** worksheet within the **MasterData** workbook. You may also want to format the columns to make it look tidy.

When you have done that, close out of the **MasterData** workbook.

Step By Step Walkthrough

Creating a Positions Import Entity

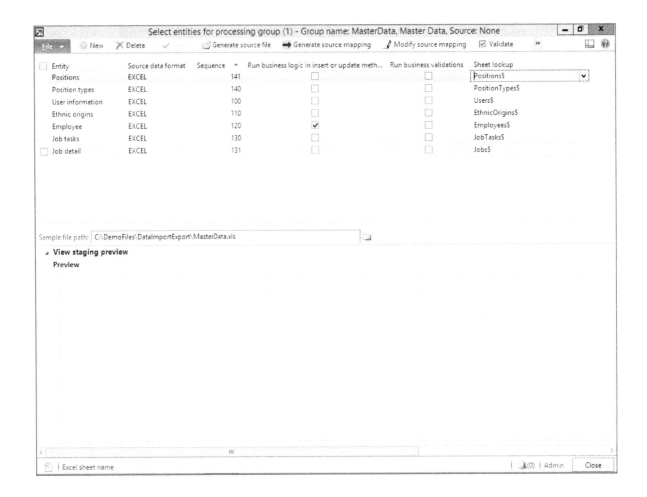

When you return back to the wizard, just click on the **Finish** button to exit from the form which will return you to the **Processing** Groups maintenance form. Click on the **Folder** icon to the right of the **Sample File Path** field.

When the file explorer opens navigate to where you saved your **MasterData** worksheet that you just created, and then click on the **Open** button.

Click on the **Sheet Lookup** dropdown list and select the **Positions$** record.

Finish off the process by clicking on the **Generate Source Mapping** button within the menu bar. If everything is linked up correctly and you have all of the key fields within your map, then you will get a quick message saying that the entity mapping was completed and you can click on the **Close** button.

 www.dynamicsaxcompanions.com
Dynamics AX Companions
- 116 -
www.blindsquirrelpublishing.com
© 2015 Blind Squirrel Publishing, LLC, All Rights Reserved
BLIND SQUIRREL
PUBLISHING

Example Data

Creating a Positions Import Entity

Now that you have the worksheet created you can start populating the worksheet with your own set of **Positions**. Here is an example of how the data should look.

HcmJob_JobId	Waterspider
HcmTitle_TitleId	Waterspider
HcmPositionType_TypeId	Full-time
HcmPositionDuration_ValidFrom	1/1/2014
HcmPositionDuration_ValidTo	12/31/2154
HcmPositionHierarchy_ParentPositionId	100280
HcmPositionHierarchyType_Name	Line

 www.dynamicsaxcompanions.com
Dynamics AX Companions
- 117 -
www.blindsquirrelpublishing.com
© 2015 Blind Squirrel Publishing, LLC , All Rights Reserved
BLIND SQUIRREL
PUBLISHING

Sample Data

Creating a Positions Import Entity

If you are looking for some sample **Position** data to load then here is a snapshot of the data that we use in the sample template.

Position Id	Description	HcmJob_Job Id	HcmTitle_Title Id	HcmPositionType_Type Id	HcmPositionDuration_Valid From	HcmPositionDuration_Valid To	HcmPositionHierarchy_ParentPosition Id	HcmPositionHierarchyType_Name
100001	Waterspider	Waterspider	Waterspider	Full-time	1/1/2014	12/31/2154	100280	Line
100002	Warehouse Worker	Warehouse Worker	Warehouse Worker	Full-time	1/1/2014	12/31/2154	100003	Line
100003	Warehouse Manager	Warehouse Manager	Warehouse Manager	Full-time	1/1/2014	12/31/2154	100320	Line
100004	Warehouse Manager	Warehouse Manager	Warehouse Manager	Full-time	1/1/2014	12/31/2154	100318	Line
100005	Value Stream Manager	Value Stream Manager	Value Stream Manager	Full-time	1/1/2014	12/31/2154	100007	Line
100006	Treasurer	Treasurer	Treasurer	Full-time	1/1/2014	12/31/2154	100105	Line
100007	Transport Coordinator	Transport Coordinator	Transport Coordinator	Full-time	1/1/2014	12/31/2154	100320	Line
100008	Store Manager	Store Manager	Store Manager - USA Central	Full-time	1/1/2014	12/31/2154	100249	Line
100009	Store Manager	Store Manager	Store Manager - USA West	Full-time	1/1/2014	12/31/2154	100247	Line
100010	Store Manager	Store Manager	Store Manager - Europe	Full-time	1/1/2014	12/31/2154	100248	Line
100011	Store Manager	Store Manager	Store Manager - Europe	Full-time	1/1/2014	12/31/2154	100248	Line
100012	Store Manager	Store Manager	Store Manager - USA East	Full-time	1/1/2014	12/31/2154	100246	Line
100013	Store Manager	Store Manager	Store Manager - USA Central	Full-time	1/1/2014	12/31/2154	100249	Line
100014	Store Manager	Store Manager	Store Manager - USA Central	Full-time	1/1/2014	12/31/2154	100249	Line
100015	Store Manager	Store Manager	Store Manager - USA West	Full-time	1/1/2014	12/31/2154	100247	Line
100016	Store Manager	Store Manager	Store Manager - USA Central	Full-time	1/1/2014	12/31/2154	100249	Line
100017	Store Manager	Store Manager	Store Manager - USA East	Full-time	1/1/2014	12/31/2154	100246	Line
100018	Store Manager	Store Manager	Store Manager - USA West	Full-time	1/1/2014	12/31/2154	100247	Line
100019	Store Manager	Store Manager	Store Manager - USA West	Full-time	1/1/2014	12/31/2154	100247	Line
100020	Store Manager	Store Manager	Store Manager - Europe	Full-time	1/1/2014	12/31/2154	100248	Line
100021	Store Manager	Store Manager	Store Manager - USA Central	Full-time	1/1/2014	12/31/2154	100249	Line
100022	Sales Associate	Sales Associate	Sales Associate - USA East	Full-time	1/1/2014	12/31/2154	100246	Line
100023	Store Manager	Store Manager	Store Manager - Europe	Full-time	1/1/2014	12/31/2154	100248	Line
100024	Store Manager	Store Manager	Store Manager - USA Central	Full-time	1/1/2014	12/31/2154	100249	Line

daxc
www.dynamicsaxcompanions.com
Dynamics AX Companions

- 119 -

www.blindsquirrelpublishing.com
© 2015 Blind Squirrel Publishing, LLC, All Rights Reserved

BLIND SQUIRREL
PUBLISHING

Creating a Main Account Categories Import Entity

Now we will move on to the entities that are related to the **General Ledger** and create the entities to load in the Chart Of Accounts. The first entity that we will configure will be the **Main Account Categories** which will be used by the **Main Accounts** entity in the next step.

Step By Step Walkthrough

Creating a Main Account Categories Import Entity

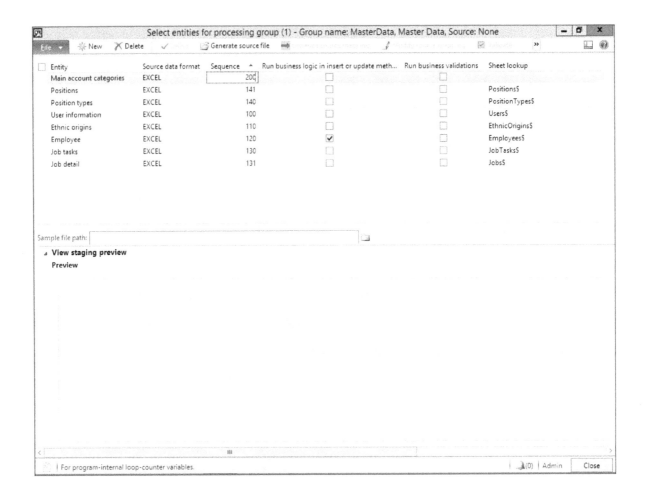

To do this, open the **Processing Group Entities** maintenance form and click on the **New** button within the menu bar to create a new record. Then click on the **Entity** dropdown list and find the **Main Account Categories** Entity type.

Click on the **Source Data Format** dropdown list and select the **EXCEL** format, and then set the **Sequence** number to **200**.

Now we want to create the mapping that we will be using to import in all of the data. To do this click on the **Generate Source File** button in the menu bar and when the **Wizard** appears, click on the **Next** button to start setting things up.

When the **Display Data** page is shown you will be able to see all of the default fields in the entity map.

Sample Data

Creating a Main Account Categories Import Entity

Here are the fields that you will want to have within your **Main Account Category** import definition if you want to use the sample company import template that we provide.

Present in source	Sequence	Field name	Mandatory	Field type	Field size
Yes	1	AccountCategory	Yes	String	20
Yes	2	AccountCategoryRef	Yes	Integer	11
Yes	3	Description	No	String	60
Yes	4	AccountType	No	String	15
Yes	5	Closed	No	String	6

Step By Step Walkthrough

Creating a Main Account Categories Import Entity

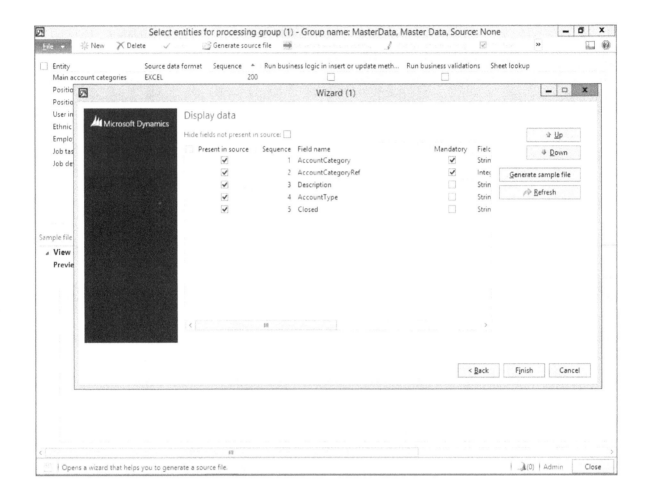

Find each of the fields in the template and then just click on the **Present In Source** checkbox, which will enable to field to be used within the template. If you need to re-order any of the fields then select the field and then click on the **Up** or **Down** buttons to rearrange them.

Once you have all of the fields selected and you have them in the right order then click on the **Generate Sample File** button.

Step By Step Walkthrough

Creating a Main Account Categories Import Entity

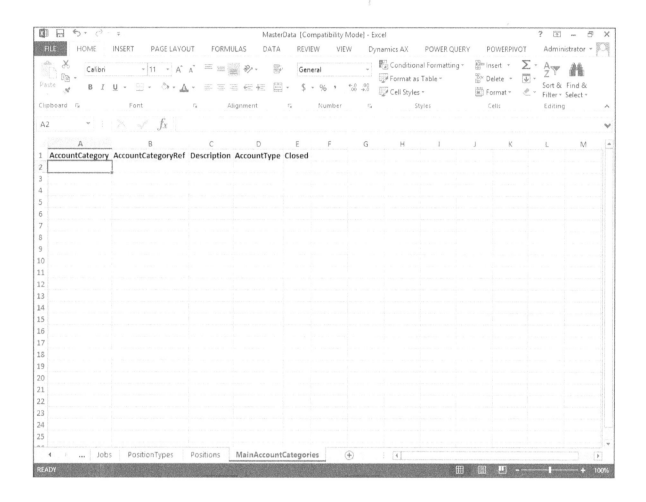

This will create another Excel Workbook for you just like before and the first sheet will already be set up with the fields that you need for the **Main Account Categories** import.

Open up the **MasterData** template that you created in the previous step and add a new Worksheet to the workbook by clicking on the **+** button and rename it to **MainAccountCategories.**

Now return to the workbook that was automatically generated by the wizard and select the auto-generated columns and copy them (**CTRL+C**) and paste (**CTRL+V**) them into the **MainAccountCategories** worksheet within the **MasterData** workbook. You may also want to format the columns to make it look tidy.

When you have done that, close out of the **MasterData** workbook.

Step By Step Walkthrough

Creating a Main Account Categories Import Entity

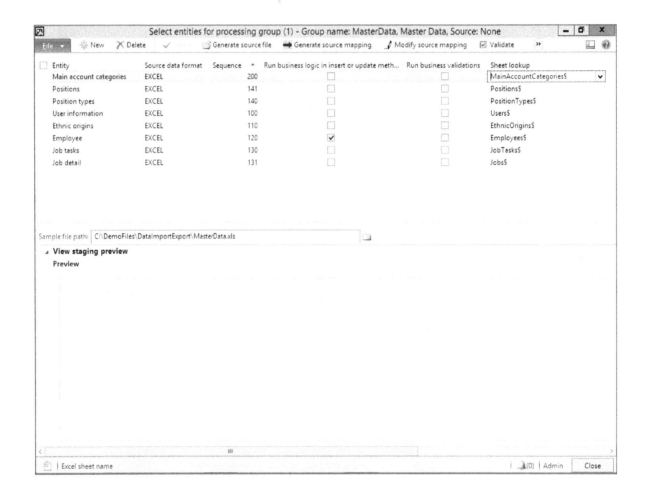

When you return back to the wizard, just click on the **Finish** button to exit from the form which will return you to the **Processing** Groups maintenance form. Click on the **Folder** icon to the right of the **Sample File Path** field.

When the file explorer opens navigate to where you saved your **MasterData** worksheet that you just created, and then click on the **Open** button.

Click on the **Sheet Lookup** dropdown list and select the **MainAccountCategories$** record.

Finish off the process by clicking on the **Generate Source Mapping** button within the menu bar. If everything is linked up correctly and you have all of the key fields within your map, then you will get a quick message saying that the entity mapping was completed and you can click on the **Close** button.

Example Data

Creating a Main Account Categories Import Entity

Now that you have the worksheet created you can start populating the worksheet with your own set of **Main Account Categories**. Here is an example of how the data should look.

AccountCategory	CASH
AccountCategoryRef	1
Description	Cash
AccountType	
Closed	No

www.dynamicsaxcompanions.com
Dynamics AX Companions

- 127 -

www.blindsquirrelpublishing.com
© 2015 Blind Squirrel Publishing, LLC, All Rights Reserved

BLIND SQUIRREL
PUBLISHING

Sample Data

Creating a Main Account Categories Import Entity

If you are looking for some sample **Main Account Category** data to load then here is a snapshot of the data that we use in the sample template.

AccountCategory	AccountCategoryRef	Description	AccountType	Closed
CASH	1	Cash		No
CASHEQUIV	2	Cash Equivalents		No
SHORTTERMINVEST	3	Short-term investments		No
AR	4	Accounts Receivable		No
INV	5	Inventory		No
NOTESREC	6	Notes Receivables		No
WIP	7	Work in Process		No
PREPAIDEXP	8	Prepaid Expenses		No
OTHERCA	9	Other Current Assets		No
LONGTERMINVEST	10	Long-term investments		No
PPE	11	Property Plant and Equipment		No
ACCUDEP	12	Accumulated Depreciation		No
INTANASSET	13	Intangible Assets		No
OTHERASSET	14	Other Assets		No
AP	15	Accounts Payable		No
NOTESPAY	16	Notes Payable		No
CURRENTMATLTD	17	Current maturities on long-term debt		No
TAXPAY	18	Taxes Payable		No
INTPAY	19	Interest Payable		No
DIVPAY	20	Dividends Payable		No
LEASEPAY	21	Leases Payable (Current)		No
SINKPAY	22	Sinking Fund Payable (Current)		No
OTHERCURLIA	23	Other Current Liabilities		No
LONGTERMDEBT	24	Long-term debt		No

Creating a Main Account Import Entity

Now we will configure the **Main Account** entity which will automatically be attached to the existing **Chart Of Accounts**.

www.dynamicsaxcompanions.com
Dynamics AX Companions

- 129 -

www.blindsquirrelpublishing.com
© 2015 Blind Squirrel Publishing, LLC, All Rights Reserved   BLIND SQUIRREL
                                                                         PUBLISHING

Step By Step Walkthrough

Creating a Main Account Import Entity

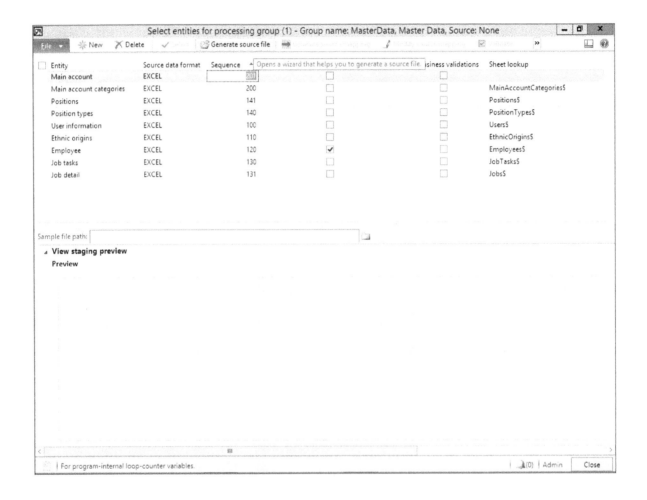

Return to the **Processing Group Entities** maintenance form and click on the **New** button within the menu bar to create a new record. Then click on the **Entity** dropdown list and find the **Main Account** Entity type.

Click on the **Source Data Format** dropdown list and select the **EXCEL** format, and then set the **Sequence** number to **201**.

Now we want to create the mapping that we will be using to import in all of the data. To do this click on the **Generate Source File** button in the menu bar and when the **Wizard** appears, click on the **Next** button to start setting things up.

When the **Display Data** page is shown you will be able to see all of the default fields in the entity map.

   www.dynamicsaxcompanions.com
Dynamics AX Companions
- 130 -
www.blindsquirrelpublishing.com
© 2015 Blind Squirrel Publishing, LLC, All Rights Reserved
BLIND SQUIRREL
PUBLISHING

Sample Data

Creating a Main Account Import Entity

Here are the fields that you will want to have within your **Main Acocunt** import definition if you want to use the sample company import template that we provide.

Present in source	Sequence	Field name	Mandatory	Field type	Field size
Yes	1	ChartOfAccounts	No	String	60
Yes	2	MainAccountId	Yes	String	20
Yes	3	Name	Yes	String	60
Yes	4	Type	No	String	16
Yes	5	AccountCategory	No	String	20

Step By Step Walkthrough

Creating a Main Account Import Entity

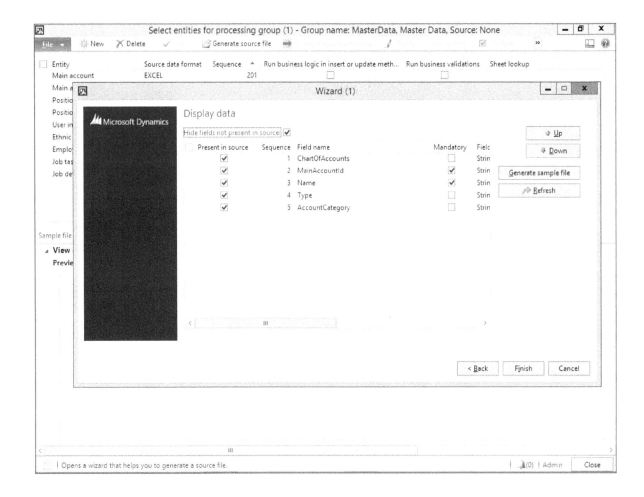

Find each of the fields in the template and then just click on the **Present In Source** checkbox, which will enable to field to be used within the template. If you need to re-order any of the fields then select the field and then click on the **Up** or **Down** buttons to rearrange them.

Once you have all of the fields selected and you have them in the right order then click on the **Generate Sample File** button.

Step By Step Walkthrough

Creating a Main Account Import Entity

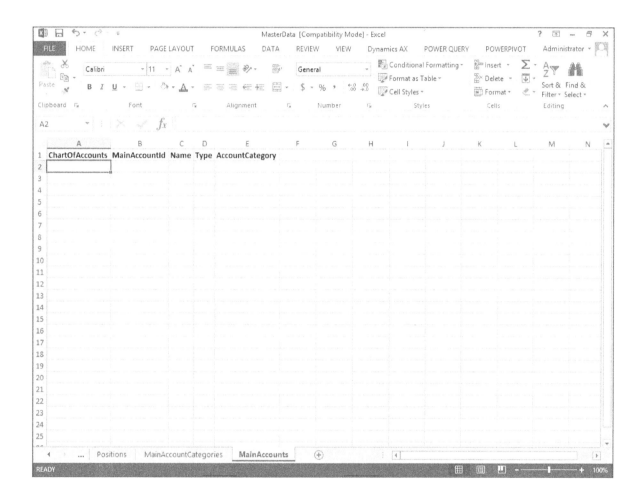

This will create another Excel Workbook for you just like before and the first sheet will already be set up with the fields that you need for the **Main Accounts** import.

Open up the **MasterData** template that you created in the previous step and add a new Worksheet to the workbook by clicking on the + button and rename it to **MainAccounts.**

Now return to the workbook that was automatically generated by the wizard and select the auto-generated columns and copy them (**CTRL+C**) and paste (**CTRL+V**) them into the **MainAccounts** worksheet within the **MasterData** workbook. You may also want to format the columns to make it look tidy.

When you have done that, close out of the **MasterData** workbook.

dαxc   www.dynamicsaxcompanions.com
Dynamics AX Companions

- 133 -

www.blindsquirrelpublishing.com
© 2015 Blind Squirrel Publishing, LLC, All Rights Reserved

BLIND SQUIRREL
PUBLISHING

Step By Step Walkthrough

Creating a Main Account Import Entity

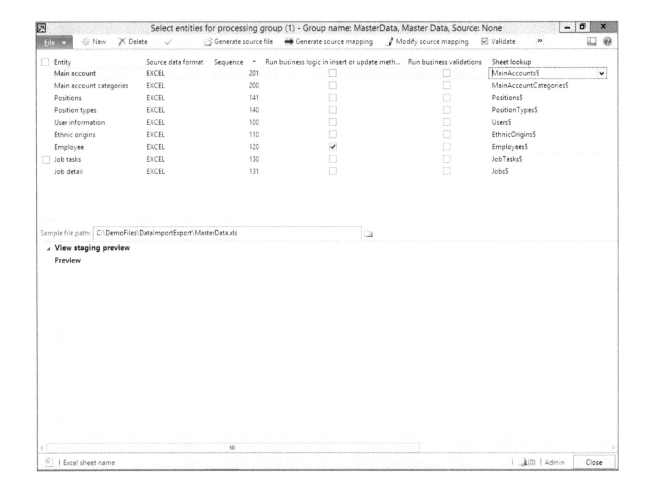

When you return back to the wizard, just click on the **Finish** button to exit from the form which will return you to the **Processing** Groups maintenance form. Click on the **Folder** icon to the right of the **Sample File Path** field.

When the file explorer opens navigate to where you saved your **MasterData** worksheet that you just created, and then click on the **Open** button.

Click on the **Sheet Lookup** dropdown list and select the **MainAccounts$** record.

Finish off the process by clicking on the **Generate Source Mapping** button within the menu bar. If everything is linked up correctly and you have all of the key fields within your map, then you will get a quick message saying that the entity mapping was completed and you can click on the **Close** button.

Example Data

Creating a Main Account Import Entity

Now that you have the worksheet created you can start populating the worksheet with your own set of **Main Accounts**. Here is an example of how the data should look.

ChartOfAccounts	Standard
MainAccountId	110110
Name	Bank Account - USD
Type	Balance sheet
AccountCategory	CASH

www.dynamicsaxcompanions.com
Dynamics AX Companions

- 135 -

www.blindsquirrelpublishing.com
© 2015 Blind Squirrel Publishing, LLC, All Rights Reserved

BLIND SQUIRREL
PUBLISHING

Sample Data

Creating a Main Account Import Entity

If you are looking for some sample **Main Account** data to load then here is a snapshot of the data that we use in the sample template.

ChartOfAccounts	MainAccountId	Name	Type	AccountCategory
Standard	110110	Bank Account - USD	Balance sheet	CASH
Standard	110120	Bank Account - CNY	Balance sheet	CASH
Standard	110130	Bank Account - EUR	Balance sheet	CASH
Standard	110140	Bank Account - RUB	Balance sheet	CASH
Standard	110141	Bank Account - DKK	Balance sheet	
Standard	110150	Bank Account - GBP	Balance sheet	CASH
Standard	110151	USD Cash Advances Account	Balance sheet	CASH
Standard	110152	EUR Cash Advances Account	Balance sheet	CASH
Standard	110153	CAD Cash Advances Account	Balance sheet	CASH
Standard	110154	Yuan Cash Advances Account	Balance sheet	CASH
Standard	110155	All Other Cash Advances Account	Balance sheet	CASH
Standard	110156	Future Bank	Balance sheet	
Standard	110157	Scandinavian Trade Bank DKK	Balance sheet	
Standard	110158	Scandinavian Trade Bank EUR	Balance sheet	
Standard	110160	Bank Account - Payroll	Balance sheet	CASH
Standard	110170	Cash in bank - US (Fixed asset purch)	Balance sheet	CASH
Standard	110180	Petty Cash	Balance sheet	CASH
Standard	119000	TOTAL CASH & CASH EQUIVALENTS	Total	
Standard	120100	Bonds	Balance sheet	SHORTTERMINVEST
Standard	120200	Other Marketable Securities	Balance sheet	LONGTERMINVEST
Standard	120300	Bill of Exchange (BOE)	Balance sheet	SHORTTERMINVEST
Standard	120400	BOE Remitted for Collection	Balance sheet	SHORTTERMINVEST

	BOE Remitted for		
Standard	120500 Discount	Balance sheet	SHORTTERMINVEST
Standard	120600 Protested BOE	Balance sheet	SHORTTERMINVEST

Creating a Line of Business Import Entity

Now we will move on to configure the entities for some of the **Customer** data. Before we load the customers though we will want to configure some of the codes that will be associated with the customer records. We will start by creating an Entity for the **Lines Of Business**.

Step By Step Walkthrough

Creating a Line of Business Import Entity

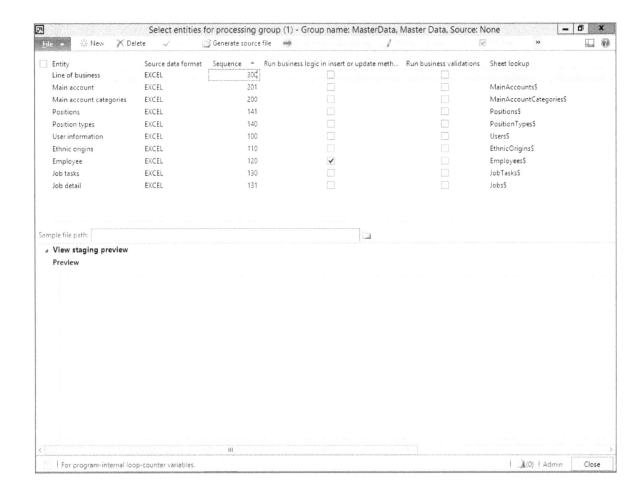

Return to the **Processing Group Entities** maintenance form and click on the **New** button within the menu bar to create a new record. Then click on the **Entity** dropdown list and find the **Line of Business** Entity type.

Click on the **Source Data Format** dropdown list and select the **EXCEL** format, and then set the **Sequence** number to **300**.

Now we want to create the mapping that we will be using to import in all of the data. To do this click on the **Generate Source File** button in the menu bar and when the **Wizard** appears, click on the **Next** button to start setting things up.

When the **Display Data** page is shown you will be able to see all of the default fields in the entity map.

www.dynamicsaxcompanions.com
Dynamics AX Companions

- 140 -

www.blindsquirrelpublishing.com
© 2015 Blind Squirrel Publishing, LLC, All Rights Reserved

BLIND SQUIRREL
PUBLISHING

Sample Data

Creating a Line of Business Import Entity

Here are the fields that you will want to have within your **Line Of Business** import definition if you want to use the sample company import template that we provide.

Present in source	Sequence	Field name	Mandatory	Field type	Field size
Yes	1	LineOfBusinessId	Yes	String	10
Yes	2	Description	No	String	60

Step By Step Walkthrough

Creating a Line of Business Import Entity

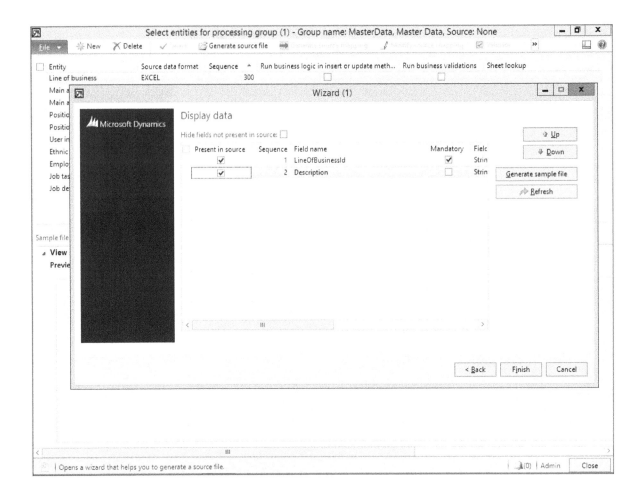

Find each of the fields in the template and then just click on the **Present In Source** checkbox, which will enable to field to be used within the template. If you need to re-order any of the fields then select the field and then click on the **Up** or **Down** buttons to rearrange them.

Once you have all of the fields selected and you have them in the right order then click on the **Generate Sample File** button.

   www.dynamicsaxcompanions.com
Dynamics AX Companions

- 142 -

www.blindsquirrelpublishing.com
© 2015 Blind Squirrel Publishing, LLC , All Rights Reserved

BLIND SQUIRREL
PUBLISHING

Step By Step Walkthrough

Creating a Line of Business Import Entity

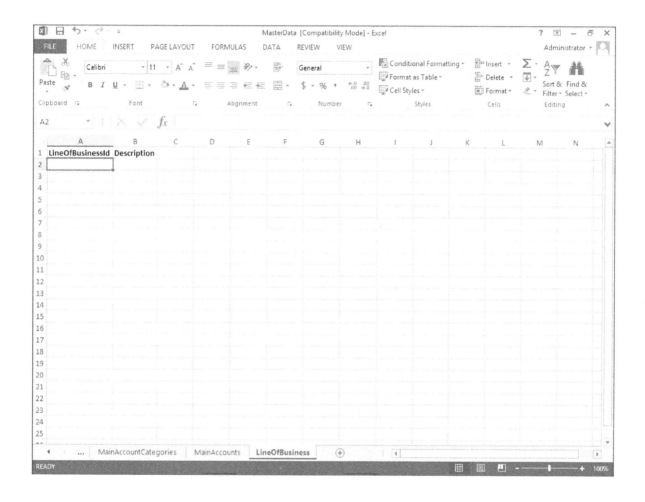

This will create another Excel Workbook for you just like before and the first sheet will already be set up with the fields that you need for the **Line Of Business** import.

Open up the **MasterData** template that you created in the previous step and add a new Worksheet to the workbook by clicking on the **+** button and rename it to **LineOfBusiness.**

Now return to the workbook that was automatically generated by the wizard and select the auto-generated columns and copy them (**CTRL+C**) and paste (**CTRL+V**) them into the **LineOfBusiness** worksheet within the **MasterData** workbook. You may also want to format the columns to make it look tidy.

When you have done that, close out of the **MasterData** workbook.

Step By Step Walkthrough

Creating a Line of Business Import Entity

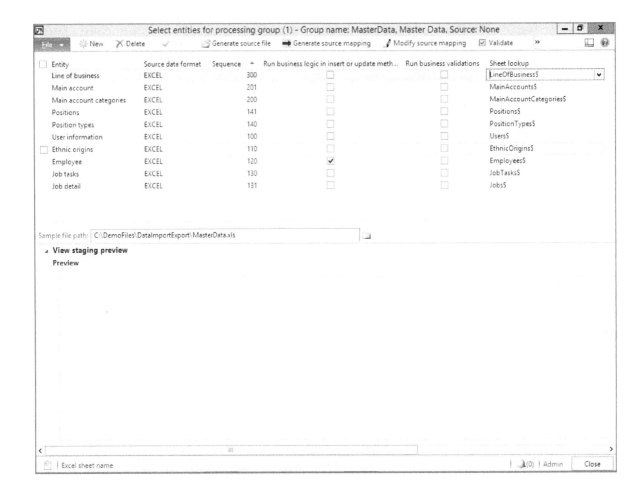

When you return back to the wizard, just click on the **Finish** button to exit from the form which will return you to the **Processing** Groups maintenance form. Click on the **Folder** icon to the right of the **Sample File Path** field.

When the file explorer opens navigate to where you saved your **MasterData** worksheet that you just created, and then click on the **Open** button.

Click on the **Sheet Lookup** dropdown list and select the **LineOfBusiness$** record.

Finish off the process by clicking on the **Generate Source Mapping** button within the menu bar. If everything is linked up correctly and you have all of the key fields within your map, then you will get a quick message saying that the entity mapping was completed and you can click on the **Close** button.

Example Data

Creating a Line of Business Import Entity

Now that you have the worksheet created you can start populating the worksheet with your own set of **Lines of Business**. Here is an example of how the data should look.

LineOfBusinessId	1000
Description	Hospitality

www.dynamicsaxcompanions.com
Dynamics AX Companions
- 145 -
www.blindsquirrelpublishing.com
© 2015 Blind Squirrel Publishing, LLC, All Rights Reserved
BLIND SQUIRREL
PUBLISHING

Sample Data

Creating a Line of Business Import Entity

If you are looking for some sample **Line Of Business** data to load then here is a snapshot of the data that we use in the sample template.

LineOfBusinessId	Description
1000	Hospitality
1003	Training Centers
1004	Education
1100	Entertainment
1200	Travel
1202	Emerging markets
2100	Wholesalers
2400	Lumber & wood products
2650	Paperboard containers & boxes
2851	Paints, varnishes, & lacquers
3080	Miscellaneous plastics products
3100	Retailers
3452	Nuts, bolts, screws, & rivets
3600	Electronic equipment
3672	Printed circuit boards
4100	Internet
7380	Miscellaneous business services

Creating a Customer Groups Import Entity

Next we will need to configure the **Customer Groups** entity. We need to have this because the Customers will not be imported if the **Customer Groups** have not been loaded.

www.dynamicsaxcompanions.com
Dynamics AX Companions

- 147 -

www.blindsquirrelpublishing.com
© 2015 Blind Squirrel Publishing, LLC, All Rights Reserved

BLIND SQUIRREL
PUBLISHING

Step By Step Walkthrough

Creating a Customer Groups Import Entity

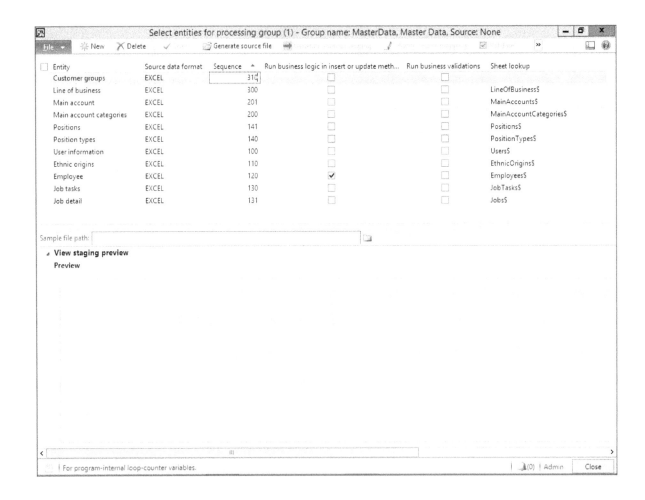

To do this, return to the **Processing Group Entities** maintenance form and click on the **New** button within the menu bar to create a new record. Then click on the **Entity** dropdown list and find the **Customer Groups** Entity type.

Click on the **Source Data Format** dropdown list and select the **EXCEL** format, and then set the **Sequence** number to **310**.

Now we want to create the mapping that we will be using to import in all of the data. To do this click on the **Generate Source File** button in the menu bar and when the **Wizard** appears, click on the **Next** button to start setting things up.

When the **Display Data** page is shown you will be able to see all of the default fields in the entity map.

Sample Data

Creating a Customer Groups Import Entity

Here are the fields that you will want to have within your **Customer Groups** import definition if you want to use the sample company import template that we provide.

Present in source	Sequence	Field name	Mandatory	Field type	Field size
Yes	1	CustGroup	Yes	String	10
Yes	2	Name	No	String	60
Yes	3	PaymTermId	No	String	10
Yes	4	ClearingPeriod	No	String	10
Yes	5	TaxGroupId	No	String	10
Yes	6	PriceIncludeSalesTax	No	String	6

www.blindsquirrelpublishing.com
© 2015 Blind Squirrel Publishing, LLC , All Rights Reserved
BLIND SQUIRREL
PUBLISHING

Step By Step Walkthrough

Creating a Customer Groups Import Entity

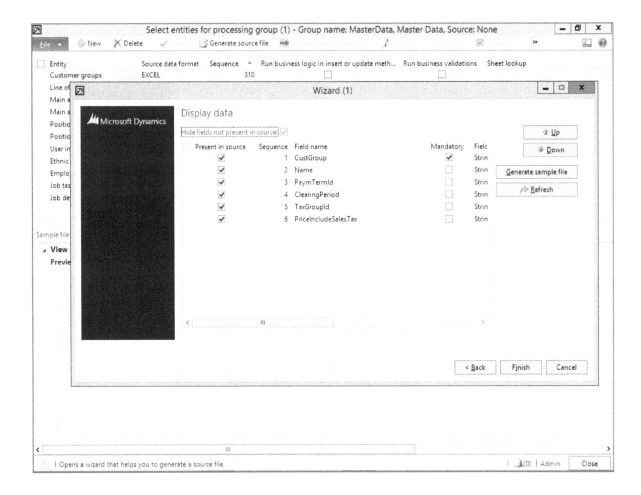

Find each of the fields in the template and then just click on the **Present In Source** checkbox, which will enable to field to be used within the template. If you need to re-order any of the fields then select the field and then click on the **Up** or **Down** buttons to rearrange them.

Once you have all of the fields selected and you have them in the right order then click on the **Generate Sample File** button.

Step By Step Walkthrough

Creating a Customer Groups Import Entity

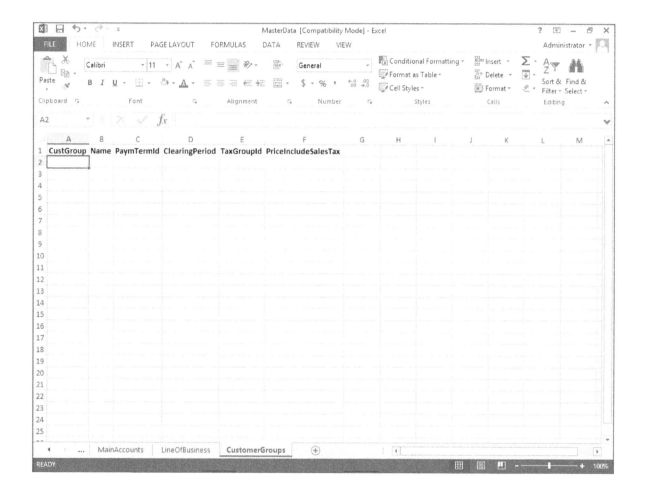

This will create another Excel Workbook for you just like before and the first sheet will already be set up with the fields that you need for the **Customer Groups** import.

Open up the **MasterData** template that you created in the previous step and add a new Worksheet to the workbook by clicking on the **+** button and rename it to **CustomerGroups.**

Now return to the workbook that was automatically generated by the wizard and select the auto-generated columns and copy them (**CTRL+C**) and paste (**CTRL+V**) them into the **CustomerGroups** worksheet within the **MasterData** workbook. You may also want to format the columns to make it look tidy.

When you have done that, close out of the **MasterData** workbook.

daxc
www.dynamicsaxcompanions.com
Dynamics AX Companions

- 151 -

www.blindsquirrelpublishing.com
© 2015 Blind Squirrel Publishing, LLC , All Rights Reserved

BLIND SQUIRREL
PUBLISHING

Step By Step Walkthrough

Creating a Customer Groups Import Entity

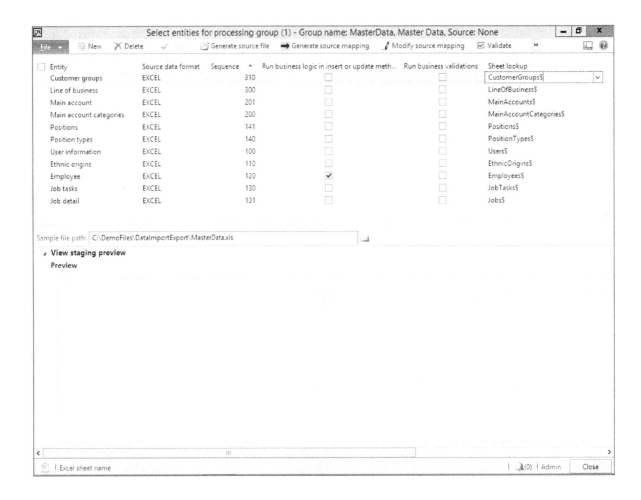

When you return back to the wizard, just click on the **Finish** button to exit from the form which will return you to the **Processing** Groups maintenance form. Click on the **Folder** icon to the right of the **Sample File Path** field.

When the file explorer opens navigate to where you saved your **MasterData** worksheet that you just created, and then click on the **Open** button.

Click on the **Sheet Lookup** dropdown list and select the **CustomerGroups$** record.

Finish off the process by clicking on the **Generate Source Mapping** button within the menu bar. If everything is linked up correctly and you have all of the key fields within your map, then you will get a quick message saying that the entity mapping was completed and you can click on the **Close** button.

Example Data

Creating a Customer Groups Import Entity

Now that you have the worksheet created you can start populating the worksheet with your own set of **Customer Groups**. Here is an example of how the data should look.

CustGroup	RETAIL
Name	Retail Customers
PaymTermId	Net30
ClearingPeriod	Net30
TaxGroupId	
PriceIncludeSalesTax	

 www.dynamicsaxcompanions.com
Dynamics AX Companions

- 153 -

www.blindsquirrelpublishing.com
© 2015 Blind Squirrel Publishing, LLC , All Rights Reserved

BLIND SQUIRREL
PUBLISHING

Sample Data

Creating a Customer Groups Import Entity

If you are looking for some sample **Customer Group** data to load then here is a snapshot of the data that we use in the sample template.

CustGroup	Name	PaymTermId	ClearingPeriod	TaxGroupId	PriceIncludeSalesTax
RETAIL	Retail Customers	Net30	Net30		
WHOLESALE	Wholesale customers	Net30	Net30		
MAJOR	Major customers	Net30	Net30		
INTERNET	Internet customers	Net10	Net10		
OTHER	Other customers	Net10	Net10		
INTERCOMPANY	Intercompany customers	Net10	Net10		

 www.dynamicsaxcompanions.com
Dynamics AX Companions

- 154 -

www.blindsquirrelpublishing.com
© 2015 Blind Squirrel Publishing, LLC , All Rights Reserved

 BLIND SQUIRREL
PUBLISHING

Creating a Customers Import Entity

Now we will create an Entity for the **Customers** so that we can get all of the customers and address details loaded in through the Import Framework.

Step By Step Walkthrough

Creating a Customers Import Entity

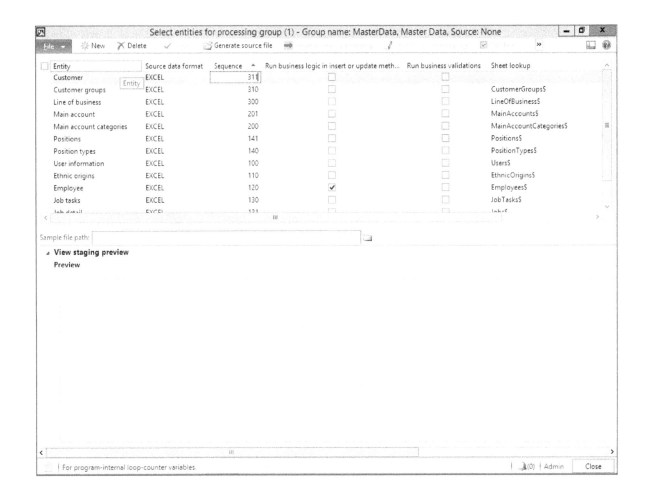

To do this, open the **Processing Group Entities** maintenance form and click on the **New** button within the menu bar to create a new record. Then click on the **Entity** dropdown list and find the **Customers** Entity type.

Click on the **Source Data Format** dropdown list and select the **EXCEL** format, and then set the **Sequence** number to **311**.

Now we want to create the mapping that we will be using to import in all of the data. To do this click on the **Generate Source File** button in the menu bar and when the **Wizard** appears, click on the **Next** button to start setting things up.

When the **Display Data** page is shown you will be able to see all of the default fields in the entity map.

Sample Data

Creating a Customers Import Entity

Here are the fields that you will want to have within your **Customers** import definition if you want to use the sample company import template that we provide.

Present in source	Sequence	Field name	Mandatory	Field type	Field size
Yes	1	AccountNum	Yes	String	20
Yes	2	AccountStatement	No	String	20
Yes	3	Name	No	String	100
Yes	4	Street	No	String	250
Yes	5	City	No	String	60
Yes	6	State	No	String	10
Yes	7	ZipCode	No	String	10
Yes	8	CountryRegionId	Yes	String	10
Yes	9	CustGroup	Yes	String	10
Yes	10	Currency	Yes	String	3

Step By Step Walkthrough

Creating a Customers Import Entity

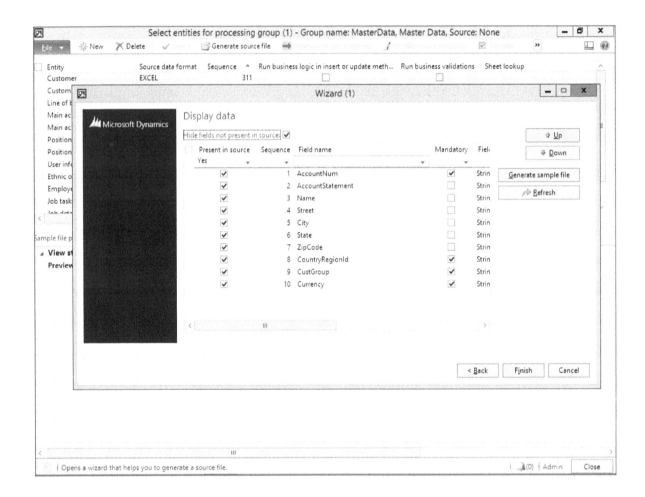

Find each of the fields in the template and then just click on the **Present In Source** checkbox, which will enable to field to be used within the template. If you need to re-order any of the fields then select the field and then click on the **Up** or **Down** buttons to rearrange them.

Once you have all of the fields selected and you have them in the right order then click on the **Generate Sample File** button.

Step By Step Walkthrough

Creating a Customers Import Entity

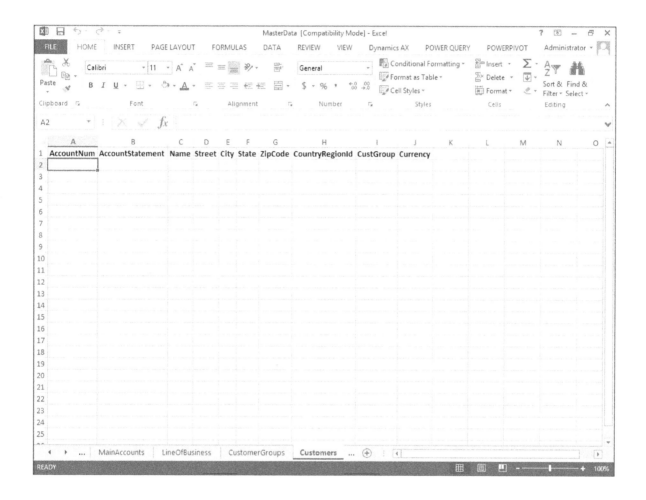

This will create another Excel Workbook for you just like before and the first sheet will already be set up with the fields that you need for the **Customer** import.

Open up the **MasterData** template that you created in the previous step and add a new Worksheet to the workbook by clicking on the **+** button and rename it to **Customers.**

Now return to the workbook that was automatically generated by the wizard and select the auto-generated columns and copy them (**CTRL+C**) and paste (**CTRL+V**) them into the **Customers** worksheet within the **MasterData** workbook. You may also want to format the columns to make it look tidy.

When you have done that, close out of the **MasterData** workbook.

Step By Step Walkthrough

Creating a Customers Import Entity

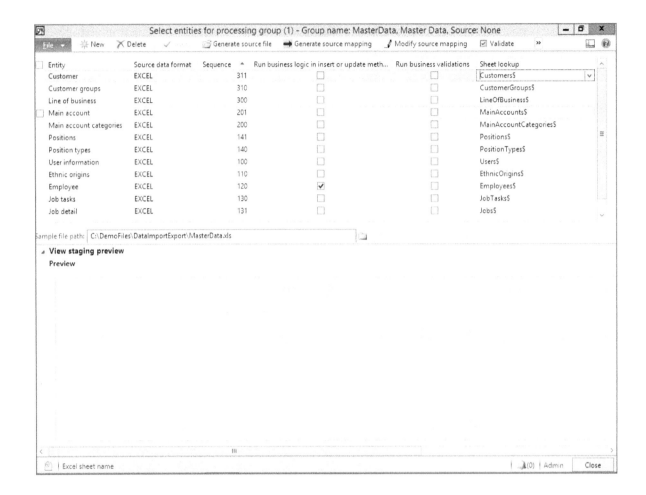

When you return back to the wizard, just click on the **Finish** button to exit from the form which will return you to the **Processing** Groups maintenance form. Click on the **Folder** icon to the right of the **Sample File Path** field.

When the file explorer opens navigate to where you saved your **MasterData** worksheet that you just created, and then click on the **Open** button.

Click on the **Sheet Lookup** dropdown list and select the **Customers$** record.

Finish off the process by clicking on the **Generate Source Mapping** button within the menu bar. If everything is linked up correctly and you have all of the key fields within your map, then you will get a quick message saying that the entity mapping was completed and you can click on the **Close** button.

Example Data

Creating a Customers Import Entity

Now that you have the worksheet created you can start populating the worksheet with your own set of **Customers**. Here is an example of how the data should look.

AccountNum	100002
AccountStatement	
Name	Nordstrom
Street	P.O. Box 870
City	Seattle
State	WA
ZipCode	98111
CountryRegionId	USA
CustGroup	RETAIL
Currency	USD

 www.dynamicsaxcompanions.com
Dynamics AX Companions

- 161 -

www.blindsquirrelpublishing.com
© 2015 Blind Squirrel Publishing, LLC, All Rights Reserved

BLIND SQUIRREL
PUBLISHING

Sample Data

Creating a Customers Import Entity

If you are looking for some sample **Customer** data to load then here is a snapshot of the data that we use in the sample template.

AccountNum	AccountStatement Name	Street	City	State	ZipCode	CountryRegionId	CustGroup	Currency
100002	Nordstrom	P.O. Box 870	Seattle	WA	98111	USA	RETAIL	USD
100003	Lazarus	P.O. Boc 415770	Cincinnati	OH	45241	USA	RETAIL	USD
100004	Sterns /Inv. Procesing	P.O. Box 415778	Cincinnatti	OH	45241	USA	RETAIL	USD
100005	Cramers Kiddie Shoppes			PA	19124	USA	RETAIL	USD
100006	Richs/ Dept 0480 $		Cincinnatti	OH	45241	USA	RETAIL	USD
100007	Kidding Around	1260 Springfield Avenue	New Providence	NJ	7974	USA	RETAIL	USD
100008	Kids Closet	1226 Connecticut Ave.N.W	Washington	DC	20036	USA	RETAIL	USD
100009	Modecraft Fashions (Old Acct)	1830 Route 130 N.	Burlington	NJ	8016	USA	RETAIL	USD
100010	Younkers Dept Store	P.O. Box 1495	Des Moines	IA	50397	USA	RETAIL	USD
100011	As/Jordan Marsh Vndr #549	P.O. Box 415774	Cincinnati	OH	45241	USA	RETAIL	USD
100012	Burdines	P.O. Box 415783	Cincinnati	OH	45241	USA	RETAIL	USD
100013	Cramers Kiddie Shop Inc	4533 Frankford Avenue	Phila	PA	19124	USA	RETAIL	USD
100014	Gayfers / Maison Blache	Mercantile Stores Dpt #30	Fairfield	OH	45014	USA	RETAIL	USD
100015	Castner Knott Co.Dept 030	C/O Mercantile Stores Co	Fairfield	OH	45014	USA	RETAIL	USD
100016	Childrenswear House Inc	1170 Northern Blvd	Manhasset	NY	11030	USA	RETAIL	USD
100017	Macys					USA	RETAIL	USD
100018	Von Maur*	6565 Brady Street	Davenport	IA	52806	USA	RETAIL	USD

100019	Macy/Bullocks Accts	P.O. Box 37610	Phoenix	AZ	85069 USA		RETAIL	USD
100020	Burkes So. Dakota Inc.	314 S. Main	Sioux Falls	SD	57102 USA		RETAIL	USD

Creating a Customer Addresses Import Entity

In addition to the **Customers** entity, we will also create a child entity for the **Customer Addresses** so that we can import in any secondary addresses that we may have for the customers.

Step By Step Walkthrough

Creating a Customer Addresses Import Entity

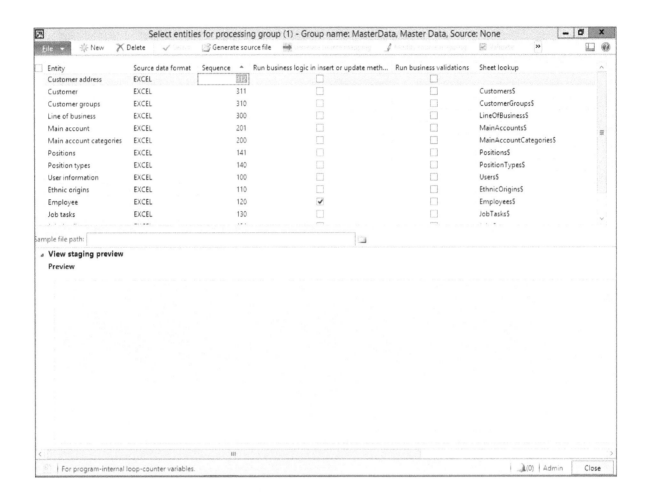

To do this, return to the **Processing Group Entities** maintenance form and click on the **New** button within the menu bar to create a new record. Then click on the **Entity** dropdown list and find the **Customer Address** Entity type.

Click on the **Source Data Format** dropdown list and select the **EXCEL** format, and then set the **Sequence** number to **312**.

Now we want to create the mapping that we will be using to import in all of the data. To do this click on the **Generate Source File** button in the menu bar and when the **Wizard** appears, click on the **Next** button to start setting things up.

When the **Display Data** page is shown you will be able to see all of the default fields in the entity map.

Sample Data

Creating a Customer Addresses Import Entity

Here are the fields that you will want to have within your **Customer Addresses** import definition if you want to use the sample company import template that we provide.

Present in source	Sequence	Field name	Mandatory	Field type	Field size
Yes	1	CustAccountNum	Yes	String	20
Yes	2	AddressName	Yes	String	60
Yes	3	LocationRole	Yes	String	100
Yes	4	Street	No	String	250
Yes	5	City	No	String	60
Yes	6	State	No	String	10
Yes	7	ZipCode	No	String	10
Yes	8	CountryRegionId	Yes	String	10

Step By Step Walkthrough

Creating a Customer Addresses Import Entity

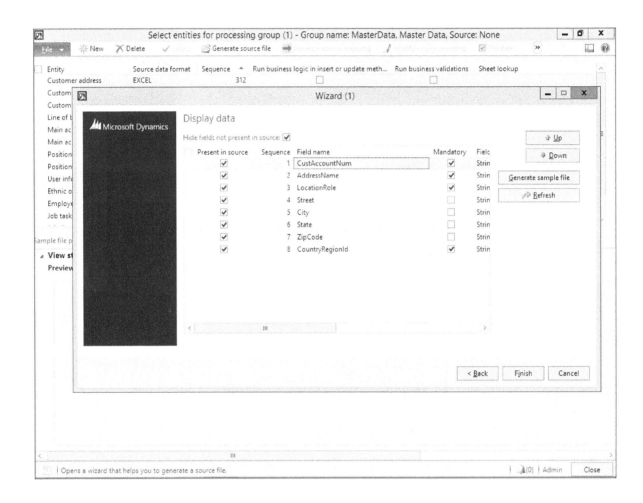

Find each of the fields in the template and then just click on the **Present In Source** checkbox, which will enable to field to be used within the template. If you need to re-order any of the fields then select the field and then click on the **Up** or **Down** buttons to rearrange them.

Once you have all of the fields selected and you have them in the right order then click on the **Generate Sample File** button.

Step By Step Walkthrough

Creating a Customer Addresses Import Entity

This will create another Excel Workbook for you just like before and the first sheet will already be set up with the fields that you need for the **Customer Addresses** import.

Open up the **MasterData** template that you created in the previous step and add a new Worksheet to the workbook by clicking on the + button and rename it to **CustomerAddresses.**

Now return to the workbook that was automatically generated by the wizard and select the auto-generated columns and copy them (**CTRL+C**) and paste (**CTRL+V**) them into the **CustomerAddresses** worksheet within the **MasterData** workbook. You may also want to format the columns to make it look tidy.

When you have done that, close out of the **MasterData** workbook.

www.dynamicsaxcompanions.com
Dynamics AX Companions
     - 169 -
www.blindsquirrelpublishing.com
© 2015 Blind Squirrel Publishing, LLC , All Rights Reserved
BLIND SQUIRREL
PUBLISHING

Step By Step Walkthrough

Creating a Customer Addresses Import Entity

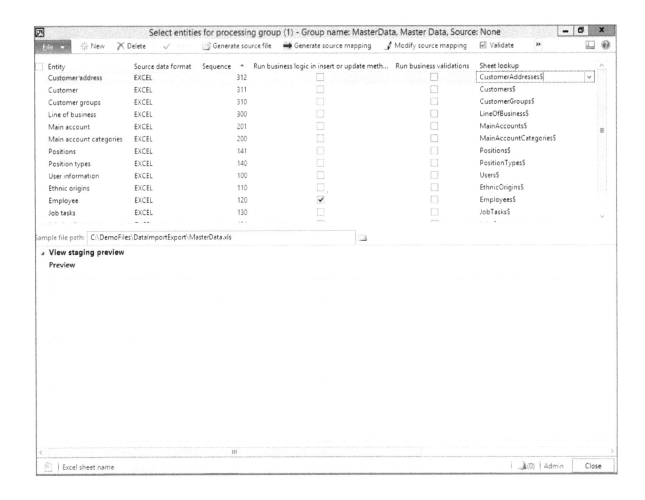

When you return back to the wizard, just click on the **Finish** button to exit from the form which will return you to the **Processing** Groups maintenance form. Click on the **Folder** icon to the right of the **Sample File Path** field.

When the file explorer opens navigate to where you saved your **MasterData** worksheet that you just created, and then click on the **Open** button.

Click on the **Sheet Lookup** dropdown list and select the **CustomerAddresses$** record.

Finish off the process by clicking on the **Generate Source Mapping** button within the menu bar. If everything is linked up correctly and you have all of the key fields within your map, then you will get a quick message saying that the entity mapping was completed and you can click on the **Close** button.

Creating a Vendor Groups Import Entity

Next we will start configuring all of the entities so that we can import in all of the **Vendor** details. To start off we will create an entity for the **Vendor Groups** which will be required in order to set up all of the **Vendor** records.

www.dynamicsaxcompanions.com
Dynamics AX Companions

- 171 -

www.blindsquirrelpublishing.com
© 2015 Blind Squirrel Publishing, LLC, All Rights Reserved

BLIND SQUIRREL
PUBLISHING

Step By Step Walkthrough

Creating a Vendor Groups Import Entity

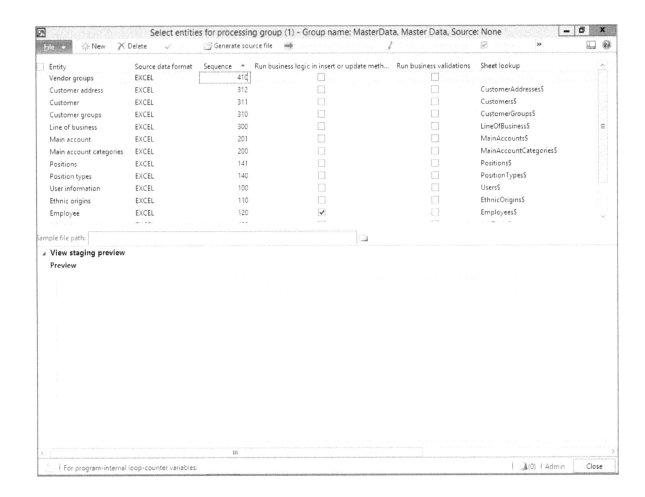

To do this, open the **Processing Group Entities** maintenance form and click on the **New** button within the menu bar to create a new record. Then click on the **Entity** dropdown list and find the **Vendor Groups** Entity type.

Click on the **Source Data Format** dropdown list and select the **EXCEL** format, and then set the **Sequence** number to **410**.

Now we want to create the mapping that we will be using to import in all of the data. To do this click on the **Generate Source File** button in the menu bar and when the **Wizard** appears, click on the **Next** button to start setting things up.

When the **Display Data** page is shown you will be able to see all of the default fields in the entity map.

www.dynamicsaxcompanions.com
Dynamics AX Companions
- 172 -
www.blindsquirrelpublishing.com
© 2015 Blind Squirrel Publishing, LLC, All Rights Reserved
BLIND SQUIRREL
PUBLISHING

Sample Data

Creating a Vendor Groups Import Entity

Here are the fields that you will want to have within your **Vendor Groups** import definition if you want to use the sample company import template that we provide.

Present in source	Sequence	Field name	Mandatory	Field type	Field size
Yes	1	VendGroup	Yes	String	10
Yes	2	Name	No	String	60
Yes	3	PaymTermId	No	String	10
Yes	4	ClearingPeriod	No	String	10
Yes	5	TaxGroupId	No	String	10

Step By Step Walkthrough

Creating a Vendor Groups Import Entity

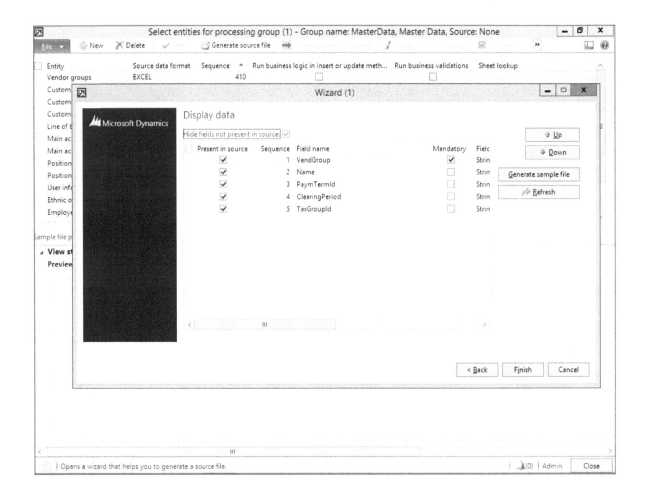

Find each of the fields in the template and then just click on the **Present In Source** checkbox, which will enable to field to be used within the template. If you need to re-order any of the fields then select the field and then click on the **Up** or **Down** buttons to rearrange them.

Once you have all of the fields selected and you have them in the right order then click on the **Generate Sample File** button.

Step By Step Walkthrough

Creating a Vendor Groups Import Entity

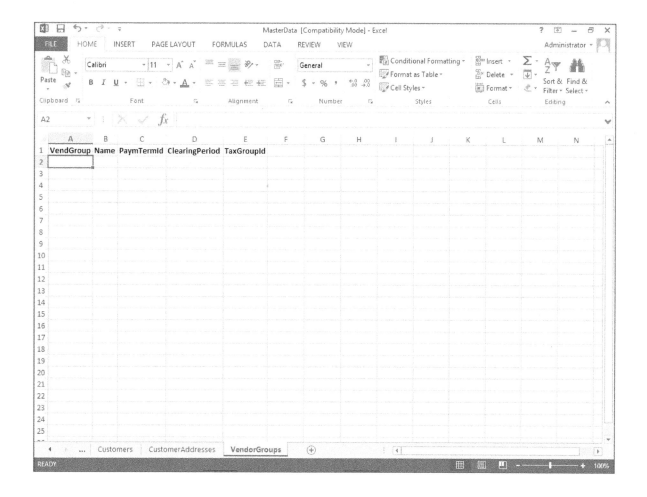

This will create another Excel Workbook for you just like before and the first sheet will already be set up with the fields that you need for the **Vendor Groups** import.

Open up the **MasterData** template that you created in the previous step and add a new Worksheet to the workbook by clicking on the **+** button and rename it to **VendorGroups.**

Now return to the workbook that was automatically generated by the wizard and select the auto-generated columns and copy them (**CTRL+C**) and paste (**CTRL+V**) them into the **VendorGroups** worksheet within the **MasterData** workbook. You may also want to format the columns to make it look tidy.

When you have done that, close out of the **MasterData** workbook.

Step By Step Walkthrough

Creating a Vendor Groups Import Entity

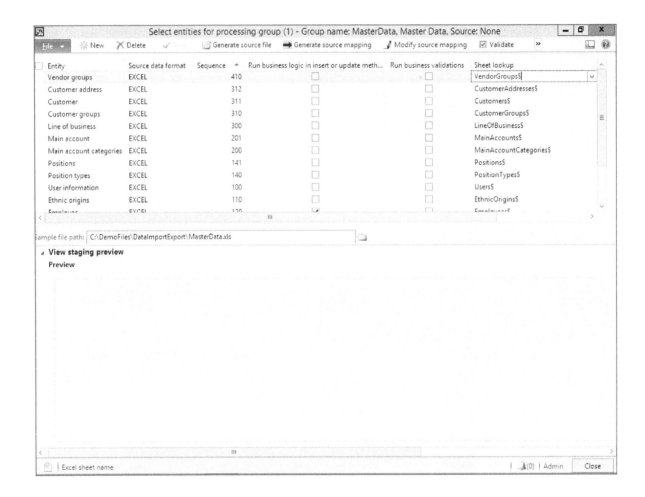

When you return back to the wizard, just click on the **Finish** button to exit from the form which will return you to the **Processing** Groups maintenance form. Click on the **Folder** icon to the right of the **Sample File Path** field.

When the file explorer opens navigate to where you saved your **MasterData** worksheet that you just created, and then click on the **Open** button.

Click on the **Sheet Lookup** dropdown list and select the **VendorGroups$** record.

Finish off the process by clicking on the **Generate Source Mapping** button within the menu bar. If everything is linked up correctly and you have all of the key fields within your map, then you will get a quick message saying that the entity mapping was completed and you can click on the **Close** button.

Example Data

Creating a Vendor Groups Import Entity

Now that you have the worksheet created you can start populating the worksheet with your own set of **Vendor Groups**. Here is an example of how the data should look.

VendGroup	ARMORY
Name	Armory Vendors
PaymTermId	NET30
ClearingPeriod	NET30
TaxGroupId	

Sample Data

Creating a Vendor Groups Import Entity

If you are looking for some sample **Vendor Group** data to load then here is a snapshot of the data that we use in the sample template.

VendGroup	Name	PaymTermId	ClearingPeriod	TaxGroupId
ARMORY	Armory Vendors	NET30	NET30	
CONFIDENTL	Confidential Vendors	NET30	NET10	
CORP				
CREDITCARD	Credit Card Only Vendors	NET30	NET10	
DEFAULT	General Vendors	NET30	NET10	
DISCOUNTS	Discount Vendors	NET30	NET10	
DOMESTIC	Domestic	NET30	NET10	
EAST				
EMGGLOBAL				
EMPLOYEE	Employees	NET30	NET10	
EXPENSE	Misc. Expense Vendors	NET30	NET10	
FREIGHT	Freight Providers	NET30	NET10	
GROCERY	Grocery Vendors	NET30	NET30	
HEALTHCARE	Healthcare Vendors	NET30	NET30	
INACTIVE	Inactive Vendors	NET30	NET10	
INTERCO	Intercompany Vendors	NET10	NET10	
INTERNL				

daxc   www.dynamicsaxcompanions.com
Dynamics AX Companions

- 178 -

www.blindsquirrelpublishing.com
© 2015 Blind Squirrel Publishing, LLC , All Rights Reserved

BLIND SQUIRREL
PUBLISHING

INTL	International Vendors	NET30	NET10
NP			
NPG			
NULL			
ONHOLD	On Hold Vendors	NET30	NET10
OTHER	Orther Vendors	NET30	NET10
PARTS	Parts Vendors	NET30	NET30
PREPAY	Prepayment Vendors	NET30	NET10
PRIORITY	Priority Vendors	NET30	NET10
SERVICES	Services Vendors	NET30	NET30
TAX	Tax Authorities	ME15	NET10
WEST			
WIRE	Wire Only Vendors	NET30	NET10

www.blindsquirrelpublishing.com
© 2015 Blind Squirrel Publishing, LLC , All Rights Reserved
BLIND SQUIRREL
PUBLISHING

Creating a Vendors Import Entity

Now we will create an import entity for the **Vendors**.

www.dynamicsaxcompanions.com
Dynamics AX Companions

- 181 -

www.blindsquirrelpublishing.com
© 2015 Blind Squirrel Publishing, LLC , All Rights Reserved

BLIND SQUIRREL
PUBLISHING

Step By Step Walkthrough

Creating a Vendors Import Entity

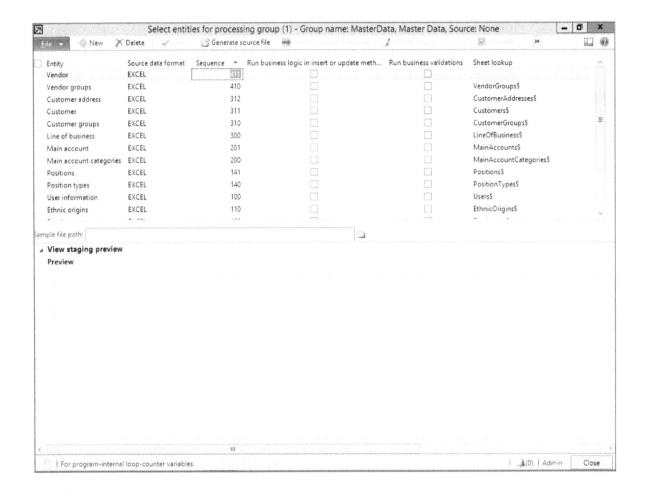

To do this, open the **Processing Group Entities** maintenance form and click on the **New** button within the menu bar to create a new record. Then click on the **Entity** dropdown list and find the **Vendors** Entity type.

Click on the **Source Data Format** dropdown list and select the **EXCEL** format, and then set the **Sequence** number to **411**.

Now we want to create the mapping that we will be using to import in all of the data. To do this click on the **Generate Source File** button in the menu bar and when the **Wizard** appears, click on the **Next** button to start setting things up.

When the **Display Data** page is shown you will be able to see all of the default fields in the entity map.

Sample Data

Creating a Vendors Import Entity

Here are the fields that you will want to have within your **Vendors** import definition if you want to use the sample company import template that we provide.

Present in source	Sequence	Field name	Mandatory	Field type	Field size
Yes	1	AccountNum	Yes	String	20
Yes	2	Name	No	String	100
Yes	3	Street	No	String	250
Yes	4	City	No	String	60
Yes	5	State	No	String	10
Yes	6	ZipCode	No	String	10
Yes	7	CountryRegionId	No	String	10
Yes	8	Currency	Yes	String	3
Yes	9	VendGroup	Yes	String	10

Step By Step Walkthrough

Creating a Vendors Import Entity

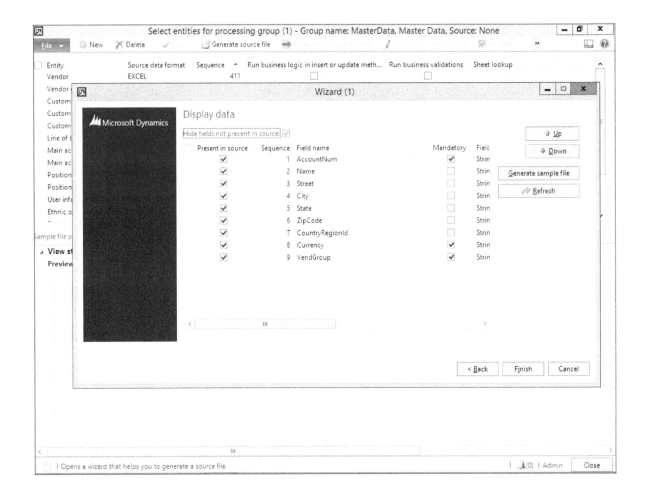

Find each of the fields in the template and then just click on the **Present In Source** checkbox, which will enable to field to be used within the template. If you need to re-order any of the fields then select the field and then click on the **Up** or **Down** buttons to rearrange them.

Once you have all of the fields selected and you have them in the right order then click on the **Generate Sample File** button.

Step By Step Walkthrough

Creating a Vendors Import Entity

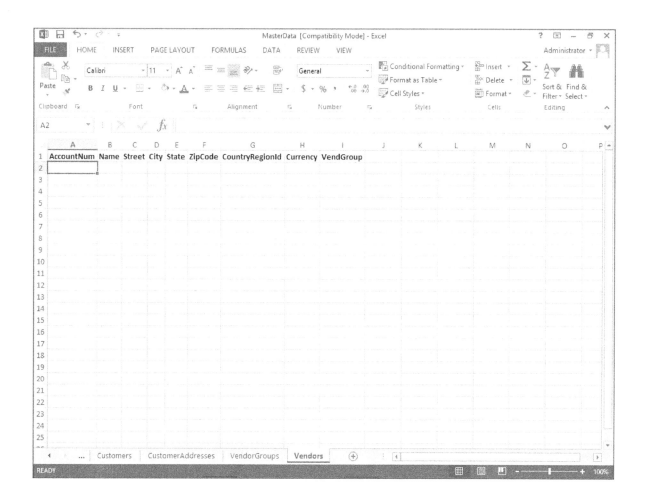

This will create another Excel Workbook for you just like before and the first sheet will already be set up with the fields that you need for the **Vendors** import.

Open up the **MasterData** template that you created in the previous step and add a new Worksheet to the workbook by clicking on the **+** button and rename it to **Vendors.**

Now return to the workbook that was automatically generated by the wizard and select the auto-generated columns and copy them (**CTRL+C**) and paste (**CTRL+V**) them into the **Vendors** worksheet within the **MasterData** workbook. You may also want to format the columns to make it look tidy.

When you have done that, close out of the **MasterData** workbook.

daxc www.dynamicsaxcompanions.com
Dynamics AX Companions

- 185 -

www.blindsquirrelpublishing.com
© 2015 Blind Squirrel Publishing, LLC, All Rights Reserved

 BLIND SQUIRREL
PUBLISHING

Step By Step Walkthrough

Creating a Vendors Import Entity

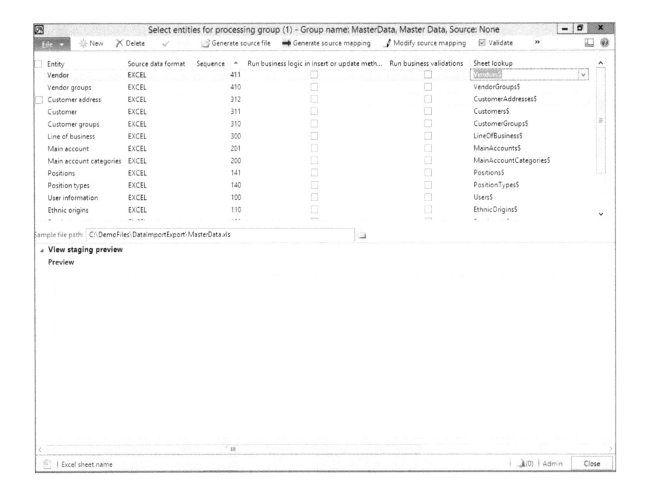

When you return back to the wizard, just click on the **Finish** button to exit from the form which will return you to the **Processing** Groups maintenance form. Click on the **Folder** icon to the right of the **Sample File Path** field.

When the file explorer opens navigate to where you saved your **MasterData** worksheet that you just created, and then click on the **Open** button.

Click on the **Sheet Lookup** dropdown list and select the **Vendors$** record.

Finish off the process by clicking on the **Generate Source Mapping** button within the menu bar. If everything is linked up correctly and you have all of the key fields within your map, then you will get a quick message saying that the entity mapping was completed and you can click on the **Close** button.

Example Data

Creating a Vendors Import Entity

Now that you have the worksheet created you can start populating the worksheet with your own set of **Vendors**. Here is an example of how the data should look.

AccountNum	100002
Name	Acme Corporation
Street	2894 Grand Via
City	Place Corners
State	WV
ZipCode	26004
CountryRegionId	USA
Currency	USD
VendGroup	SERVICES

Sample Data

Creating a Vendors Import Entity

If you are looking for some sample **Vendors** data to load then here is a snapshot of the data that we use in the sample template.

AccountNum	Name	Street	City	State	ZipCode	CountryRegionId	Currency	VendGroup
100002	Acme Corporation	2894 Grand Via	Place Corners	WV	26004	USA	USD	SERVICES
100003	Adipose Industries	2295 Sleepy Bear Valley	Tabasco	TN	38028	USA	USD	SERVICES
100004	Advanced Idea Mechanics	8716 Cinder Canyon	Bethune	DC	20066	USA	USD	SERVICES
100005	AmerTek	5137 Rustic Maze	Egorkovskoi	VT	5659	USA	USD	SERVICES
100006	Anim-X	2266 Bright Spring Mountain	Cracker City	NE	68400	USA	USD	SERVICES
100007	ARCAM Corporation	1940 Green Drive	Connoquenessing	NC	28219	USA	USD	SERVICES
100008	Beyond Corporation ©	61 Colonial Towers	South Lake	VA	23001	USA	USD	SERVICES
100009	Bonk Business	5670 Indian Pony Crest	Dicktown	ID	83977	USA	USD	SERVICES
100010	Bonsai Kitten	3088 Noble Blossom Estates	Helltown	NC	27169	USA	USD	SERVICES
100011	Brand Corporation	2210 Merry Zephyr Bay	New Munich	MA	1206	USA	USD	SERVICES

100012	Brilliant Industries	3530 Fallen Grove	Kinikinik	MT	59205	USA	USD	SERVICES
100013	Buy More	9026 Quiet Pine Landing	Ronkonkoma	MN	55328	USA	USD	SERVICES
100014	BuyTigers.com	8807 Foggy Shadow Mall	Peace Dale	NJ	7799	USA	USD	SERVICES
100015	Carver Media Group Network	8852 Emerald Butterfly Chase	Tenth Legion	DE	19956	USA	USD	SERVICES
100016	CHOAM	1726 Little End	Ho	AL	36248	USA	USD	SERVICES
100017	List of Cinco Family products	5901 Silver Wagon Mount	Sivili Chuchg	AL	36627	USA	USD	SERVICES
100018	Clothes Over Bro's	4330 Iron Pike	Rhump	NJ	7996	USA	USD	SERVICES
100019	Company	9815 Wishing Edge	Shin Hollow	AZ	86257	USA	USD	SERVICES
100020	The Company	3914 Shady Farms	Elevenmile Homestead	MI	48763	USA	USD	SERVICES
100021	ConHugeCo	8529 Amber Knoll	Anamoose	ND	58807	USA	USD	SERVICES
100022	Contoso	4862 Hidden Gardens	Lunenburg	IA	52516	USA	USD	SERVICES
100023	Cross Technological Enterprises	1188 Harvest Common	Cee Vee	IA	50974	USA	USD	SERVICES
100024	Crosstime Traffic	3227 Broad Place	Soft Shell	NV	89318	USA	USD	SERVICES
100025	Crudgington Brewery	4636 Gentle Downs	Kodiak	MD	21019	USA	USD	SERVICES

Creating a Vendor Addresses Import Entity

Just as with the **Customers** we will also create an entity for the **Vendors Addresses** so that we can import in any additional addresses against the **Vendors**.

Step By Step Walkthrough

Creating a Vendor Addresses Import Entity

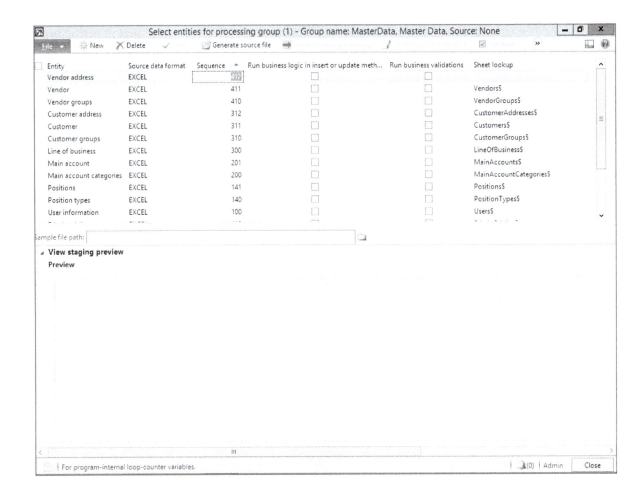

To do this, return to the **Processing Group Entities** maintenance form and click on the **New** button within the menu bar to create a new record. Then click on the **Entity** dropdown list and find the **Vendor Address** Entity type.

Click on the **Source Data Format** dropdown list and select the **EXCEL** format, and then set the **Sequence** number to **412**.

Now we want to create the mapping that we will be using to import in all of the data. To do this click on the **Generate Source File** button in the menu bar and when the **Wizard** appears, click on the **Next** button to start setting things up.

When the **Display Data** page is shown you will be able to see all of the default fields in the entity map.

Sample Data

Creating a Vendor Addresses Import Entity

Here are the fields that you will want to have within your **Vendor Addresses** import definition if you want to use the sample company import template that we provide.

Present in source	Sequence	Field name	Mandatory	Field type	Field size
Yes	1	VendAccountNum	Yes	String	20
Yes	2	AddressName	Yes	String	60
Yes	3	LocationRole	Yes	String	100
Yes	4	Street	No	String	250
Yes	5	City	No	String	60
Yes	6	State	No	String	10
Yes	7	ZipCode	No	String	10
Yes	8	CountryRegionId	Yes	String	10

Step By Step Walkthrough

Creating a Vendor Addresses Import Entity

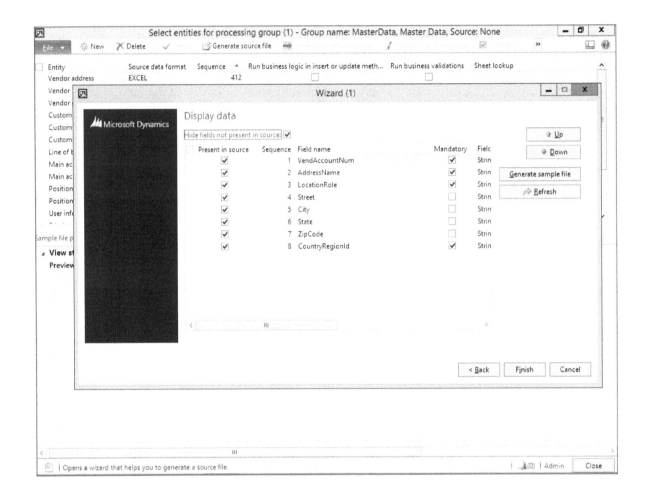

Find each of the fields in the template and then just click on the **Present In Source** checkbox, which will enable to field to be used within the template. If you need to re-order any of the fields then select the field and then click on the **Up** or **Down** buttons to rearrange them.

Once you have all of the fields selected and you have them in the right order then click on the **Generate Sample File** button.

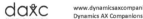
www.dynamicsaxcompanions.com
Dynamics AX Companions
- 194 -
www.blindsquirrelpublishing.com
© 2015 Blind Squirrel Publishing, LLC, All Rights Reserved
BLIND SQUIRREL
PUBLISHING

Step By Step Walkthrough

Creating a Vendor Addresses Import Entity

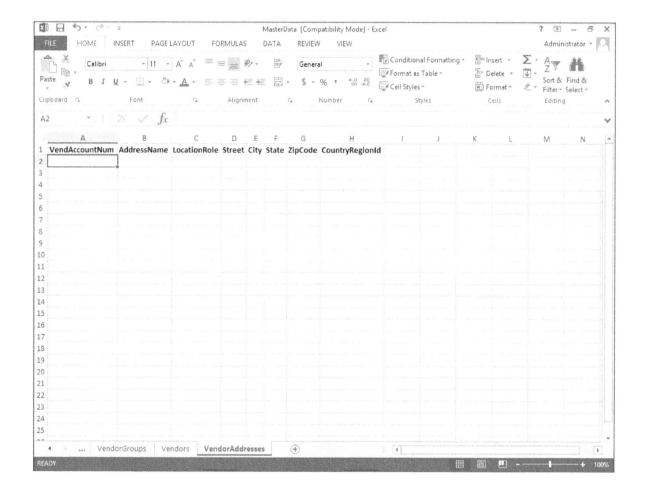

This will create another Excel Workbook for you just like before and the first sheet will already be set up with the fields that you need for the **Vendor Addresses** import.

Open up the **MasterData** template that you created in the previous step and add a new Worksheet to the workbook by clicking on the **+** button and rename it to **VendorAddresses.**

Now return to the workbook that was automatically generated by the wizard and select the auto-generated columns and copy them (**CTRL+C**) and paste (**CTRL+V**) them into the **VendorAddresses** worksheet within the **MasterData** workbook. You may also want to format the columns to make it look tidy.

When you have done that, close out of the **MasterData** workbook.

Step By Step Walkthrough

Creating a Vendor Addresses Import Entity

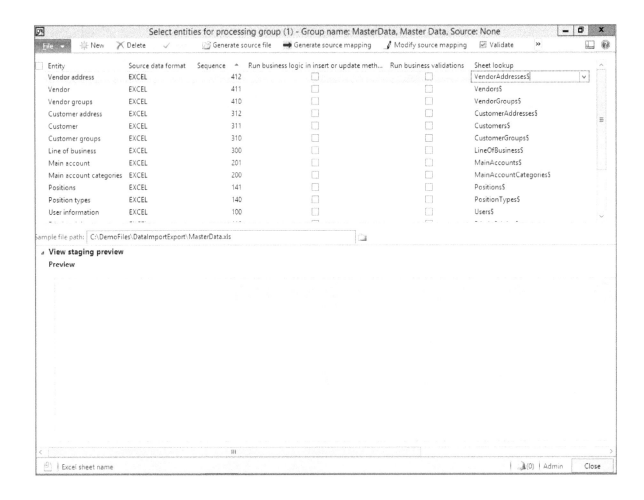

When you return back to the wizard, just click on the **Finish** button to exit from the form which will return you to the **Processing** Groups maintenance form. Click on the **Folder** icon to the right of the **Sample File Path** field.

When the file explorer opens navigate to where you saved your **MasterData** worksheet that you just created, and then click on the **Open** button.

Click on the **Sheet Lookup** dropdown list and select the **VendorAddresses$** record.

Finish off the process by clicking on the **Generate Source Mapping** button within the menu bar. If everything is linked up correctly and you have all of the key fields within your map, then you will get a quick message saying that the entity mapping was completed and you can click on the **Close** button.

 www.dynamicsaxcompanions.com
Dynamics AX Companions
- 196 -
www.blindsquirrelpublishing.com
© 2015 Blind Squirrel Publishing, LLC, All Rights Reserved
BLIND SQUIRREL PUBLISHING

Creating a Contacts Import Entity

In addition to importing in the **Customers** and **Vendors** there is one more entity that we will configure and that is the **Contacts.** This will allow us to create contacts against the customers and vendors and have address information associated with the contact records as well – just in case you want to use the inbuilt Dynamics contact management features.

daxc
www.dynamicsaxcompanions.com
Dynamics AX Companions

- 197 -

www.blindsquirrelpublishing.com
© 2015 Blind Squirrel Publishing, LLC, All Rights Reserved

BLIND SQUIRREL
PUBLISHING

Step By Step Walkthrough

Creating a Contacts Import Entity

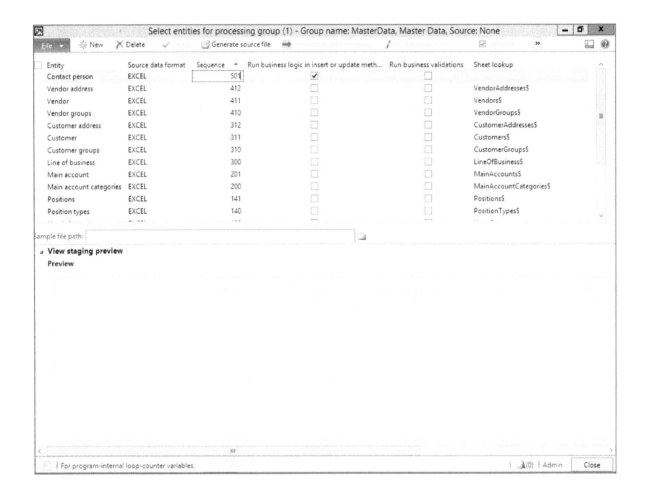

To do this, return to the **Processing Group Entities** maintenance form and click on the **New** button within the menu bar to create a new record. Then click on the **Entity** dropdown list and find the **Contact Person** Entity type.

Click on the **Source Data Format** dropdown list and select the **EXCEL** format, and then set the **Sequence** number to **501**.

Now we want to create the mapping that we will be using to import in all of the data. To do this click on the **Generate Source File** button in the menu bar and when the **Wizard** appears, click on the **Next** button to start setting things up.

When the **Display Data** page is shown you will be able to see all of the default fields in the entity map.

Sample Data

Creating a Contacts Import Entity

Here are the fields that you will want to have within your **Contacts** import definition if you want to use the sample company import template that we provide.

Present in source	Sequence	Field name	Mandatory	Field type	Field size
Yes	1	DirPartyTable_ContactForName	Yes	String	100
Yes	2	ContactPersonId	Yes	String	20
Yes	3	DirPartyTable_FirstName	No	String	25
Yes	4	DirPartyTable_LastName	No	String	25
Yes	5	Phone	No	String	200
Yes	6	Email	No	String	300
Yes	7	Title	No	String	30
Yes	8	Street	No	String	250
Yes	9	City	No	String	60
Yes	10	State	No	String	10
Yes	11	ZipCode	No	String	10
Yes	12	CountryRegionId	Yes	String	10

Step By Step Walkthrough

Creating a Contacts Import Entity

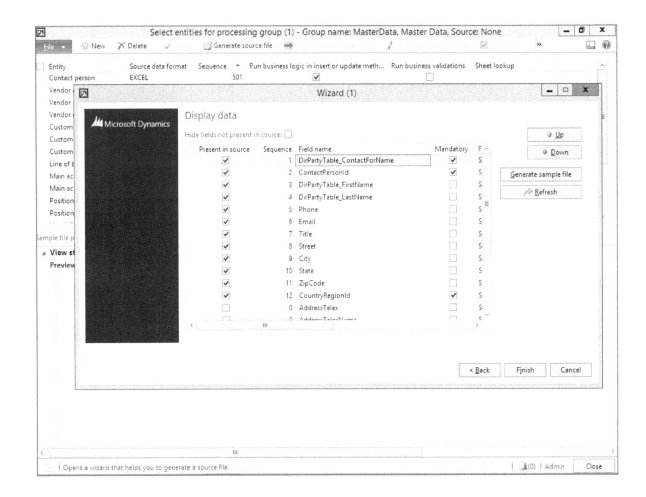

Find each of the fields in the template and then just click on the **Present In Source** checkbox, which will enable to field to be used within the template. If you need to re-order any of the fields then select the field and then click on the **Up** or **Down** buttons to rearrange them.

Once you have all of the fields selected and you have them in the right order then click on the **Generate Sample File** button.

Step By Step Walkthrough

Creating a Contacts Import Entity

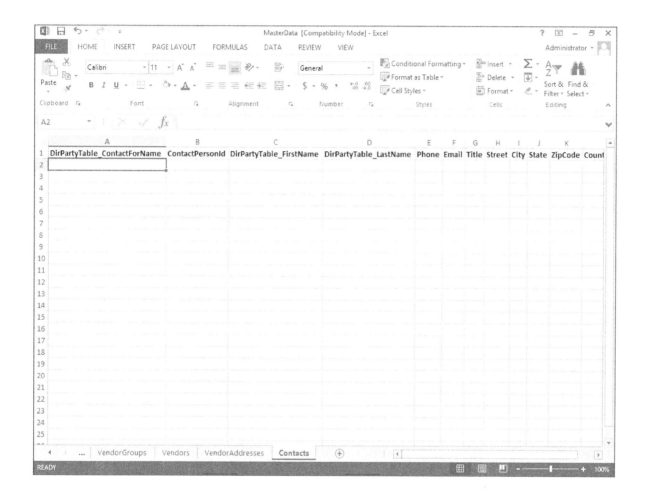

This will create another Excel Workbook for you just like before and the first sheet will already be set up with the fields that you need for the **Contacts** import.

Open up the **MasterData** template that you created in the previous step and add a new Worksheet to the workbook by clicking on the **+** button and rename it to **Contacts.**

Now return to the workbook that was automatically generated by the wizard and select the auto-generated columns and copy them (**CTRL+C**) and paste (**CTRL+V**) them into the **Contacts** worksheet within the **MasterData** workbook. You may also want to format the columns to make it look tidy.

When you have done that, close out of the **MasterData** workbook.

Step By Step Walkthrough

Creating a Contacts Import Entity

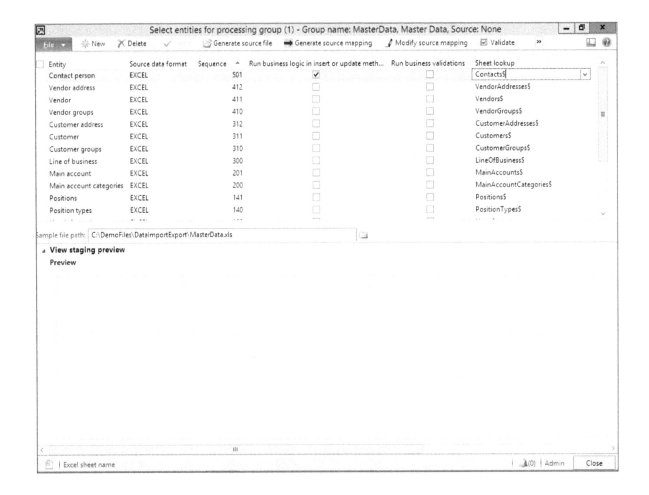

When you return back to the wizard, just click on the **Finish** button to exit from the form which will return you to the **Processing** Groups maintenance form. Click on the **Folder** icon to the right of the **Sample File Path** field.

When the file explorer opens navigate to where you saved your **MasterData** worksheet that you just created, and then click on the **Open** button.

Click on the **Sheet Lookup** dropdown list and select the **Contacts$** record.

Finish off the process by clicking on the **Generate Source Mapping** button within the menu bar. If everything is linked up correctly and you have all of the key fields within your map, then you will get a quick message saying that the entity mapping was completed and you can click on the **Close** button.

Creating a Units Of Measure Import Entity

Now we will move on to configure the **Product** entities. Before we do that though, if you have any Units Of Measure that are not standard within the default Dynamics AX configuration then you will want to load them in as well. So we will create a new entity for the **Units**.

Step By Step Walkthrough

Creating a Units Of Measure Import Entity

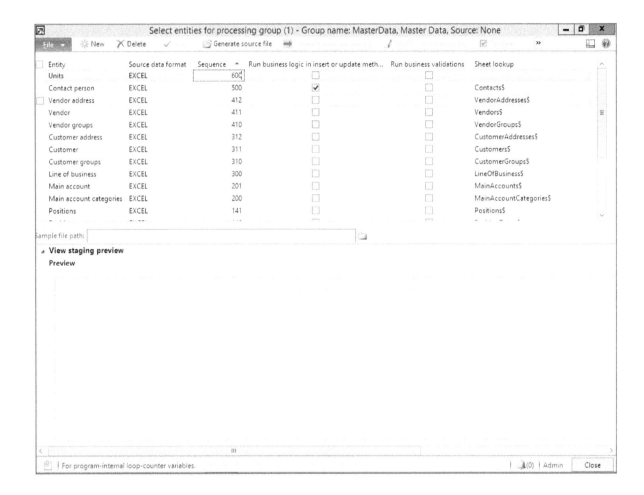

To do this, open the **Processing Group Entities** maintenance form and click on the **New** button within the menu bar to create a new record. Then click on the **Entity** dropdown list and find the **Units** Entity type.

Click on the **Source Data Format** dropdown list and select the **EXCEL** format, and then set the **Sequence** number to **600**.

Now we want to create the mapping that we will be using to import in all of the data. To do this click on the **Generate Source File** button in the menu bar and when the **Wizard** appears, click on the **Next** button to start setting things up.

When the **Display Data** page is shown you will be able to see all of the default fields in the entity map.

Sample Data

Creating a Units Of Measure Import Entity

Here are the fields that you will want to have within your **Units** import definition if you want to use the sample company import template that we provide.

Present in source	Sequence	Field name	Mandatory	Field type	Field size
Yes	1	Symbol	Yes	String	10

 BLIND SQUIRREL PUBLISHING

Step By Step Walkthrough

Creating a Units Of Measure Import Entity

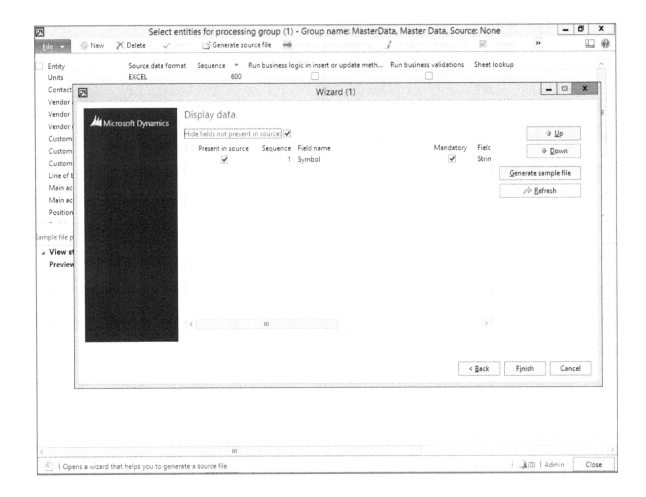

Find each of the fields in the template and then just click on the **Present In Source** checkbox, which will enable to field to be used within the template. If you need to re-order any of the fields then select the field and then click on the **Up** or **Down** buttons to rearrange them.

Once you have all of the fields selected and you have them in the right order then click on the **Generate Sample File** button.

Step By Step Walkthrough

Creating a Units Of Measure Import Entity

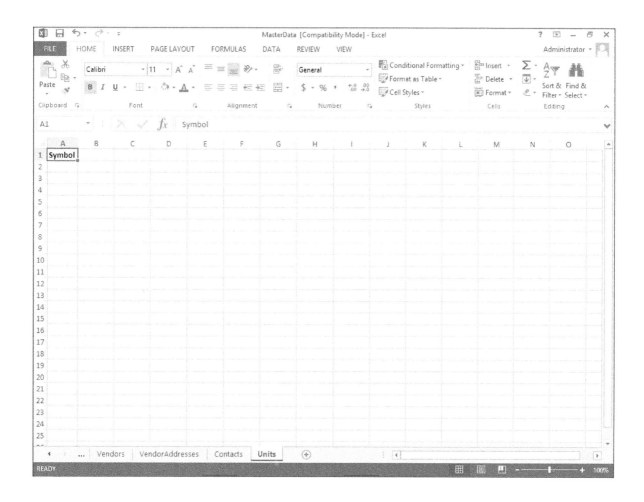

This will create another Excel Workbook for you just like before and the first sheet will already be set up with the fields that you need for the **Units Of Measure** import.

Open up the **MasterData** template that you created in the previous step and add a new Worksheet to the workbook by clicking on the **+** button and rename it to **Units.**

Now return to the workbook that was automatically generated by the wizard and select the auto-generated columns and copy them (**CTRL+C**) and paste (**CTRL+V**) them into the **Units** worksheet within the **MasterData** workbook. You may also want to format the columns to make it look tidy.

When you have done that, close out of the **MasterData** workbook.

Step By Step Walkthrough

Creating a Units Of Measure Import Entity

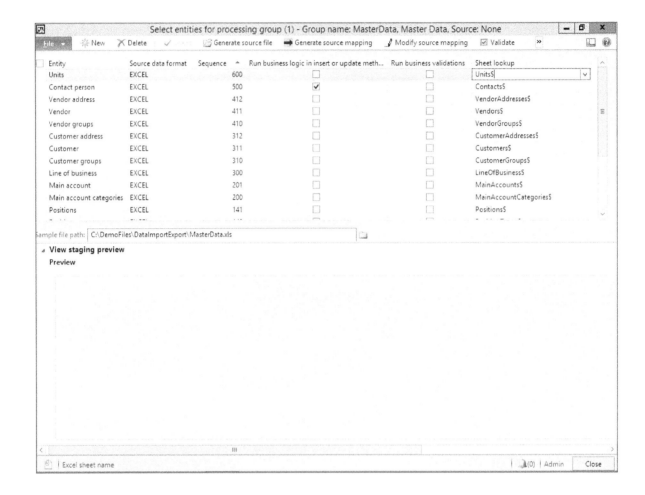

When you return back to the wizard, just click on the **Finish** button to exit from the form which will return you to the **Processing** Groups maintenance form. Click on the **Folder** icon to the right of the **Sample File Path** field.

When the file explorer opens navigate to where you saved your **MasterData** worksheet that you just created, and then click on the **Open** button.

Click on the **Sheet Lookup** dropdown list and select the **Units$** record.

Finish off the process by clicking on the **Generate Source Mapping** button within the menu bar. If everything is linked up correctly and you have all of the key fields within your map, then you will get a quick message saying that the entity mapping was completed and you can click on the **Close** button.

Example Data

Creating a Units Of Measure Import Entity

Now that you have the worksheet created you can start populating the worksheet with your own set of **Units Of Measure**. Here is an example of how the data should look.

Symbol	
	ea

www.dynamicsaxcompanions.com
Dynamics AX Companions

- 209 -

www.blindsquirrelpublishing.com
© 2015 Blind Squirrel Publishing, LLC, All Rights Reserved

BLIND SQUIRREL
PUBLISHING

Sample Data

Creating a Units Of Measure Import Entity

If you are looking for some sample **Units Of Measure** data to load then here is a snapshot of the data that we use in the sample template.

Symbol
ea

Creating a Products Import Entity

Now we will create an entity for the **Products** so that we can import in all of the **Released Products**. Luckily we only need to use one entity for this and it will update both the release and master records.

www.dynamicsaxcompanions.com
Dynamics AX Companions

- 211 -

www.blindsquirrelpublishing.com
© 2015 Blind Squirrel Publishing, LLC , All Rights Reserved

BLIND SQUIRREL
PUBLISHING

Step By Step Walkthrough

Creating a Products Import Entity

To do this, return to the **Processing Group Entities** maintenance form and click on the **New** button within the menu bar to create a new record. Then click on the **Entity** dropdown list and find the **Product** Entity type.

Click on the **Source Data Format** dropdown list and select the **EXCEL** format, and then set the **Sequence** number to **610**.

Now we want to create the mapping that we will be using to import in all of the data. To do this click on the **Generate Source File** button in the menu bar and when the **Wizard** appears, click on the **Next** button to start setting things up.

When the **Display Data** page is shown you will be able to see all of the default fields in the entity map.

Sample Data

Creating a Products Import Entity

Here are the fields that you will want to have within your **Products** import definition if you want to use the sample company import template that we provide.

Present in source	Sequence	Field name	Mandatory	Field type	Field size
Yes	1	DisplayProductNumber	Yes	String	70
Yes	2	EcoResProductTranslation_LanguageId	Yes	String	7
Yes	3	EcoResProductTranslation_Name	Yes	String	60
Yes	4	ItemId	Yes	String	20
Yes	5	ProductSubType	Yes	String	20
Yes	6	ProductType	Yes	String	20
Yes	7	EcoResProductDimensionGroup_Name	No	String	10
Yes	8	EcoResStorageDimensionGroup_Name	No	String	10
Yes	9	EcoResTrackingDimensionGroup_Name	No	String	10
Yes	10	InventTableModuleInvent_Price	No	Real	31
Yes	11	InventTableModuleInvent_UnitId	No	String	10
Yes	12	InventTableModulePurch_Price	No	Real	31
Yes	13	InventTableModulePurch_UnitId	No	String	10
Yes	14	InventTableModulePurch_TaxItemGroupId	No	String	10
Yes	15	InventTableModuleSales_Price	No	Real	31
Yes	16	InventTableModuleSales_UnitId	No	String	10
Yes	17	InventTableModuleSales_TaxItemGroupId	No	String	10
Yes	18	ItemGroupId	No	String	10
Yes	19	ModelGroupId	No	String	10
Yes	20	SearchName	No	String	20
Yes	21	CostGroupId	No	String	10
Yes	22	CostModel	No	String	6
Yes	23	NameAlias	No	String	20
Yes	24	BOMCalcGroupId	No	String	10
Yes	25	BOMUnitId	No	String	10

www.dynamicsaxcompanions.com
Dynamics AX Companions
- 213 -
www.blindsquirrelpublishing.com
© 2015 Blind Squirrel Publishing, LLC, All Rights Reserved
BLIND SQUIRREL
PUBLISHING

Step By Step Walkthrough

Creating a Products Import Entity

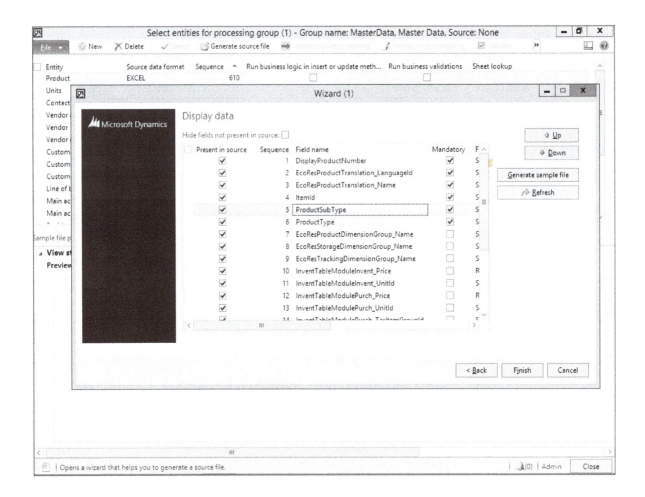

Find each of the fields in the template and then just click on the **Present In Source** checkbox, which will enable to field to be used within the template. If you need to re-order any of the fields then select the field and then click on the **Up** or **Down** buttons to rearrange them.

Once you have all of the fields selected and you have them in the right order then click on the **Generate Sample File** button.

www.dynamicsaxcompanions.com
Dynamics AX Companions
- 214 -
www.blindsquirrelpublishing.com
© 2015 Blind Squirrel Publishing, LLC , All Rights Reserved
BLIND SQUIRREL
PUBLISHING

Step By Step Walkthrough

Creating a Products Import Entity

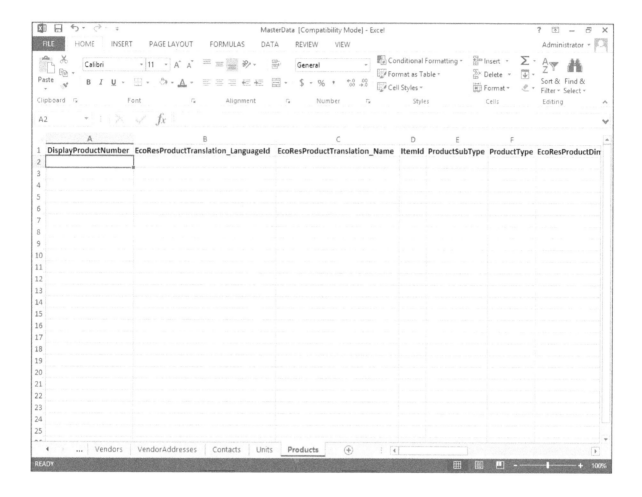

This will create another Excel Workbook for you just like before and the first sheet will already be set up with the fields that you need for the **Products** import.

Open up the **MasterData** template that you created in the previous step and add a new Worksheet to the workbook by clicking on the **+** button and rename it to **Products.**

Now return to the workbook that was automatically generated by the wizard and select the auto-generated columns and copy them (**CTRL+C**) and paste (**CTRL+V**) them into the **Products** worksheet within the **MasterData** workbook. You may also want to format the columns to make it look tidy.

When you have done that, close out of the **MasterData** workbook.

Step By Step Walkthrough

Creating a Products Import Entity

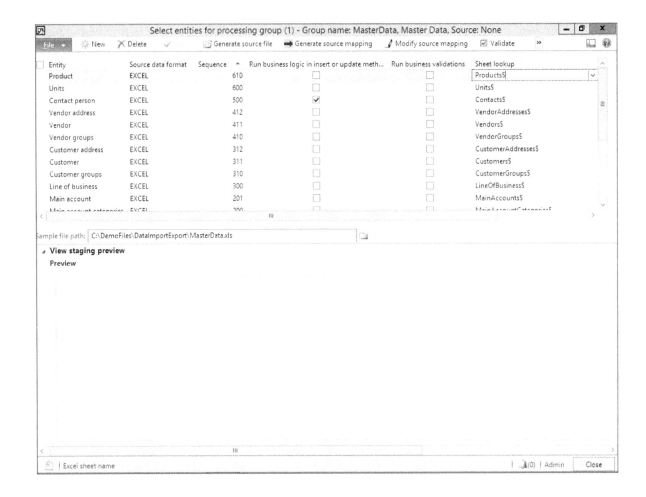

When you return back to the wizard, just click on the **Finish** button to exit from the form which will return you to the **Processing** Groups maintenance form. Click on the **Folder** icon to the right of the **Sample File Path** field.

When the file explorer opens navigate to where you saved your **MasterData** worksheet that you just created, and then click on the **Open** button.

Click on the **Sheet Lookup** dropdown list and select the **Products$** record.

Finish off the process by clicking on the **Generate Source Mapping** button within the menu bar. If everything is linked up correctly and you have all of the key fields within your map, then you will get a quick message saying that the entity mapping was completed and you can click on the **Close** button.

Example Data

Creating a Products Import Entity

Now that you have the worksheet created you can start populating the worksheet with your own set of **Products**. Here is an example of how the data should look.

DisplayProductNumber	0050209O
EcoResProductTranslation_LanguageId	en-us
EcoResProductTranslation_Name	Honeywell 005-02044-0029+O Encoder
ItemId	0050209O
ProductSubType	Product
ProductType	Item
EcoResProductDimensionGroup_Name	WH
EcoResStorageDimensionGroup_Name	NONE
EcoResTrackingDimensionGroup_Name	NONE
InventTableModuleInvent_Price	1
InventTableModuleInvent_UnitId	ea
InventTableModulePurch_Price	1
InventTableModulePurch_UnitId	ea
InventTableModulePurch_TaxItemGroupId	
InventTableModuleSales_Price	1
InventTableModuleSales_UnitId	ea
InventTableModuleSales_TaxItemGroupId	
ItemGroupId	
ModelGroupId	
SearchName	005-02044-0029+O
CostGroupId	
CostModel	
NameAlias	Honeywell 005-02044-0029+O Encoder
BOMCalcGroupId	
BOMUnitId	ea

www.dynamicsaxcompanions.com
Dynamics AX Companions
- 217 -
www.blindsquirrelpublishing.com
© 2015 Blind Squirrel Publishing, LLC, All Rights Reserved
BLIND SQUIRREL
PUBLISHING

Creating a Product Categories Import Entity

So that we can classify all of the products within the product category hierarchies we will now create an entity for the **Product Categories**. This entity allows you to create a category tree structure that we will then link to the products in the next step.

daxc

www.dynamicsaxcompanions.com
Dynamics AX Companions

- 219 -

www.blindsquirrelpublishing.com
© 2015 Blind Squirrel Publishing, LLC, All Rights Reserved

BLIND SQUIRREL
PUBLISHING

Step By Step Walkthrough

Creating a Product Categories Import Entity

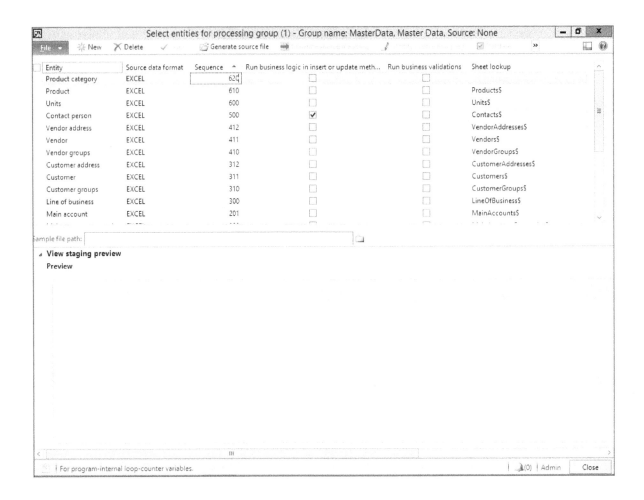

To do this, return to the **Processing Group Entities** maintenance form and click on the **New** button within the menu bar to create a new record. Then click on the **Entity** dropdown list and find the **Product Category** Entity type.

Click on the **Source Data Format** dropdown list and select the **EXCEL** format, and then set the **Sequence** number to **620**.

Now we want to create the mapping that we will be using to import in all of the data. To do this click on the **Generate Source File** button in the menu bar and when the **Wizard** appears, click on the **Next** button to start setting things up.

When the **Display Data** page is shown you will be able to see all of the default fields in the entity map.

Sample Data

Creating a Product Categories Import Entity

Here are the fields that you will want to have within your **Product Categories** import definition if you want to use the sample company import template that we provide.

Present in source	Sequence	Field name	Mandatory	Field type	Field size
Yes	1	EcoResCategory_Name	Yes	String	254
Yes	2	EcoResCategoryHierarchy_Name	Yes	String	128
Yes	3	Product_DisplayProductNumber	Yes	String	70

Step By Step Walkthrough

Creating a Product Categories Import Entity

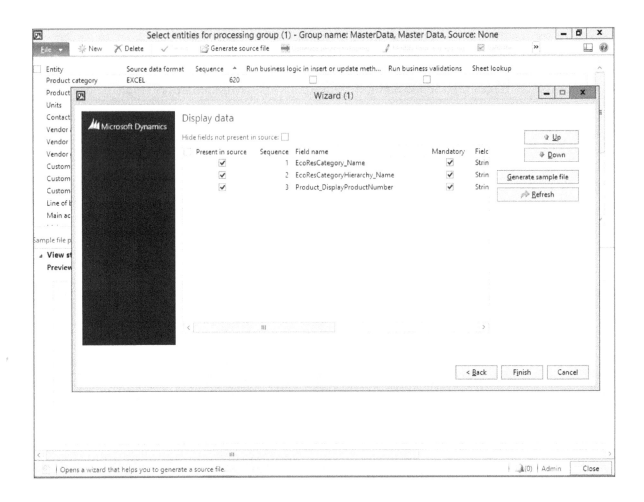

Find each of the fields in the template and then just click on the **Present In Source** checkbox, which will enable to field to be used within the template. If you need to re-order any of the fields then select the field and then click on the **Up** or **Down** buttons to rearrange them.

Once you have all of the fields selected and you have them in the right order then click on the **Generate Sample File** button.

Step By Step Walkthrough

Creating a Product Categories Import Entity

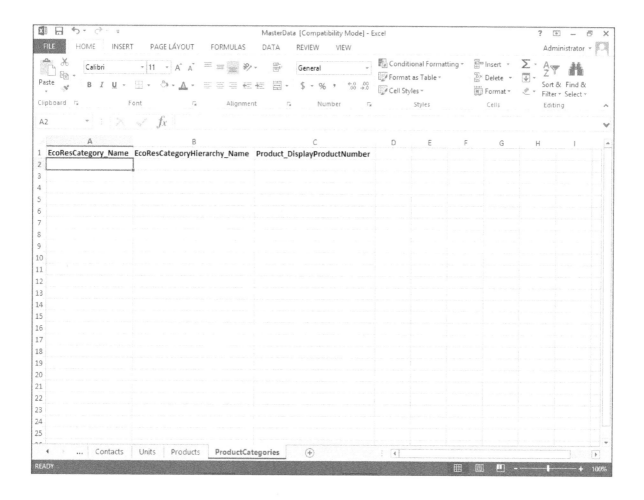

This will create another Excel Workbook for you just like before and the first sheet will already be set up with the fields that you need for the **Product Category** import.

Open up the **MasterData** template that you created in the previous step and add a new Worksheet to the workbook by clicking on the **+** button and rename it to **ProductCategories.**

Now return to the workbook that was automatically generated by the wizard and select the auto-generated columns and copy them (**CTRL+C**) and paste (**CTRL+V**) them into the **ProductCategories** worksheet within the **MasterData** workbook. You may also want to format the columns to make it look tidy.

When you have done that, close out of the **MasterData** workbook.

Step By Step Walkthrough

Creating a Product Categories Import Entity

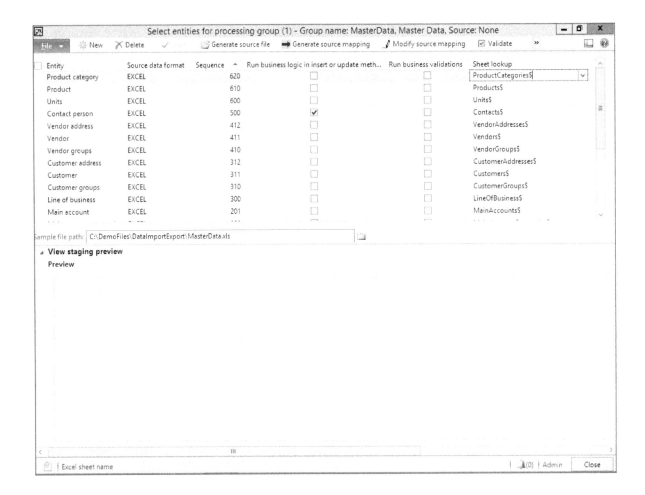

When you return back to the wizard, just click on the **Finish** button to exit from the form which will return you to the **Processing** Groups maintenance form. Click on the **Folder** icon to the right of the **Sample File Path** field.

When the file explorer opens navigate to where you saved your **MasterData** worksheet that you just created, and then click on the **Open** button.

Click on the **Sheet Lookup** dropdown list and select the **ProductCategories$** record.

Finish off the process by clicking on the **Generate Source Mapping** button within the menu bar. If everything is linked up correctly and you have all of the key fields within your map, then you will get a quick message saying that the entity mapping was completed and you can click on the **Close** button.

Example Data

Creating a Product Categories Import Entity

Now that you have the worksheet created you can start populating the worksheet with your own set of **Product Categories**. Here is an example of how the data should look.

CategoryHierarchy Name	Marketplace ALL
Code	
ParentName	

www.dynamicsaxcompanions.com
Dynamics AX Companions

- 225 -

www.blindsquirrelpublishing.com
© 2015 Blind Squirrel Publishing, LLC, All Rights Reserved

BLIND SQUIRREL
PUBLISHING

Sample Data

Creating a Product Categories Import Entity

If you are looking for some sample **Product Category** data to load then here is a snapshot of the data that we use in the sample template.

CategoryHierarchy	Name	Code	ParentName
Marketplace	ALL		
Marketplace	Animals & Pet Supplies		ALL
Marketplace	Live Animals		Animals & Pet Supplies
Marketplace	Pet Supplies		Animals & Pet Supplies
Marketplace	Bird Supplies		Pet Supplies
Marketplace	Bird Cage Accessories		Bird Supplies
Marketplace	Bird Cage Bird Baths		Bird Cage Accessories
Marketplace	Bird Cage Food & Water Dishes		Bird Cage Accessories
Marketplace	Bird Cages & Stands		Bird Supplies
Marketplace	Bird Food		Bird Supplies
Marketplace	Bird Gyms & Playstands		Bird Supplies
Marketplace	Bird Ladders & Perches		Bird Supplies
Marketplace	Bird Toys		Bird Supplies
Marketplace	Bird Treats		Bird Supplies
Marketplace	Cat Supplies		Pet Supplies
Marketplace	Cat Apparel		Cat Supplies
Marketplace	Cat Beds		Cat Supplies

Marketplace	Cat Food	Cat Supplies
Marketplace	Cat Furniture	Cat Supplies
Marketplace	Cat Furniture Accessories	Cat Supplies
Marketplace	Cat Litter	Cat Supplies
Marketplace	Cat Litter Box Liners	Cat Supplies
Marketplace	Cat Litter Box Mats	Cat Supplies
Marketplace	Cat Litter Boxes	Cat Supplies

daxc
www.dynamicsaxcompanions.com
Dynamics AX Companions

- 227 -

www.blindsquirrelpublishing.com
© 2015 Blind Squirrel Publishing, LLC , All Rights Reserved

BLIND SQUIRREL
PUBLISHING

Creating a Product Category Hierarchy Import Entity

Once the **Product Categories** have been configured for importing then you will need to import in the links between the products and the categories. This is done through the **Product Category Hierarchy** entity which we will now configure.

www.dynamicsaxcompanions.com
Dynamics AX Companions

- 229 -

www.blindsquirrelpublishing.com
© 2015 Blind Squirrel Publishing, LLC, All Rights Reserved

BLIND SQUIRREL
PUBLISHING

Step By Step Walkthrough

Creating a Product Category Hierarchy Import Entity

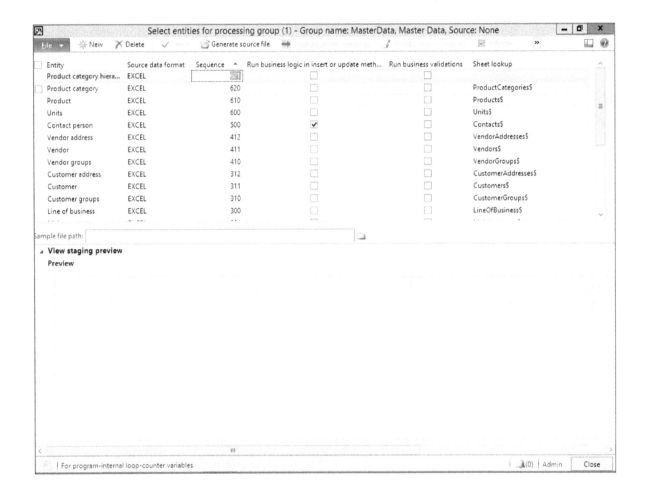

To do this, open the **Processing Group Entities** maintenance form and click on the **New** button within the menu bar to create a new record. Then click on the **Entity** dropdown list and find the **Product Category Hierarchy** Entity type.

Click on the **Source Data Format** dropdown list and select the **EXCEL** format, and then set the **Sequence** number to **621**.

Now we want to create the mapping that we will be using to import in all of the data. To do this click on the **Generate Source File** button in the menu bar and when the **Wizard** appears, click on the **Next** button to start setting things up.

When the **Display Data** page is shown you will be able to see all of the default fields in the entity map.

Sample Data

Creating a Product Category Hierarchy Import Entity

Here are the fields that you will want to have within your **Product Category Hierarchy** import definition if you want to use the sample company import template that we provide.

Present in source	Sequence	Field name	Mandatory	Field type	Field size
Yes	1	EcoResCategory_Name	Yes	String	254
Yes	2	EcoResCategoryHierarchy_Name	Yes	String	128

Step By Step Walkthrough

Creating a Product Category Hierarchy Import Entity

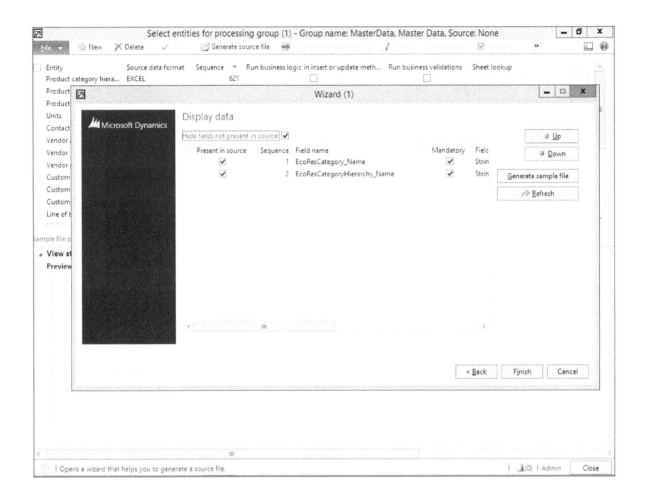

Find each of the fields in the template and then just click on the **Present In Source** checkbox, which will enable to field to be used within the template. If you need to re-order any of the fields then select the field and then click on the **Up** or **Down** buttons to rearrange them.

Once you have all of the fields selected and you have them in the right order then click on the **Generate Sample File** button.

Step By Step Walkthrough

Creating a Product Category Hierarchy Import Entity

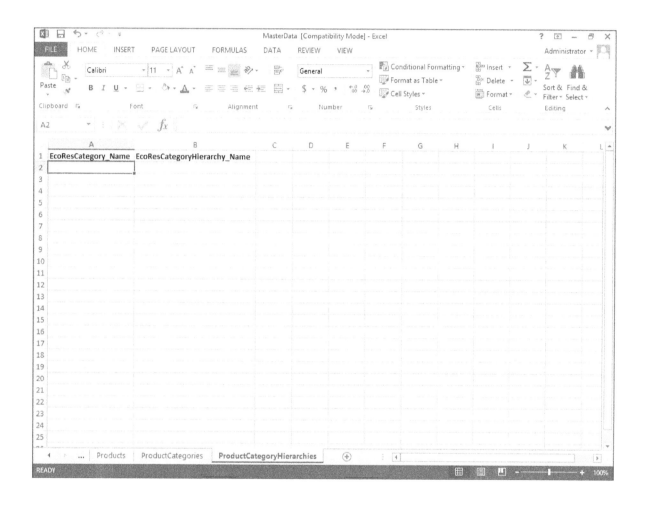

This will create another Excel Workbook for you just like before and the first sheet will already be set up with the fields that you need for the **Product Category Hierarchy** import.

Open up the **MasterData** template that you created in the previous step and add a new Worksheet to the workbook by clicking on the + button and rename it to **ProductCategoryHierarchy.**

Now return to the workbook that was automatically generated by the wizard and select the auto-generated columns and copy them (**CTRL+C**) and paste (**CTRL+V**) them into the **ProductCategoryHierarchies** worksheet within the **MasterData** workbook. You may also want to format the columns to make it look tidy.

When you have done that, close out of the **MasterData** workbook.

Step By Step Walkthrough

Creating a Product Category Hierarchy Import Entity

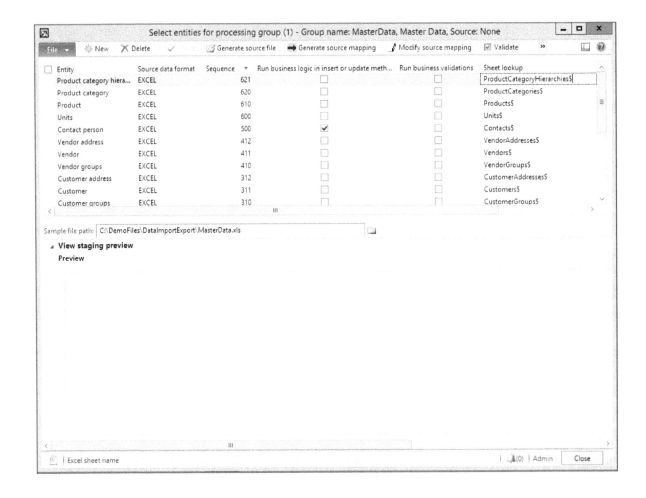

When you return back to the wizard, just click on the **Finish** button to exit from the form which will return you to the **Processing** Groups maintenance form. Click on the **Folder** icon to the right of the **Sample File Path** field.

When the file explorer opens navigate to where you saved your **MasterData** worksheet that you just created, and then click on the **Open** button.

Click on the **Sheet Lookup** dropdown list and select the **ProductCategoryHierarchies$** record.

Finish off the process by clicking on the **Generate Source Mapping** button within the menu bar. If everything is linked up correctly and you have all of the key fields within your map, then you will get a quick message saying that the entity mapping was completed and you can click on the **Close** button.

Creating a BOM Version Import Entity

If you want to import in the **Bills Of Material** through the Data Import Export Framework then we need to create a couple of entities. The first one is the **BOM Version** which just creates a BOM header and associates it with a **Product**.

daxc
www.dynamicsaxcompanions.com
Dynamics AX Companions

- 235 -

www.blindsquirrelpublishing.com
© 2015 Blind Squirrel Publishing, LLC , All Rights Reserved

BLIND SQUIRREL
PUBLISHING

Step By Step Walkthrough

Creating a BOM Version Import Entity

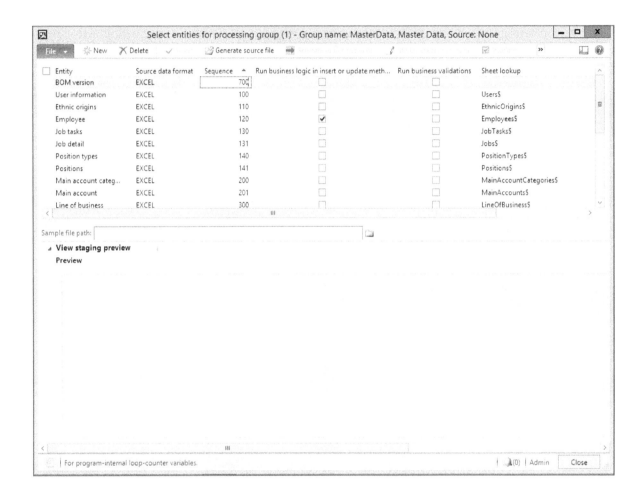

To do this, return to the **Processing Group Entities** maintenance form and click on the **New** button within the menu bar to create a new record. Then click on the **Entity** dropdown list and find the **BOM Version** Entity type.

Click on the **Source Data Format** dropdown list and select the **EXCEL** format, and then set the **Sequence** number to **700**.

Now we want to create the mapping that we will be using to import in all of the data. To do this click on the **Generate Source File** button in the menu bar and when the **Wizard** appears, click on the **Next** button to start setting things up.

When the **Display Data** page is shown you will be able to see all of the default fields in the entity map.

Sample Data

Creating a BOM Version Import Entity

Here are the fields that you will want to have within your **BOM Version** import definition if you want to use the sample company import template that we provide.

Present in source	Sequence	Field name	Mandatory	Field type	Field size
Yes	1	BOM_BOMId	Yes	String	20
Yes	2	ItemId	Yes	String	20
Yes	3	BOM_Name	No	String	60

Step By Step Walkthrough

Creating a BOM Version Import Entity

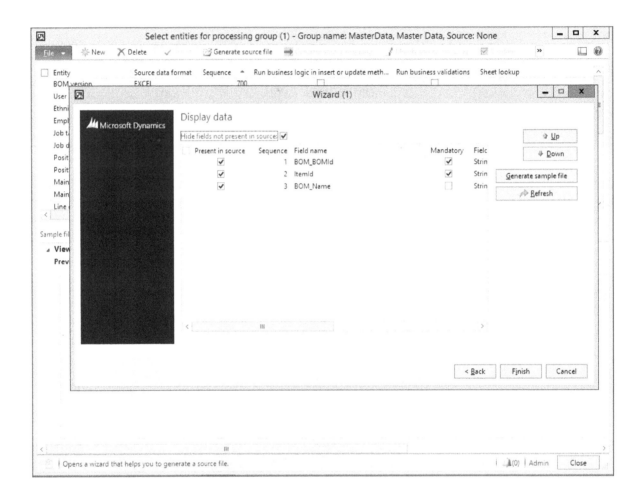

Find each of the fields in the template and then just click on the **Present In Source** checkbox, which will enable to field to be used within the template. If you need to re-order any of the fields then select the field and then click on the **Up** or **Down** buttons to rearrange them.

Once you have all of the fields selected and you have them in the right order then click on the **Generate Sample File** button.

Step By Step Walkthrough

Creating a BOM Version Import Entity

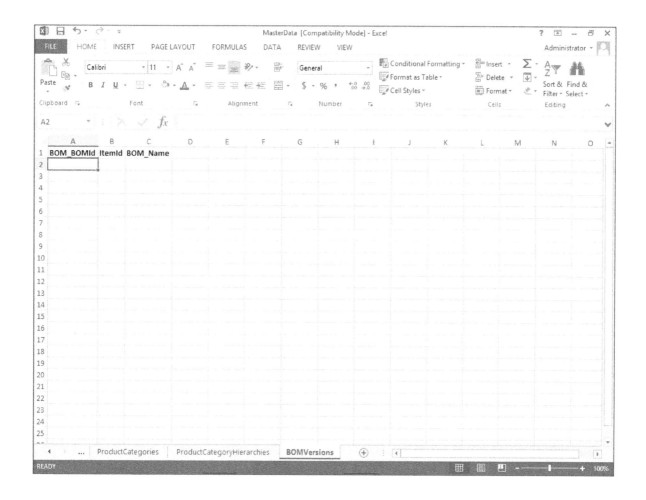

This will create another Excel Workbook for you just like before and the first sheet will already be set up with the fields that you need for the **BOM Version** import.

Open up the **MasterData** template that you created in the previous step and add a new Worksheet to the workbook by clicking on the **+** button and rename it to **BOMVersions.**

Now return to the workbook that was automatically generated by the wizard and select the auto-generated columns and copy them (**CTRL+C**) and paste (**CTRL+V**) them into the **BOMVersions** worksheet within the **MasterData** workbook. You may also want to format the columns to make it look tidy.

When you have done that, close out of the **MasterData** workbook.

Step By Step Walkthrough

Creating a BOM Version Import Entity

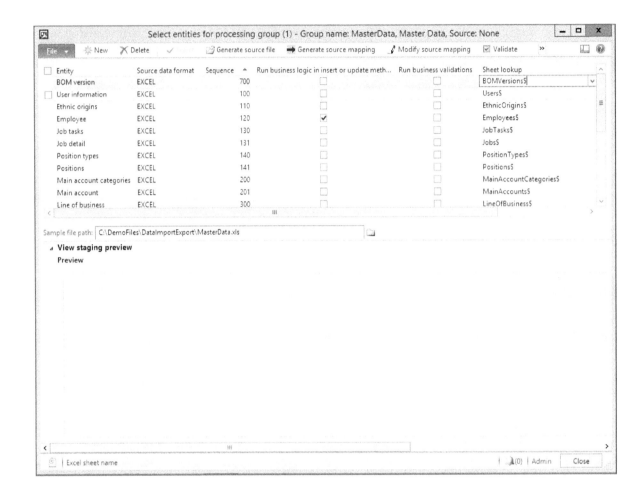

When you return back to the wizard, just click on the **Finish** button to exit from the form which will return you to the **Processing** Groups maintenance form. Click on the **Folder** icon to the right of the **Sample File Path** field.

When the file explorer opens navigate to where you saved your **MasterData** worksheet that you just created, and then click on the **Open** button.

Click on the **Sheet Lookup** dropdown list and select the **BOMVersions$** record.

Finish off the process by clicking on the **Generate Source Mapping** button within the menu bar. If everything is linked up correctly and you have all of the key fields within your map, then you will get a quick message saying that the entity mapping was completed and you can click on the **Close** button.

Example Data

Creating a BOM Version Import Entity

Now that you have the worksheet created you can start populating the worksheet with your own set of **BOM Versions**. Here is an example of how the data should look.

BOM_BOMId	KM-SS-62TS4-BL
ItemId	KM-SS-62TS4-BL
BOM_Name	KM-SS-62TS4-BL

Sample Data

Creating a BOM Version Import Entity

If you are looking for some sample **BOM Version** data to load then here is a snapshot of the
data that we use in the sample template.

BOM_BOMId	ItemId	BOM_Name
KM-SS-62TS4-BL	KM-SS-62TS4-BL	KM-SS-62TS4-BL

BLIND SQUIRREL
PUBLISHING

Creating a BOM Import Entity

Once you have the entity configured for the **BOM Version** you will also want to create an import entity for the **BOM** lines.

daxc
www.dynamicsaxcompanions.com
Dynamics AX Companions

- 243 -

www.blindsquirrelpublishing.com
© 2015 Blind Squirrel Publishing, LLC , All Rights Reserved

BLIND SQUIRREL
PUBLISHING

Step By Step Walkthrough

Creating a BOM Import Entity

To do this, open the **Processing Group Entities** maintenance form and click on the **New** button within the menu bar to create a new record. Then click on the **Entity** dropdown list and find the **BOM** Entity type.

Click on the **Source Data Format** dropdown list and select the **EXCEL** format, and then set the **Sequence** number to **701**.

Now we want to create the mapping that we will be using to import in all of the data. To do this click on the **Generate Source File** button in the menu bar and when the **Wizard** appears, click on the **Next** button to start setting things up.

When the **Display Data** page is shown you will be able to see all of the default fields in the entity map.

www.dynamicsaxcompanions.com
Dynamics AX Companions

- 244 -

www.blindsquirrelpublishing.com
© 2015 Blind Squirrel Publishing, LLC, All Rights Reserved

BLIND SQUIRREL
PUBLISHING

Sample Data

Creating a BOM Import Entity

Here are the fields that you will want to have within your **BOM** import definition if you want to use the sample company import template that we provide.

Present in source	Sequence	Field name	Mandatory	Field type	Field size
Yes	1	BOM_BOMId	Yes	String	20
Yes	2	LineNum	Yes	Real	31
Yes	3	ItemId	Yes	String	20
Yes	4	BOMQty	No	Real	31
Yes	5	UnitId	Yes	String	10

Step By Step Walkthrough

Creating a BOM Import Entity

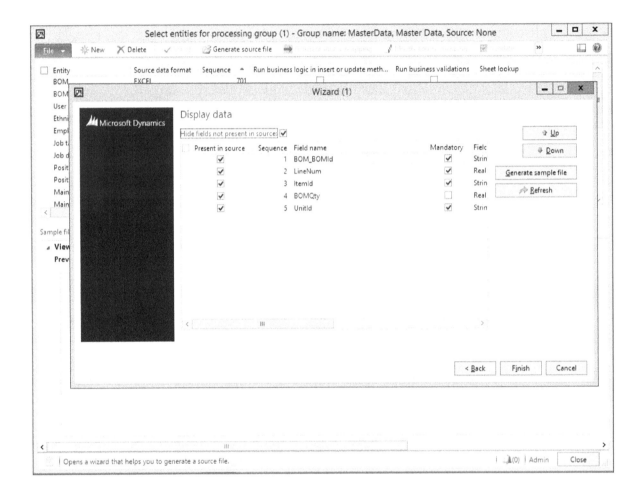

Find each of the fields in the template and then just click on the **Present In Source** checkbox, which will enable to field to be used within the template. If you need to re-order any of the fields then select the field and then click on the **Up** or **Down** buttons to rearrange them.

Once you have all of the fields selected and you have them in the right order then click on the **Generate Sample File** button.

Step By Step Walkthrough

Creating a BOM Import Entity

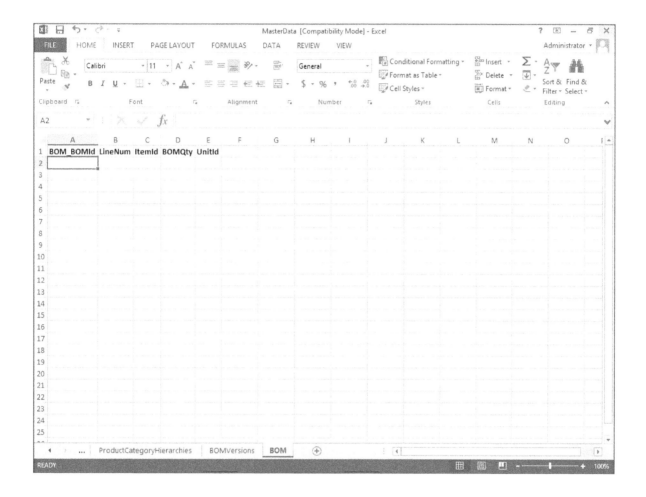

This will create another Excel Workbook for you just like before and the first sheet will already be set up with the fields that you need for the **BOM** import.

Open up the **MasterData** template that you created in the previous step and add a new Worksheet to the workbook by clicking on the **+** button and rename it to **BOM.**

Now return to the workbook that was automatically generated by the wizard and select the auto-generated columns and copy them (**CTRL+C**) and paste (**CTRL+V**) them into the **BOM** worksheet within the **MasterData** workbook. You may also want to format the columns to make it look tidy.

When you have done that, close out of the **MasterData** workbook.

Step By Step Walkthrough

Creating a BOM Import Entity

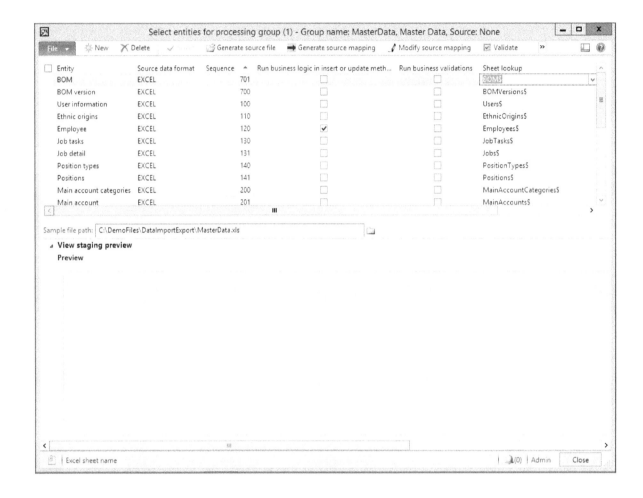

When you return back to the wizard, just click on the **Finish** button to exit from the form which will return you to the **Processing** Groups maintenance form. Click on the **Folder** icon to the right of the **Sample File Path** field.

When the file explorer opens navigate to where you saved your **MasterData** worksheet that you just created, and then click on the **Open** button.

Click on the **Sheet Lookup** dropdown list and select the **BOM$** record.

Finish off the process by clicking on the **Generate Source Mapping** button within the menu bar. If everything is linked up correctly and you have all of the key fields within your map, then you will get a quick message saying that the entity mapping was completed and you can click on the **Close** button.

Creating a Route Import Entity

Next we will want to create the import entities for the **Route** details. Just like the **BOM** this has a number of different entities that we need to create in order to link them correctly to the Product. To start off we will want to create an entity for the **Route** header.

daxc
www.dynamicsaxcompanions.com
Dynamics AX Companions

- 249 -

www.blindsquirrelpublishing.com
© 2015 Blind Squirrel Publishing, LLC, All Rights Reserved

BLIND SQUIRREL
PUBLISHING

Step By Step Walkthrough

Creating a Route Import Entity

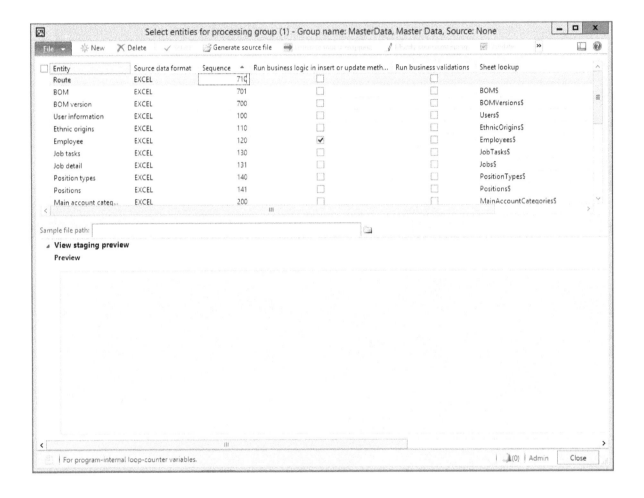

To do this, open the **Processing Group Entities** maintenance form and click on the **New** button within the menu bar to create a new record. Then click on the **Entity** dropdown list and find the **Route** Entity type.

Click on the **Source Data Format** dropdown list and select the **EXCEL** format, and then set the **Sequence** number to **710**.

Now we want to create the mapping that we will be using to import in all of the data. To do this click on the **Generate Source File** button in the menu bar and when the **Wizard** appears, click on the **Next** button to start setting things up.

When the **Display Data** page is shown you will be able to see all of the default fields in the entity map.

Sample Data

Creating a Route Import Entity

Here are the fields that you will want to have within your **Route** import definition if you want to use the sample company import template that we provide.

Present in source	Sequence	Field name	Mandatory	Field type	Field size
Yes	1	RouteId	Yes	String	20
Yes	2	ItemId	Yes	String	20
Yes	3	Route_Name	No	String	60
Yes	4	InventSiteId	No	String	10
Yes	5	Active	Yes	String	6

daxc
www.dynamicsaxcompanions.com
Dynamics AX Companions

- 251 -

www.blindsquirrelpublishing.com
© 2015 Blind Squirrel Publishing, LLC , All Rights Reserved

BLIND SQUIRREL
PUBLISHING

Step By Step Walkthrough

Creating a Route Import Entity

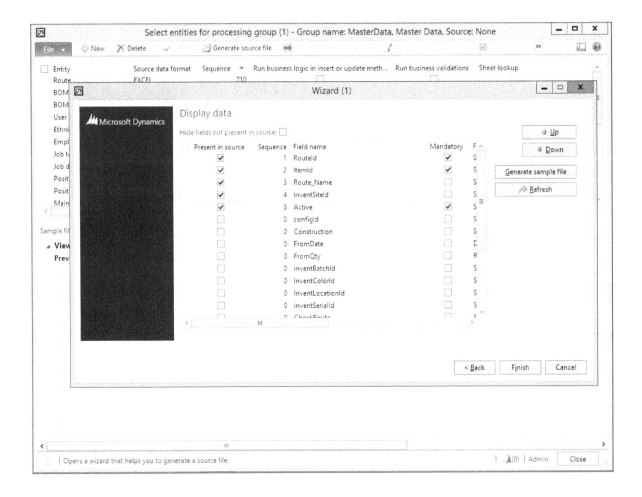

Find each of the fields in the template and then just click on the **Present In Source** checkbox, which will enable to field to be used within the template. If you need to re-order any of the fields then select the field and then click on the **Up** or **Down** buttons to rearrange them.

Once you have all of the fields selected and you have them in the right order then click on the **Generate Sample File** button.

Step By Step Walkthrough

Creating a Route Import Entity

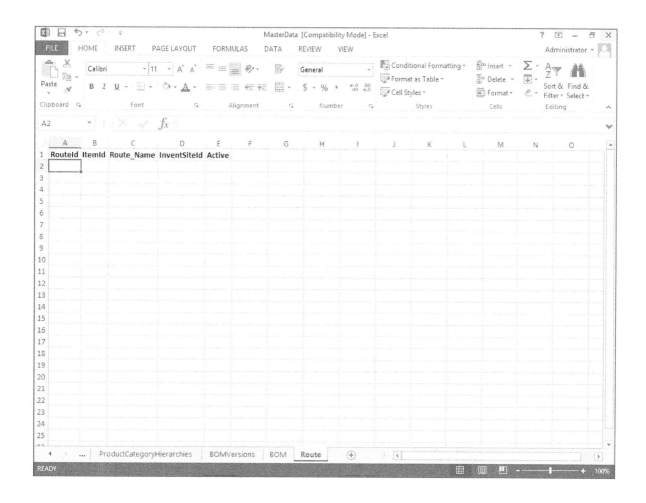

This will create another Excel Workbook for you just like before and the first sheet will already be set up with the fields that you need for the **Route** import.

Open up the **MasterData** template that you created in the previous step and add a new Worksheet to the workbook by clicking on the **+** button and rename it to **Route.**

Now return to the workbook that was automatically generated by the wizard and select the auto-generated columns and copy them (**CTRL+C**) and paste (**CTRL+V**) them into the **Route** worksheet within the **MasterData** workbook. You may also want to format the columns to make it look tidy.

When you have done that, close out of the **MasterData** workbook.

da&c
www.dynamicsaxcompanions.com
Dynamics AX Companions

- 253 -

www.blindsquirrelpublishing.com
© 2015 Blind Squirrel Publishing, LLC, All Rights Reserved

BLIND SQUIRREL
PUBLISHING

Step By Step Walkthrough

Creating a Route Import Entity

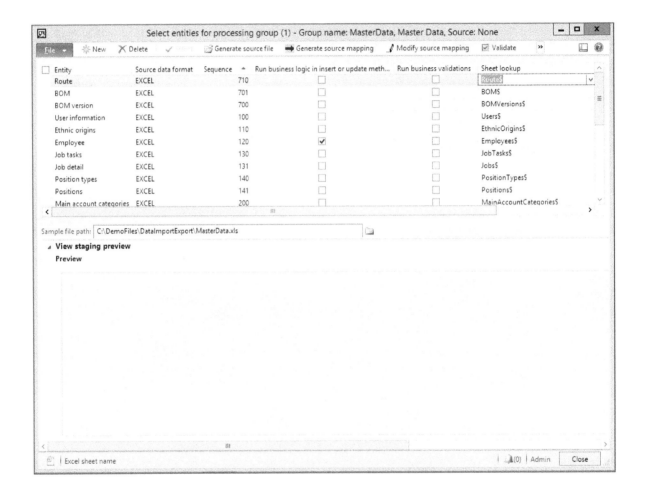

When you return back to the wizard, just click on the **Finish** button to exit from the form which will return you to the **Processing** Groups maintenance form. Click on the **Folder** icon to the right of the **Sample File Path** field.

When the file explorer opens navigate to where you saved your **MasterData** worksheet that you just created, and then click on the **Open** button.

Click on the **Sheet Lookup** dropdown list and select the **Routes$** record.

Finish off the process by clicking on the **Generate Source Mapping** button within the menu bar. If everything is linked up correctly and you have all of the key fields within your map, then you will get a quick message saying that the entity mapping was completed and you can click on the **Close** button.

Example Data

Creating a Route Import Entity

Now that you have the worksheet created you can start populating the worksheet with your own set of **Routes**. Here is an example of how the data should look.

RouteId	KM-SS-62TS4-BL
Route_Name	KM-SS-62TS4-BL
ItemId	KM-SS-62TS4-BL
InventSiteId	10
Active	No

Sample Data

Creating a Route Import Entity

If you are looking for some sample **Route** data to load then here is a snapshot of the data that we use in the sample template.

RouteId	Route_Name	ItemId	InventSiteId	Active
KM-SS-62TS4-BL	KM-SS-62TS4-BL	KM-SS-62TS4-BL	10	No

dαℵc   www.dynamicsaxcompanions.com
Dynamics AX Companions

- 256 -

www.blindsquirrelpublishing.com
© 2015 Blind Squirrel Publishing, LLC, All Rights Reserved

BLIND SQUIRREL
PUBLISHING

Creating a Route Relation Import Entity

Next we will want to create an entity for the **Route Relation** which will allow us to load in all of the operational steps for the route.

Step By Step Walkthrough

Creating a Route Relation Import Entity

To do this, open the **Processing Group Entities** maintenance form and click on the **New** button within the menu bar to create a new record. Then click on the **Entity** dropdown list and find the **Route Relation** Entity type.

Click on the **Source Data Format** dropdown list and select the **EXCEL** format, and then set the **Sequence** number to **711**.

Now we want to create the mapping that we will be using to import in all of the data. To do this click on the **Generate Source File** button in the menu bar and when the **Wizard** appears, click on the **Next** button to start setting things up.

When the **Display Data** page is shown you will be able to see all of the default fields in the entity map.

dαxc   www.dynamicsaxcompanions.com
Dynamics AX Companions

- 258 -

www.blindsquirrelpublishing.com
© 2015 Blind Squirrel Publishing, LLC , All Rights Reserved

BLIND SQUIRREL
PUBLISHING

Sample Data

Creating a Route Relation Import Entity

Here are the fields that you will want to have within your **Route Relation** import definition if you want to use the sample company import template that we provide.

Present in source	Sequence	Field name	Mandatory	Field type	Field size
Yes	1	RouteId	Yes	String	20
Yes	2	OprPriority	No	String	20
Yes	3	OprId	Yes	String	10
Yes	4	Level	No	Integer	11
Yes	5	OprNum	Yes	Integer	11

Step By Step Walkthrough

Creating a Route Relation Import Entity

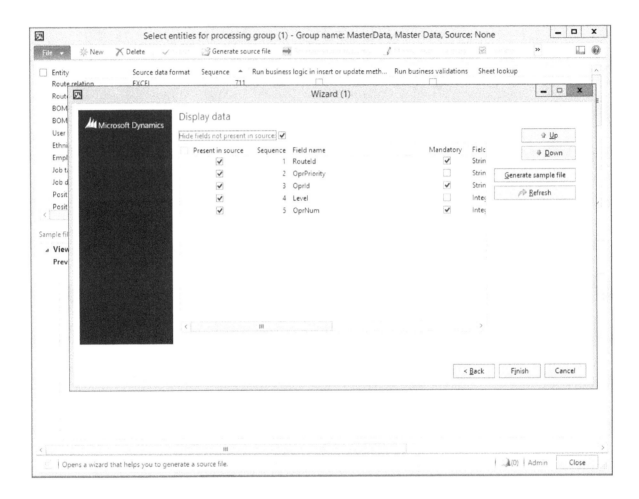

Find each of the fields in the template and then just click on the **Present In Source** checkbox, which will enable to field to be used within the template. If you need to re-order any of the fields then select the field and then click on the **Up** or **Down** buttons to rearrange them.

Once you have all of the fields selected and you have them in the right order then click on the **Generate Sample File** button.

Step By Step Walkthrough

Creating a Route Relation Import Entity

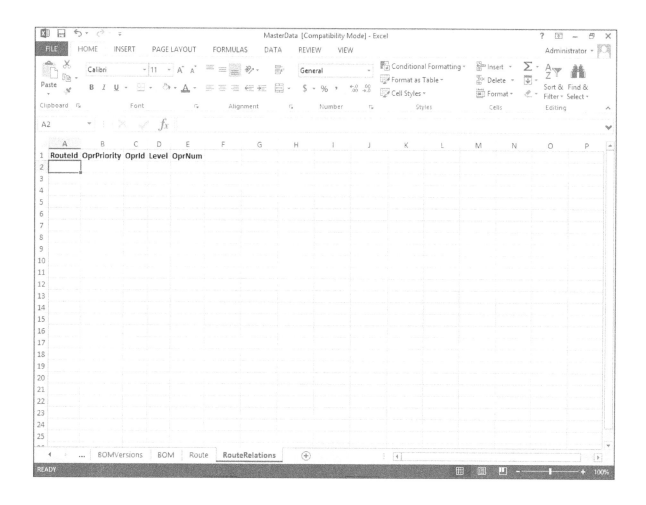

This will create another Excel Workbook for you just like before and the first sheet will already be set up with the fields that you need for the **Route Relations** import.

Open up the **MasterData** template that you created in the previous step and add a new Worksheet to the workbook by clicking on the **+** button and rename it to **ReouteRelations.**

Now return to the workbook that was automatically generated by the wizard and select the auto-generated columns and copy them (**CTRL+C**) and paste (**CTRL+V**) them into the **RouteRelations** worksheet within the **MasterData** workbook. You may also want to format the columns to make it look tidy.

When you have done that, close out of the **MasterData** workbook.

Step By Step Walkthrough

Creating a Route Relation Import Entity

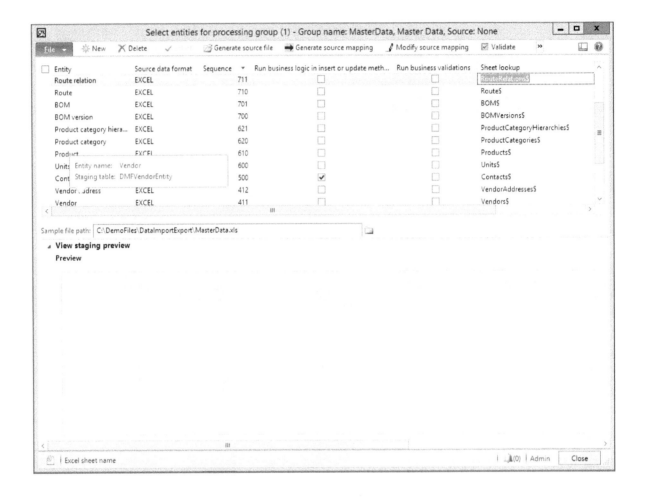

When you return back to the wizard, just click on the **Finish** button to exit from the form which will return you to the **Processing** Groups maintenance form. Click on the **Folder** icon to the right of the **Sample File Path** field.

When the file explorer opens navigate to where you saved your **MasterData** worksheet that you just created, and then click on the **Open** button.

Click on the **Sheet Lookup** dropdown list and select the **RouteRelations$** record.

Finish off the process by clicking on the **Generate Source Mapping** button within the menu bar. If everything is linked up correctly and you have all of the key fields within your map, then you will get a quick message saying that the entity mapping was completed and you can click on the **Close** button.

www.dynamicsaxcompanions.com
Dynamics AX Companions
- 262 -
www.blindsquirrelpublishing.com
© 2015 Blind Squirrel Publishing, LLC , All Rights Reserved
BLIND SQUIRREL
PUBLISHING

Example Data

Creating a Route Relation Import Entity

Now that you have the worksheet created you can start populating the worksheet with your own set of **Route Relations**. Here is an example of how the data should look.

RouteId	KM-SS-62TS4-BL
OprPriority	Primary
OprId	Sleeve Replace
Level	1
OprNum	10

www.dynamicsaxcompanions.com
Dynamics AX Companions

- 263 -

www.blindsquirrelpublishing.com
© 2015 Blind Squirrel Publishing, LLC , All Rights Reserved

BLIND SQUIRREL
PUBLISHING

Sample Data

Creating a Route Relation Import Entity

If you are looking for some sample **Route Relation** data to load then here is a snapshot of the data that we use in the sample template.

RouteId	OprPriority	OprId	Level	OprNum
KM-SS-62TS4-BL	Primary	Sleeve Replace	1	10
KM-SS-62TS4-BL	Primary	PressureTest	1	20

Creating a Route Operations Import Entity

Finally we will want to create a **Route Operations** entity which will link the **Route** with the **Product** record and tie everything together.

 www.dynamicsaxcompanions.com
Dynamics AX Companions
- 265 -
www.blindsquirrelpublishing.com
© 2015 Blind Squirrel Publishing, LLC, All Rights Reserved
BLIND SQUIRREL
PUBLISHING

Step By Step Walkthrough

Creating a Route Operations Import Entity

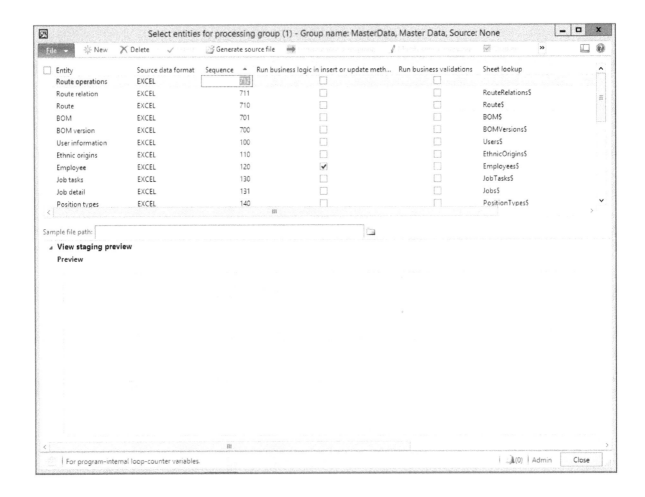

To do this, return to the **Processing Group Entities** maintenance form and click on the **New** button within the menu bar to create a new record. Then click on the **Entity** dropdown list and find the **Route Operations** Entity type.

Click on the **Source Data Format** dropdown list and select the **EXCEL** format, and then set the **Sequence** number to **712**.

Now we want to create the mapping that we will be using to import in all of the data. To do this click on the **Generate Source File** button in the menu bar and when the **Wizard** appears, click on the **Next** button to start setting things up.

When the **Display Data** page is shown you will be able to see all of the default fields in the entity map.

Sample Data

Creating a Route Operations Import Entity

Here are the fields that you will want to have within your **Route Operations** import definition if you want to use the sample company import template that we provide.

Present in source	Sequence	Field name	Mandatory	Field type	Field size
Yes	1	RouteId	No	String	20
Yes	2	RouteRelation	Yes	String	20
Yes	3	ItemRelation	Yes	String	20
Yes	4	ItemCode	No	String	10
Yes	5	SiteId	Yes	String	10
Yes	6	OprId	Yes	String	10
Yes	7	Quantity	No	Integer	11
Yes	8	Description	No	String	60
Yes	9	SetupTime	No	Real	31
Yes	10	QueueTimeBefore	No	Real	31
Yes	11	ProcessTime	No	Real	31
Yes	12	QueueTimeAfter	No	Real	31
Yes	13	OprNum	No	Integer	11
Yes	14	RouteGroupId	No	String	10

Step By Step Walkthrough

Creating a Route Operations Import Entity

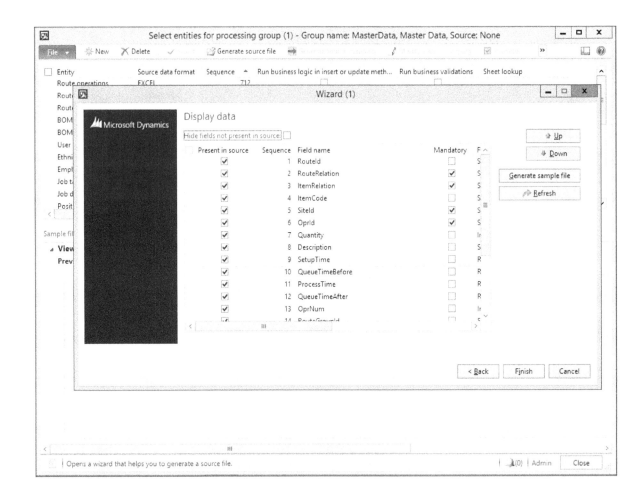

Find each of the fields in the template and then just click on the **Present In Source** checkbox, which will enable to field to be used within the template. If you need to re-order any of the fields then select the field and then click on the **Up** or **Down** buttons to rearrange them.

Once you have all of the fields selected and you have them in the right order then click on the **Generate Sample File** button.

 www.dynamicsaxcompanions.com
Dynamics AX Companions
- 268 -
www.blindsquirrelpublishing.com
© 2015 Blind Squirrel Publishing, LLC, All Rights Reserved
BLIND SQUIRREL
PUBLISHING

Step By Step Walkthrough

Creating a Route Operations Import Entity

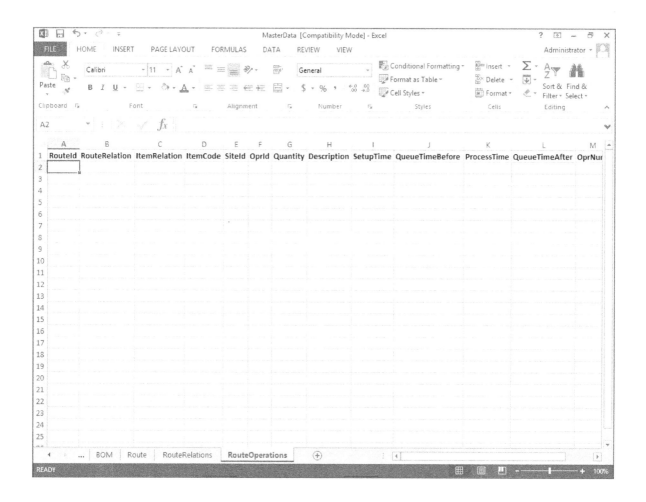

This will create another Excel Workbook for you just like before and the first sheet will already be set up with the fields that you need for the **Route Operations** import.

Open up the **MasterData** template that you created in the previous step and add a new Worksheet to the workbook by clicking on the **+** button and rename it to **RouteOperations.**

Now return to the workbook that was automatically generated by the wizard and select the auto-generated columns and copy them (**CTRL+C**) and paste (**CTRL+V**) them into the **RouteOperations** worksheet within the **MasterData** workbook. You may also want to format the columns to make it look tidy.

When you have done that, close out of the **MasterData** workbook.

daxc   www.dynamicsaxcompanions.com
Dynamics AX Companions
- 269 -
www.blindsquirrelpublishing.com
© 2015 Blind Squirrel Publishing, LLC, All Rights Reserved

BLIND SQUIRREL
PUBLISHING

Step By Step Walkthrough

Creating a Route Operations Import Entity

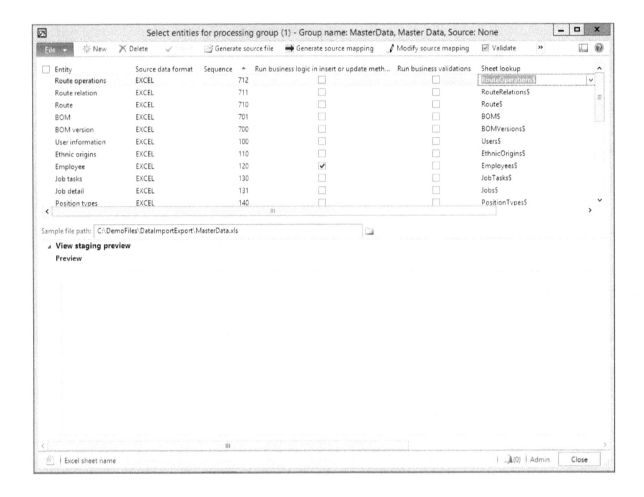

When you return back to the wizard, just click on the **Finish** button to exit from the form which will return you to the **Processing** Groups maintenance form. Click on the **Folder** icon to the right of the **Sample File Path** field.

When the file explorer opens navigate to where you saved your **MasterData** worksheet that you just created, and then click on the **Open** button.

Click on the **Sheet Lookup** dropdown list and select the **RouteOperations$** record.

Finish off the process by clicking on the **Generate Source Mapping** button within the menu bar. If everything is linked up correctly and you have all of the key fields within your map, then you will get a quick message saying that the entity mapping was completed and you can click on the **Close** button.

Example Data

Creating a Route Operations Import Entity

Now that you have the worksheet created you can start populating the worksheet with your own set of **Route Operations**. Here is an example of how the data should look.

OprId	Sleeve Replace
Quantity	1
Description	remove existing handle sleeve and replace with new Blue handle sleeve
SetupTime	0.10
QueueTimeAfter	
QueueTimeBefore	
ProcessTime	
OprNum	10
RouteGroupID	Std

www.dynamicsaxcompanions.com
Dynamics AX Companions

- 271 -

www.blindsquirrelpublishing.com
© 2015 Blind Squirrel Publishing, LLC, All Rights Reserved

BLIND SQUIRREL
PUBLISHING

Sample Data

Creating a Route Operations Import Entity

If you are looking for some sample **Route Operation** data to load then here is a snapshot of the data that we use in the sample template.

RouteID	RouteRelation	ItemRelation	ItemCode	SiteId	OprId	Quantity	Description	SetupTime	QueueTimeAfter	QueueTimeBefore	ProcessTime	OprNum	RouteGroupID
KM-SS-62TS4-BL	Route	Table	KM-SS-62TS4-BL		Sleeve Replace		remove existing handle sleeve and replace with new Blue handle sleeve						
				10		1		0.10				10	Std
KM-SS-62TS4-BL	Route	Table	KM-SS-62TS4-BL		PressureTest	1	Ensure hose can hold 1000 PSI pressure.						
				10				0.20				20	Std

Creating a Terms of Delivery Import Entity

Now we will show how you can configure the entities to load in some of the historical transactions into the system such as the **Sales Orders**. Before we do that we will want to configure a couple of codes that are required for the orders to be imported, and we will start by creating an entity for the **Terms Of Delivery**.

Step By Step Walkthrough

Creating a Terms of Delivery Import Entity

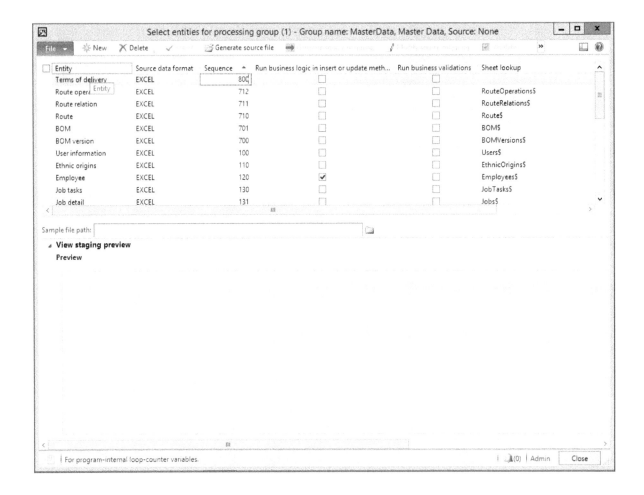

To do this, open the **Processing Group Entities** maintenance form and click on the **New** button within the menu bar to create a new record. Then click on the **Entity** dropdown list and find the **Terms Of Delivery** Entity type.

Click on the **Source Data Format** dropdown list and select the **EXCEL** format, and then set the **Sequence** number to **800**.

Now we want to create the mapping that we will be using to import in all of the data. To do this click on the **Generate Source File** button in the menu bar and when the **Wizard** appears, click on the **Next** button to start setting things up.

When the **Display Data** page is shown you will be able to see all of the default fields in the entity map.

Sample Data

Creating a Terms of Delivery Import Entity

Here are the fields that you will want to have within your **Terms Of Delivery** import definition if you want to use the sample company import template that we provide.

Present in source	Sequence	Field name	Mandatory	Field type	Field size
Yes	1	Code	Yes	String	10
Yes	2	Txt	No	String	60
Yes	3	DlvTerm	No	String	10
Yes	4	ShipCarrierApplyFreeMinimum	No	String	6
Yes	5	ShipCarrierFreeMinimum	No	Real	31
Yes	6	ShipCarrierFreightApplied	No	String	29
Yes	7	TransferChargesToOrder	No	String	6

Step By Step Walkthrough

Creating a Terms of Delivery Import Entity

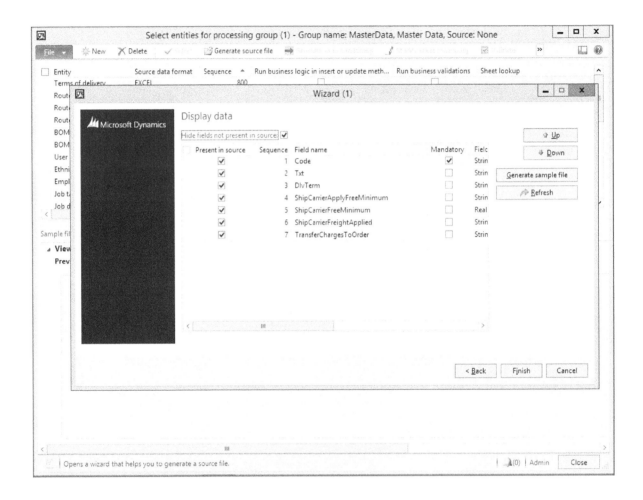

Find each of the fields in the template and then just click on the **Present In Source** checkbox, which will enable to field to be used within the template. If you need to re-order any of the fields then select the field and then click on the **Up** or **Down** buttons to rearrange them.

Once you have all of the fields selected and you have them in the right order then click on the **Generate Sample File** button.

Step By Step Walkthrough

Creating a Terms of Delivery Import Entity

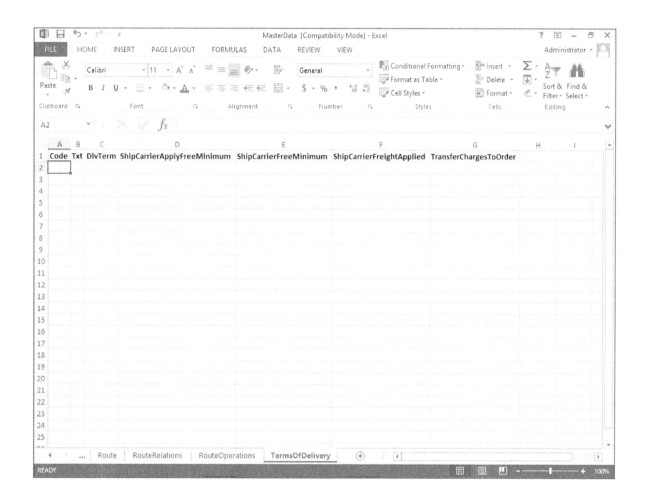

This will create another Excel Workbook for you just like before and the first sheet will already be set up with the fields that you need for the **Terms Of Delivery** import.

Open up the **MasterData** template that you created in the previous step and add a new Worksheet to the workbook by clicking on the **+** button and rename it to **TermsOfDelivery.**

Now return to the workbook that was automatically generated by the wizard and select the auto-generated columns and copy them (**CTRL+C**) and paste (**CTRL+V**) them into the **TermsOfDelivery** worksheet within the **MasterData** workbook. You may also want to format the columns to make it look tidy.

When you have done that, close out of the **MasterData** workbook.

Step By Step Walkthrough

Creating a Terms of Delivery Import Entity

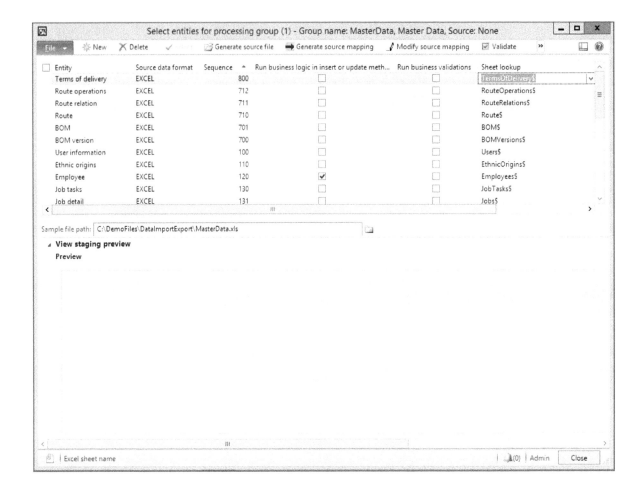

When you return back to the wizard, just click on the **Finish** button to exit from the form which will return you to the **Processing** Groups maintenance form. Click on the **Folder** icon to the right of the **Sample File Path** field.

When the file explorer opens navigate to where you saved your **MasterData** worksheet that you just created, and then click on the **Open** button.

Click on the **Sheet Lookup** dropdown list and select the **TermsOfDelivery$** record.

Finish off the process by clicking on the **Generate Source Mapping** button within the menu bar. If everything is linked up correctly and you have all of the key fields within your map, then you will get a quick message saying that the entity mapping was completed and you can click on the **Close** button.

Example Data

Creating a Terms of Delivery Import Entity

Now that you have the worksheet created you can start populating the worksheet with your own set of **Terms of Delivery**. Here is an example of how the data should look.

Code	CIF
Txt	Cost, insurance, freight
DlvTerm	Cost, insurance, freight
ShipCarrierApplyFreeMinimum	
ShipCarrierFreeMinimum	
ShipCarrierFreightApplied	
TransferChargesToOrder	

www.dynamicsaxcompanions.com
Dynamics AX Companions
   - 279 -
www.blindsquirrelpublishing.com
© 2015 Blind Squirrel Publishing, LLC , All Rights Reserved
BLIND SQUIRREL
PUBLISHING

Sample Data

Creating a Terms of Delivery Import Entity

If you are looking for some sample **Terms of Delivery** data to load then here is a snapshot of the data that we use in the sample template.

Code	Txt	DlvTerm	ShipCarrierApplyFreeMinimum	ShipCarrierFreeMinimum	ShipCarrierFreightApplied	TransferChargesToOrder
CIF	Cost, insurance, freight	Cost, insurance, freight				
DDP	Delivered duty paid	Delivered duty paid				
DES	Delivered ex ship	Delivered ex ship				
EXW	Ex works	Ex works				
FAS	Free along ship	Free along ship				
FCA	Free carrier (place)	Free carrier (place)				
FOB	Free on Board	Free on Board				

www.dynamicsaxcompanions.com
Dynamics AX Companions

- 280 -

BLIND SQUIRREL
PUBLISHING

Creating a Delivery Mode Import Entity

Another entity that we will want to configure within the import is the **Delivery Mode** entity which is required for sales orders to process.

dakc
www.dynamicsaxcompanions.com
Dynamics AX Companions

- 281 -

www.blindsquirrelpublishing.com
© 2015 Blind Squirrel Publishing, LLC, All Rights Reserved

BLIND SQUIRREL
PUBLISHING

Step By Step Walkthrough

Creating a Delivery Mode Import Entity

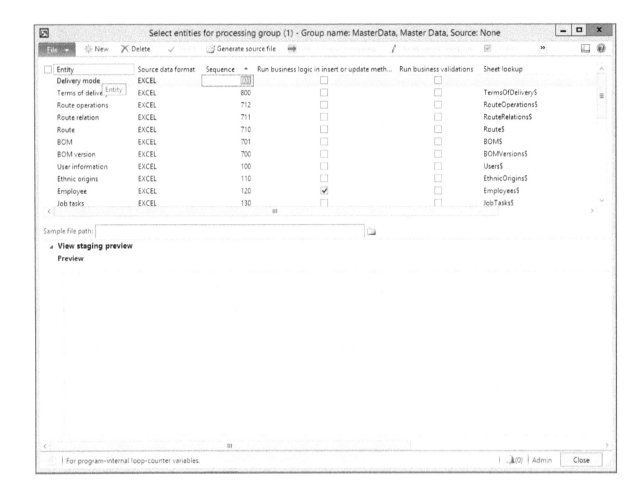

To do this return to the **Processing Group Entities** maintenance form and click on the **New** button within the menu bar to create a new record. Then click on the **Entity** dropdown list and find the **Delivery Mode** Entity type.

Click on the **Source Data Format** dropdown list and select the **EXCEL** format, and then set the **Sequence** number to **801**.

Now we want to create the mapping that we will be using to import in all of the data. To do this click on the **Generate Source File** button in the menu bar and when the **Wizard** appears, click on the **Next** button to start setting things up.

When the **Display Data** page is shown you will be able to see all of the default fields in the entity map.

Sample Data

Creating a Delivery Mode Import Entity

Here are the fields that you will want to have within your **Delivery Mode** import definition if you want to use the sample company import template that we provide.

Present in source	Sequence	Field name	Mandatory	Field type	Field size
Yes	1	Code	Yes	String	10
Yes	2	Txt	Yes	String	60
Yes	3	MarkupGroup	No	String	10
Yes	4	ShipCarrierAccountCode	No	String	20
Yes	5	ShipCarrierDlvType	No	String	20
Yes	6	ShipCarrierId	No	String	10
Yes	7	ShipCarrierName	No	String	20

Step By Step Walkthrough

Creating a Delivery Mode Import Entity

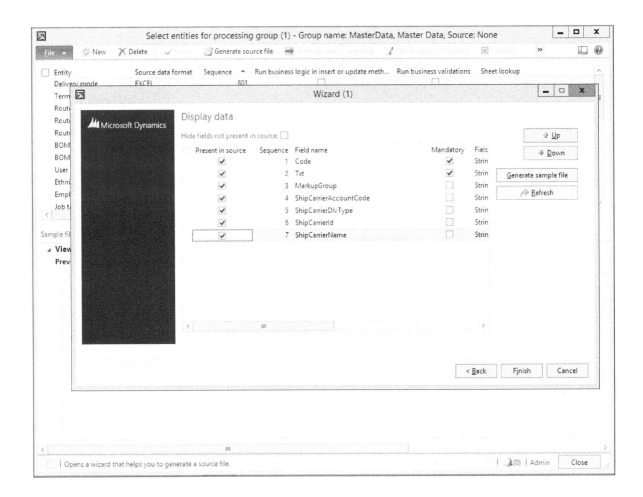

Find each of the fields in the template and then just click on the **Present In Source** checkbox, which will enable to field to be used within the template. If you need to re-order any of the fields then select the field and then click on the **Up** or **Down** buttons to rearrange them.

Once you have all of the fields selected and you have them in the right order then click on the **Generate Sample File** button.

Step By Step Walkthrough

Creating a Delivery Mode Import Entity

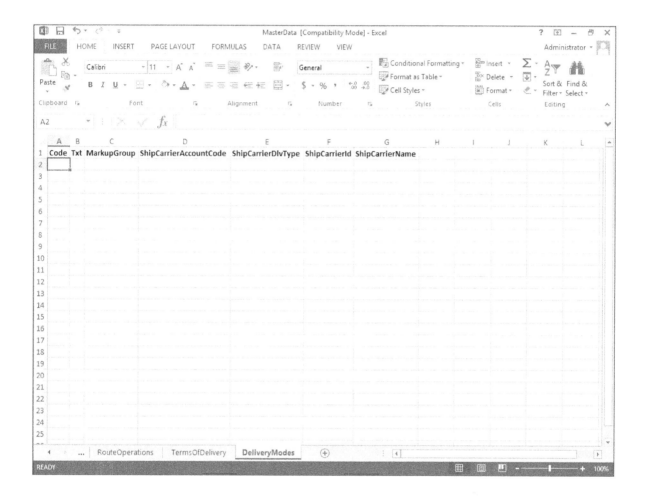

This will create another Excel Workbook for you just like before and the first sheet will already be set up with the fields that you need for the **Delivery Modes** import.

Open up the **MasterData** template that you created in the previous step and add a new Worksheet to the workbook by clicking on the **+** button and rename it to **DeliveryModes.**

Now return to the workbook that was automatically generated by the wizard and select the auto-generated columns and copy them (**CTRL+C**) and paste (**CTRL+V**) them into the **DeliveryModes** worksheet within the **MasterData** workbook. You may also want to format the columns to make it look tidy.

When you have done that, close out of the **MasterData** workbook.

Step By Step Walkthrough

Creating a Delivery Mode Import Entity

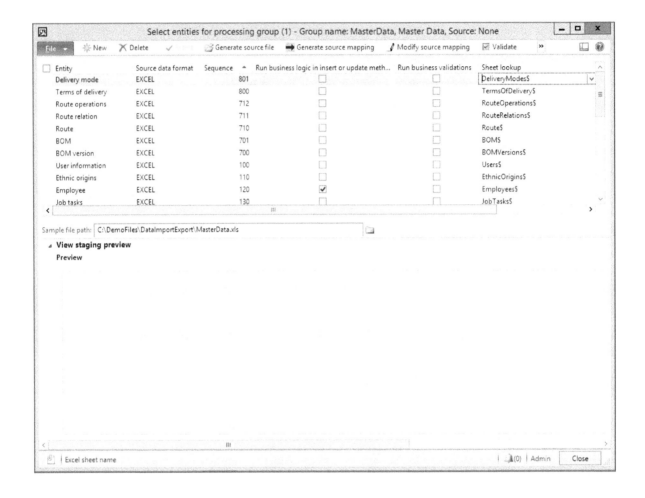

When you return back to the wizard, just click on the **Finish** button to exit from the form which will return you to the **Processing** Groups maintenance form. Click on the **Folder** icon to the right of the **Sample File Path** field.

When the file explorer opens navigate to where you saved your **MasterData** worksheet that you just created, and then click on the **Open** button.

Click on the **Sheet Lookup** dropdown list and select the **DeliveryModes$** record.

Finish off the process by clicking on the **Generate Source Mapping** button within the menu bar. If everything is linked up correctly and you have all of the key fields within your map, then you will get a quick message saying that the entity mapping was completed and you can click on the **Close** button.

Example Data

Creating a Delivery Mode Import Entity

Now that you have the worksheet created you can start populating the worksheet with your own set of **Delivery Modes**. Here is an example of how the data should look.

Code	TRUCK
Txt	Truck
MarkupGroup	
ShipCarrierAccountCode	
ShipCarrierDlvType	
ShipCarrierId	
ShipCarrierName	

www.dynamicsaxcompanions.com
Dynamics AX Companions

- 287 -

www.blindsquirrelpublishing.com
© 2015 Blind Squirrel Publishing, LLC, All Rights Reserved

BLIND SQUIRREL
PUBLISHING

Sample Data

Creating a Delivery Mode Import Entity

If you are looking for some sample **Delivery Modes** data to load then here is a snapshot of the data that we use in the sample template.

Code	Txt	MarkupGroup	ShipCarrierAccountCode	ShipCarrierDlvType	ShipCarrierId	ShipCarrierName
TRUCK	Truck					
AIR	Air					
RAIL	Rail					
OCEAN	Ocean					
PARCEL	Parcel					
CPU	Customer pickup					

www.dynamicsaxcompanions.com
Dynamics AX Companions

- 288 -

www.blindsquirrelpublishing.com
© 2015 Blind Squirrel Publishing, LLC, All Rights Reserved

BLIND SQUIRREL
PUBLISHING

Creating a Sales Order Header Import Entity

Now that we have the key codes configured for the sales orders we will create the import entities for the **Sales Orders**. There are two in this case so we will start by creating one for the **Sales Order Headers**.

Step By Step Walkthrough

Creating a Sales Order Header Import Entity

To do this, return to the **Processing Group Entities** maintenance form and click on the **New** button within the menu bar to create a new record. Then click on the **Entity** dropdown list and find the **Sales Order Header** Entity type.

Click on the **Source Data Format** dropdown list and select the **EXCEL** format, and then set the **Sequence** number to **910**.

Now we want to create the mapping that we will be using to import in all of the data. To do this click on the **Generate Source File** button in the menu bar and when the **Wizard** appears, click on the **Next** button to start setting things up.

When the **Display Data** page is shown you will be able to see all of the default fields in the entity map.

Sample Data

Creating a Sales Order Header Import Entity

Here are the fields that you will want to have within your **Sales Order Headers** import definition if you want to use the sample company import template that we provide.

Present in source	Sequence	Field name	Mandatory	Field type	Field size
Yes	1	SalesType	No	String	20
Yes	2	SalesId	Yes	String	20
Yes	3	CurrencyCode	Yes	String	3
Yes	4	CustAccount	Yes	String	20
Yes	5	CustGroup	Yes	String	10
Yes	6	InvoiceAccount	Yes	String	20
Yes	7	ShippingDateRequested	Yes	Date	30
Yes	8	LanguageId	Yes	String	7
Yes	9	DeliveryAddress	No	String	250
Yes	10	DlvMode	No	String	10
Yes	11	DlvTerm	No	String	10
Yes	12	CashDisc	No	String	10
Yes	13	SalesOriginId	No	String	10

daxc   www.dynamicsaxcompanions.com
Dynamics AX Companions

- 291 -

www.blindsquirrelpublishing.com
© 2015 Blind Squirrel Publishing, LLC , All Rights Reserved

BLIND SQUIRREL
PUBLISHING

Step By Step Walkthrough

Creating a Sales Order Header Import Entity

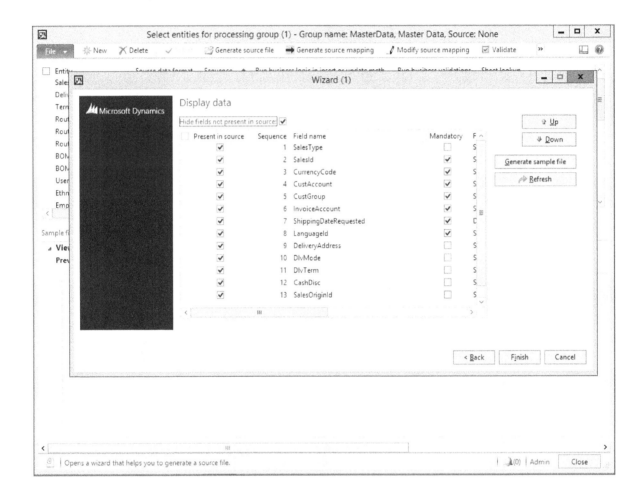

Find each of the fields in the template and then just click on the **Present In Source** checkbox, which will enable to field to be used within the template. If you need to re-order any of the fields then select the field and then click on the **Up** or **Down** buttons to rearrange them.

Once you have all of the fields selected and you have them in the right order then click on the **Generate Sample File** button.

Step By Step Walkthrough

Creating a Sales Order Header Import Entity

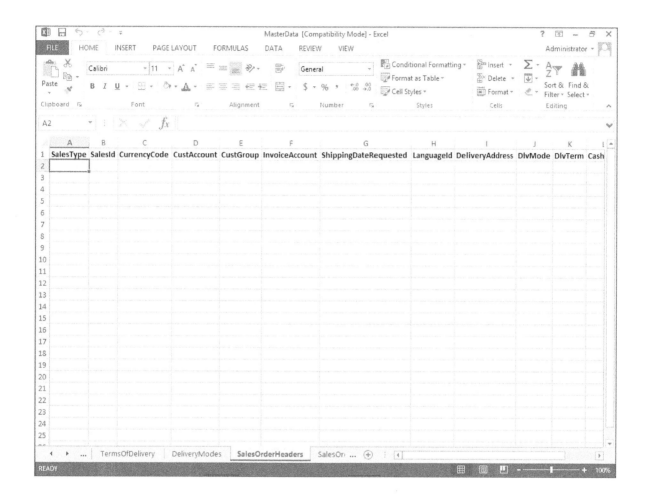

This will create another Excel Workbook for you just like before and the first sheet will already be set up with the fields that you need for the **Sales Order Header** import.

Open up the **MasterData** template that you created in the previous step and add a new Worksheet to the workbook by clicking on the + button and rename it to **SalesOrderHeaders.**

Now return to the workbook that was automatically generated by the wizard and select the auto-generated columns and copy them (**CTRL+C**) and paste (**CTRL+V**) them into the **SalesOrderHEaders** worksheet within the **MasterData** workbook. You may also want to format the columns to make it look tidy.

When you have done that, close out of the **MasterData** workbook.

www.dynamicsaxcompanions.com
Dynamics AX Companions
- 293 -
www.blindsquirrelpublishing.com
© 2015 Blind Squirrel Publishing, LLC, All Rights Reserved

BLIND SQUIRREL
PUBLISHING

Step By Step Walkthrough

Creating a Sales Order Header Import Entity

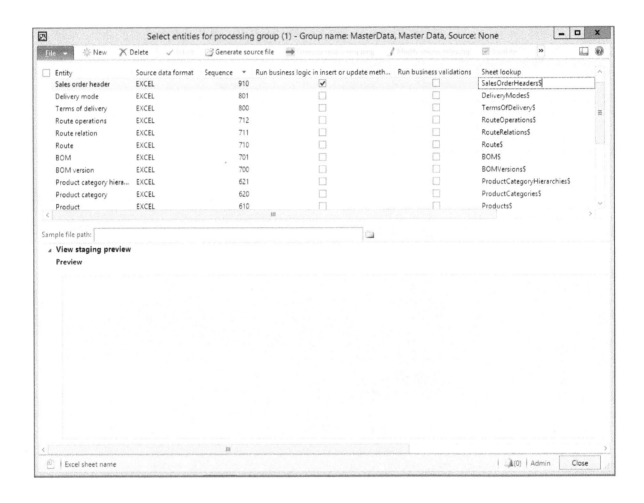

When you return back to the wizard, just click on the **Finish** button to exit from the form which will return you to the **Processing** Groups maintenance form. Click on the **Folder** icon to the right of the **Sample File Path** field.

When the file explorer opens navigate to where you saved your **MasterData** worksheet that you just created, and then click on the **Open** button.

Click on the **Sheet Lookup** dropdown list and select the **SalesOrderHeaders$** record.

Finish off the process by clicking on the **Generate Source Mapping** button within the menu bar. If everything is linked up correctly and you have all of the key fields within your map, then you will get a quick message saying that the entity mapping was completed and you can click on the **Close** button.

Example Data

Creating a Sales Order Header Import Entity

Now that you have the worksheet created you can start populating the worksheet with your own set of **Sales Order Headers**. Here is an example of how the data should look.

CurrencyCode	USD
CustAccount	10024183
CustGroup	DOMESTIC
InvoiceAccount	10024183
LanguageId	en-us
SalesId	29453
ShippingDateRequested	1/1/2015

www.dynamicsaxcompanions.com
Dynamics AX Companions

- 295 -

www.blindsquirrelpublishing.com
© 2015 Blind Squirrel Publishing, LLC , All Rights Reserved

BLIND SQUIRREL
PUBLISHING

Sample Data

Creating a Sales Order Header Import Entity

If you are looking for some sample **Sales Order Header** data to load then here is a snapshot of the data that we use in the sample template.

CurrencyCode	CustAccount	CustGroup	InvoiceAccount	LanguageId	SalesId	ShippingDateRequested
USD	10024183	DOMESTIC	10024183	en-us	29453	1/1/2015
USD	10024144	DOMESTIC	10024144	en-us	29454	1/1/2015
USD	10024140	DOMESTIC	10024140	en-us	29455	1/5/2015
USD	10024041	DOMESTIC	10024041	en-us	29456	1/6/2015

 www.dynamicsaxcompanions.com
Dynamics AX Companions
- 296 -
  BLIND SQUIRREL
PUBLISHING

Creating a Sales Order Line Import Entity

To finish off the **Sales Order** import we will not create an entity that will load in all of the **Sales Order Lines**.

daxc
www.dynamicsaxcompanions.com
Dynamics AX Companions

- 297 -

www.blindsquirrelpublishing.com
© 2015 Blind Squirrel Publishing, LLC, All Rights Reserved

BLIND SQUIRREL
PUBLISHING

Step By Step Walkthrough

Creating a Sales Order Line Import Entity

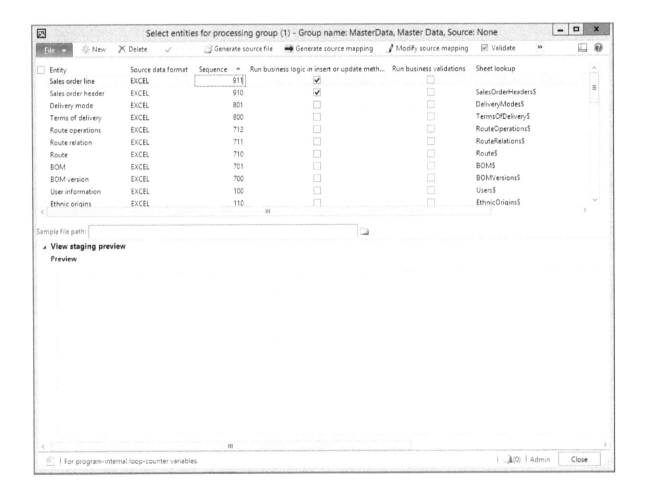

To do this, open the **Processing Group Entities** maintenance form and click on the **New** button within the menu bar to create a new record. Then click on the **Entity** dropdown list and find the **Sales Order Line** Entity type.

Click on the **Source Data Format** dropdown list and select the **EXCEL** format, and then set the **Sequence** number to **911**.

Now we want to create the mapping that we will be using to import in all of the data. To do this click on the **Generate Source File** button in the menu bar and when the **Wizard** appears, click on the **Next** button to start setting things up.

When the **Display Data** page is shown you will be able to see all of the default fields in the entity map.

www.dynamicsaxcompanions.com
Dynamics AX Companions
- 298 -
www.blindsquirrelpublishing.com
© 2015 Blind Squirrel Publishing, LLC, All Rights Reserved
BLIND SQUIRREL
PUBLISHING

Sample Data

Creating a Sales Order Line Import Entity

Here are the fields that you will want to have within your **Sales Order Lines** import definition if you want to use the sample company import template that we provide.

Present in source	Sequence	Field name	Mandatory	Field type	Field size
Yes	1	SalesId	Yes	String	20
Yes	2	LineNum	Yes	Real	31
Yes	3	CustAccount	Yes	String	20
Yes	4	CustGroup	Yes	String	10
Yes	5	ItemId	No	String	20
Yes	6	InventSiteId	No	String	10
Yes	7	wMSLocationId	No	String	10
Yes	8	InventLocationId	No	String	10
Yes	9	SalesQty	No	Real	31
Yes	10	CurrencyCode	Yes	String	3
Yes	11	ShippingDateRequested	Yes	Date	30
Yes	12	DeliveryAddress	No	String	250
Yes	13	DlvMode	No	String	10

Step By Step Walkthrough

Creating a Sales Order Line Import Entity

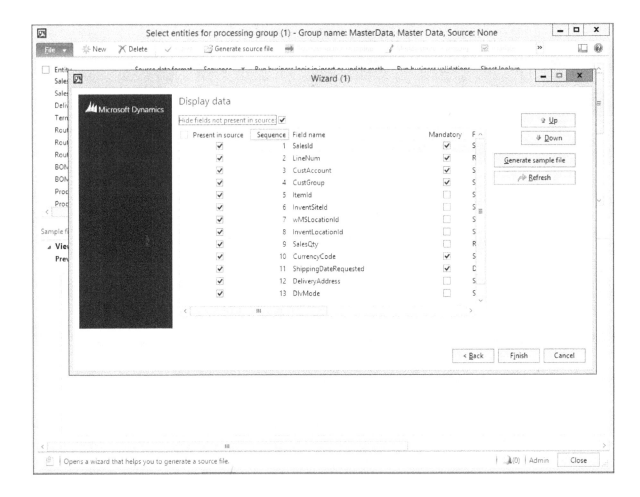

Find each of the fields in the template and then just click on the **Present In Source** checkbox, which will enable to field to be used within the template. If you need to re-order any of the fields then select the field and then click on the **Up** or **Down** buttons to rearrange them.

Once you have all of the fields selected and you have them in the right order then click on the **Generate Sample File** button.

Step By Step Walkthrough

Creating a Sales Order Line Import Entity

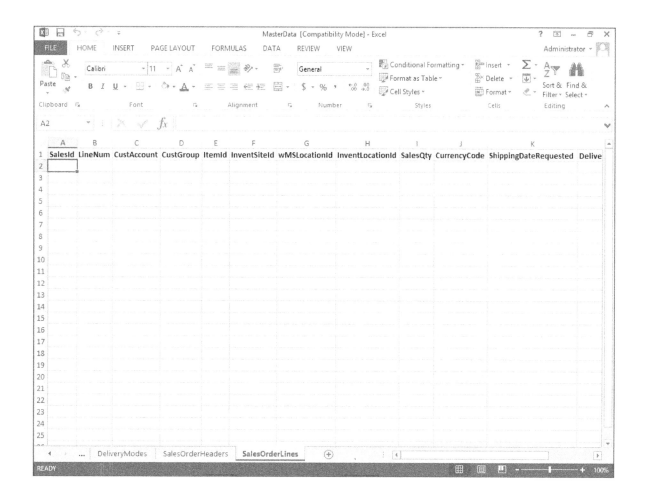

This will create another Excel Workbook for you just like before and the first sheet will already be set up with the fields that you need for the **Sales Order Line** import.

Open up the **MasterData** template that you created in the previous step and add a new Worksheet to the workbook by clicking on the + button and rename it to **SalesOrderLines.**

Now return to the workbook that was automatically generated by the wizard and select the auto-generated columns and copy them (**CTRL+C**) and paste (**CTRL+V**) them into the **SalesOrderLines** worksheet within the **MasterData** workbook. You may also want to format the columns to make it look tidy.

When you have done that, close out of the **MasterData** workbook.

www.dynamicsaxcompanions.com
Dynamics AX Companions
- 301 -
www.blindsquirrelpublishing.com
© 2015 Blind Squirrel Publishing, LLC , All Rights Reserved

BLIND SQUIRREL
PUBLISHING

Step By Step Walkthrough

Creating a Sales Order Line Import Entity

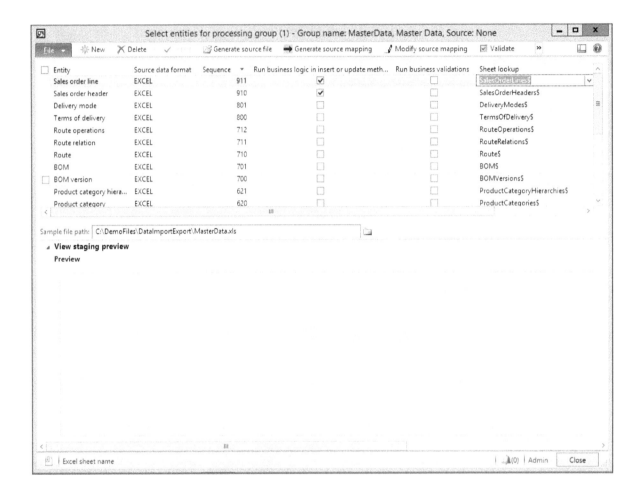

When you return back to the wizard, just click on the **Finish** button to exit from the form which will return you to the **Processing** Groups maintenance form. Click on the **Folder** icon to the right of the **Sample File Path** field.

When the file explorer opens navigate to where you saved your **MasterData** worksheet that you just created, and then click on the **Open** button.

Click on the **Sheet Lookup** dropdown list and select the **SalesOrderLines$** record.

Finish off the process by clicking on the **Generate Source Mapping** button within the menu bar. If everything is linked up correctly and you have all of the key fields within your map, then you will get a quick message saying that the entity mapping was completed and you can click on the **Close** button.

Example Data

Creating a Sales Order Line Import Entity

Now that you have the worksheet created you can start populating the worksheet with your own set of **Sales Order Lines**. Here is an example of how the data should look.

CurrencyCode	USD
CustAccount	10024183
CustGroup	DOMESTIC
LineNum	4
SalesId	29453
ShippingDateRequested	1/1/2015
ItemId	5882373
SalesQty	3
InventSiteId	2
InventLocationId	100

www.dynamicsaxcompanions.com
Dynamics AX Companions

- 303 -

www.blindsquirrelpublishing.com
© 2015 Blind Squirrel Publishing, LLC , All Rights Reserved

BLIND SQUIRREL
PUBLISHING

Sample Data

Creating a Sales Order Line Import Entity

If you are looking for some sample **Sales Order Line** data to load then here is a snapshot of the data that we use in the sample template.

CurrencyCode	CustAccount	CustGroup	LineNum	SalesId	ShippingDateRequested	ItemId	SalesQty	InventSiteId	InventLocationId
		DOMES		2945		58823			
USD	10024183	TIC	4	3	1/1/2015	73	3	2	100
		DOMES		2945		58821			
USD	10024183	TIC	3	3	1/1/2015	44	7	2	100
		DOMES		2945		58821			
USD	10024183	TIC	2	3	1/1/2015	20	20	2	100
		DOMES		2945		58826			
USD	10024183	TIC	1	3	1/1/2015	32	4	2	100
		DOMES		2945		50322			
USD	10024144	TIC	5	4	1/1/2015	80	12	2	100
		DOMES		2945		55623			
USD	10024144	TIC	4	4	1/2/2015	74	3	2	100
		DOMES		2945		58821			
USD	10024144	TIC	3	4	1/2/2015	20	16	2	100
		DOMES		2945		58826			
USD	10024144	TIC	2	4	1/2/2015	18	10	2	100
		DOMES		2945		58823			
USD	10024144	TIC	1	4	1/2/2015	73	15	2	100
		DOMES		2945		50322			
USD	10024140	TIC	3	5	1/5/2015	80	14	2	100
		DOMES		2945		58823			
USD	10024140	TIC	2	5	1/5/2015	73	19	2	100
		DOMES		2945		58825			
USD	10024140	TIC	1	5	1/5/2015	95	20	2	100
		DOMES		2945		59024			
USD	10024041	TIC	5	6	1/6/2015	39	3	2	100
		DOMES		2945		58821			
USD	10024041	TIC	4	6	1/6/2015	20	10	2	100
		DOMES		2945		58823			
USD	10024041	TIC	3	6	1/6/2015	04	16	2	100
		DOMES		2945		50324			
USD	10024041	TIC	2	6	1/6/2015	40	13	2	100
		DOMES		2945		58825			
USD	10024041	TIC	1	6	1/6/2015	95	18	2	100
		DOMES		2945		58825			
USD	10024138	TIC	1	7	1/7/2015	95	11	2	100

www.dynamicsaxcompanions.com
Dynamics AX Companions

www.blindsquirrelpublishing.com

Creating a Number Sequences Import Entity

If you are importing this data into a blank environment then you may want to have the system import in the default Journals that you want to use rather than typing them in by hand which can be a laborious task. Before we create the entity for the **Journals** though we will want to create an import that will load all of the custom number sequences that will be used by the journals – saving a lot of work if you've ever had to do this manually.

daxc
www.dynamicsaxcompanions.com
Dynamics AX Companions

- 307 -

www.blindsquirrelpublishing.com
© 2015 Blind Squirrel Publishing, LLC , All Rights Reserved

BLIND SQUIRREL
PUBLISHING

Step By Step Walkthrough

Creating a Number Sequences Import Entity

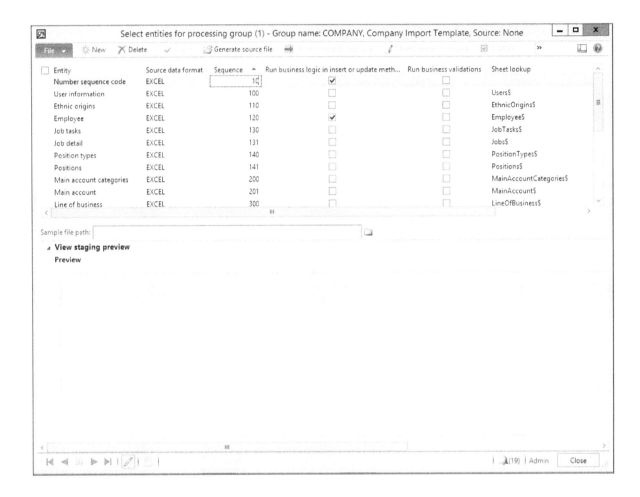

To do this, return to the **Processing Group Entities** maintenance form and click on the **New** button within the menu bar to create a new record. Then click on the **Entity** dropdown list and find the **Number Sequence Code** Entity type.

Click on the **Source Data Format** dropdown list and select the **EXCEL** format, and then set the **Sequence** number to **10**.

Now we want to create the mapping that we will be using to import in all of the data. To do this click on the **Generate Source File** button in the menu bar and when the **Wizard** appears, click on the **Next** button to start setting things up.

When the **Display Data** page is shown you will be able to see all of the default fields in the entity map.

www.dynamicsaxcompanions.com
Dynamics AX Companions
- 308 -
www.blindsquirrelpublishing.com
© 2015 Blind Squirrel Publishing, LLC, All Rights Reserved
BLIND SQUIRREL
PUBLISHING

Sample Data

Creating a Number Sequences Import Entity

Here are the fields that you will want to have within your **Number Sequences** import definition if you want to use the sample company import template that we provide.

Present in source	Sequence	Field name	Mandatory	Field type	Field size
Yes		1 NumberSequence	Yes	String	10
Yes		2 Txt	No	String	60
Yes		3 ScopeType	No	String	60
Yes		4 DataArea	No	String	4
Yes		5 Continuous	No	String	6
Yes		6 Format	No	String	20
Yes		7 Lowest	No	Integer	11
Yes		8 Highest	No	Integer	11
Yes		9 NextRec	No	Integer	11

 www.dynamicsaxcompanions.com
Dynamics AX Companions

- 309 -

www.blindsquirrelpublishing.com
© 2015 Blind Squirrel Publishing, LLC, All Rights Reserved

BLIND SQUIRREL
PUBLISHING

Step By Step Walkthrough

Creating a Number Sequences Import Entity

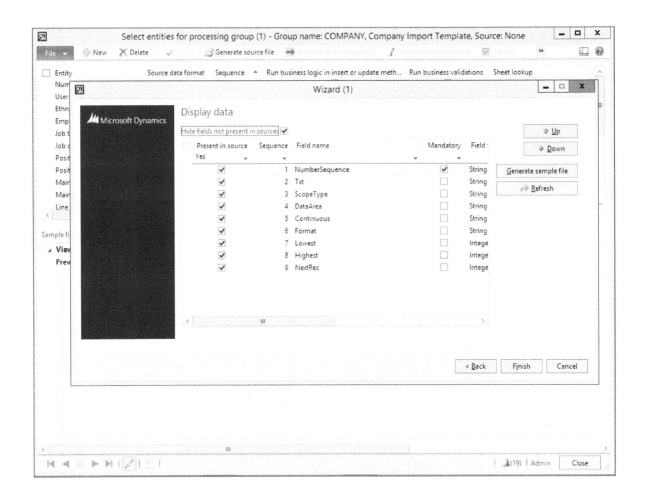

Find each of the fields in the template and then just click on the **Present In Source** checkbox, which will enable to field to be used within the template. If you need to re-order any of the fields then select the field and then click on the **Up** or **Down** buttons to rearrange them.

Once you have all of the fields selected and you have them in the right order then click on the **Generate Sample File** button.

Step By Step Walkthrough

Creating a Number Sequences Import Entity

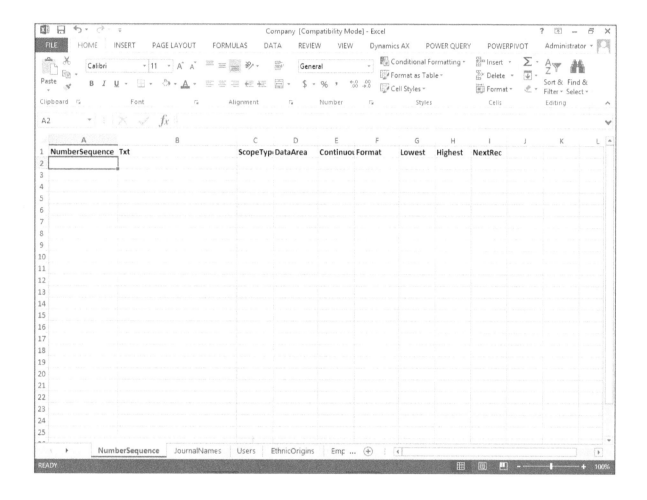

This will create another Excel Workbook for you just like before and the first sheet will already be set up with the fields that you need for the **Number Sequences** import.

Open up the **MasterData** template that you created in the previous step and add a new Worksheet to the workbook by clicking on the **+** button and rename it to **NumberSequences.**

Now return to the workbook that was automatically generated by the wizard and select the auto-generated columns and copy them (**CTRL+C**) and paste (**CTRL+V**) them into the **NumberSequences** worksheet within the **MasterData** workbook. You may also want to format the columns to make it look tidy.

When you have done that, close out of the **MasterData** workbook.

daxc   www.dynamicsaxcompanions.com
Dynamics AX Companions

- 311 -

www.blindsquirrelpublishing.com
© 2015 Blind Squirrel Publishing, LLC , All Rights Reserved

BLIND SQUIRREL
PUBLISHING

Step By Step Walkthrough

Creating a Number Sequences Import Entity

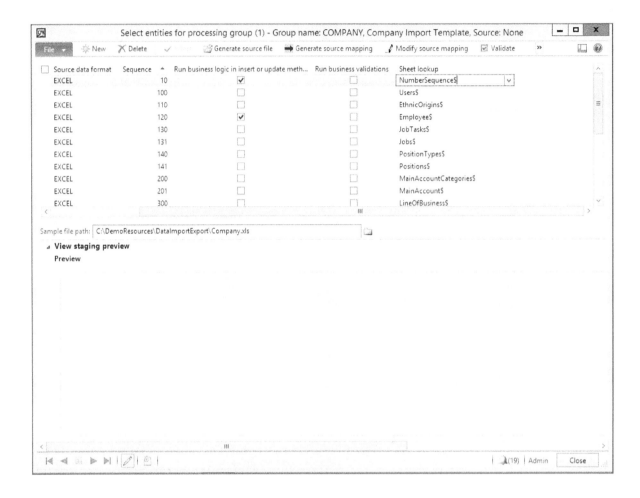

When you return back to the wizard, just click on the **Finish** button to exit from the form which will return you to the **Processing** Groups maintenance form. Click on the **Folder** icon to the right of the **Sample File Path** field.

When the file explorer opens navigate to where you saved your **MasterData** worksheet that you just created, and then click on the **Open** button.

Click on the **Sheet Lookup** dropdown list and select the **NumberSequences$** record.

Finish off the process by clicking on the **Generate Source Mapping** button within the menu bar. If everything is linked up correctly and you have all of the key fields within your map, then you will get a quick message saying that the entity mapping was completed and you can click on the **Close** button.

Example Data

Creating a Number Sequences Import Entity

Now that you have the worksheet created you can start populating the worksheet with your own set of **Number Sequences**. Here is an example of how the data should look.

NumberSequence	CustPay_01
Txt	Customer Payment
ScopeType	Company
DataArea	tof
Continuous	Y
Format	TOF-######
Lowest	1
Highest	999999
NextRec	1

Sample Data

Creating a Number Sequences Import Entity

If you are looking for some sample **Number Sequence** data to load then here is a snapshot of the data that we use in the sample template.

NumberSequence	Txt	ScopeType	DataArea	Continuous	Format	Lowest	Highest	NextRec
CustPay_01	Customer Payment	Company	tof	Y	TOF-######	1	999999	1
Alloc_01	Ledger allocations	Company	tof	Y	TOF-######	1	999999	1
APInvApp01	AP Invoice Approval	Company	tof	Y	TOF-######	1	999999	1
APInv_01	AP Invoice	Company	tof	Y	TOF-######	1	999999	1
APInvReg01	AP Invoice Register	Company	tof	Y	TOF-######	1	999999	1
ExpJrn_01	AR Consumption journal	Company	tof	Y	TOF-######	1	999999	1
BroClm_01	Broker Liability	Company	tof	Y	TOF-######	1	999999	1
Budget_01	Budget Appropriation	Company	tof	Y	TOF-######	1	999999	1
Bank_01	Check Reversal	Company	tof	Y	TOF-######	1	999999	1
DedJrn_01	Deduction journal	Company	tof	Y	TOF-######	1	999999	1
Bank_02	Deposit Reversal	Company	tof	Y	TOF-######	1	999999	1
FABud_01	FA Budget	Company	tof	Y	TOF-######	1	999999	1
FACur_01	Fixed Asset Entries - Current	Company	tof	Y	TOF-######	1	999999	1
FAOper_01	Fixed Asset Entries - Operations	Company	tof	Y	TOF-######	1	999999	1
FATax_01	Fixed Asset Entries - Tax	Company	tof	Y	TOF-######	1	999999	1
GenJrn_01	General Journal	Company	tof	Y	TOF-######	1	999999	1
IntJrn_01	Intercompany Journal	Company	tof	Y	TOF-######	1	999999	1
LOG_01	Letter of guarantee journal	Company	tof	Y	TOF-######	1	999999	1
Payroll_01	Payroll Journal	Company	tof	Y	TOF-######	1	999999	1
PerJrn_01	Periodic Journal	Company	tof	Y	TOF-######	1	999999	1
PrjJrn_01	Project Journal	Company	tof	Y	TOF-######	1	999999	1
RebAcc_01	Rebate accrual journal	Company	tof	Y	TOF-######	1	999999	1
Royalty_01	Royalty accruals	Company	tof	Y	TOF-######	1	999999	1

SrvJrn_01	Services Expenses	Company	tof	Y	TOF-######	1	999999	1
ExpJrn_01	Expense Journal	Company	tof	Y	TOF-######	1	999999	1
VendPay_01	Vendor Payment	Company	tof	Y	TOF-######	1	999999	1
WriteOff01	Write-off Journal	Company	tof	Y	TOF-######	1	999999	1

daxc
www.dynamicsaxcompanions.com
Dynamics AX Companions

- 315 -

www.blindsquirrelpublishing.com
© 2015 Blind Squirrel Publishing, LLC, All Rights Reserved

BLIND SQUIRREL
PUBLISHING

Creating a Journal Names Import Entity

Once we have our **Number Sequence** entity configured we will want to create our **Journal Names** entity which will load in all of the default Journals for us.

Step By Step Walkthrough

Creating a Journal Names Import Entity

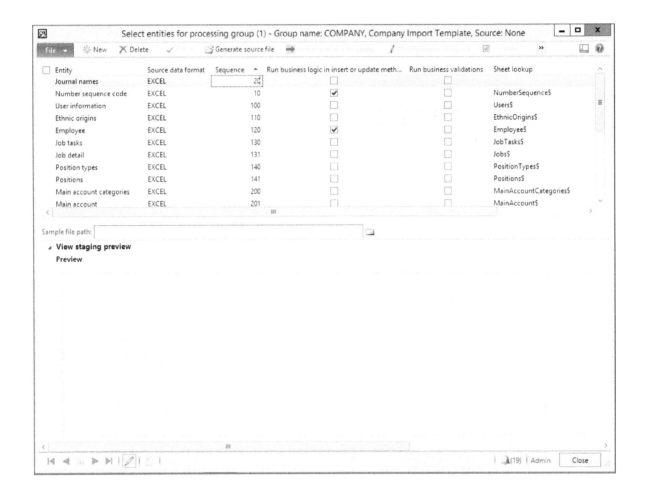

To do this, open the **Processing Group Entities** maintenance form and click on the **New** button within the menu bar to create a new record. Then click on the **Entity** dropdown list and find the **Journal Names** Entity type.

Click on the **Source Data Format** dropdown list and select the **EXCEL** format, and then set the **Sequence** number to **20**.

Now we want to create the mapping that we will be using to import in all of the data. To do this click on the **Generate Source File** button in the menu bar and when the **Wizard** appears, click on the **Next** button to start setting things up.

When the **Display Data** page is shown you will be able to see all of the default fields in the entity map.

www.dynamicsaxcompanions.com
Dynamics AX Companions   - 318 -
www.blindsquirrelpublishing.com
© 2015 Blind Squirrel Publishing, LLC , All Rights Reserved
BLIND SQUIRREL
PUBLISHING

Sample Data

Creating a Journal Names Import Entity

Here are the fields that you will want to have within your **Journal Names** import definition if you want to use the sample company import template that we provide.

Present in source	Sequence	Field name	Mandatory	Field type	Field size
Yes		1 JournalName	Yes	String	10
Yes		2 Name	No	String	60
Yes		3 JournalType	No	String	33
Yes		4 NumberSequence	No	String	10
Yes		5 OffsetAccountType	No	String	12

daxc www.dynamicsaxcompanions.com
Dynamics AX Companions
- 319 -
www.blindsquirrelpublishing.com
© 2015 Blind Squirrel Publishing, LLC , All Rights Reserved
BLIND SQUIRREL PUBLISHING

Step By Step Walkthrough

Creating a Journal Names Import Entity

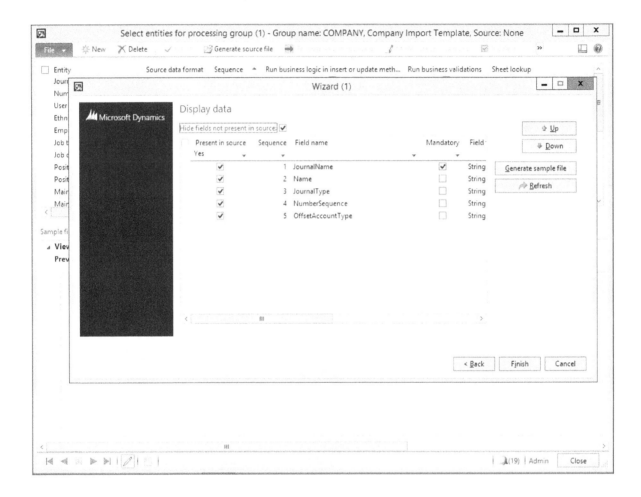

Find each of the fields in the template and then just click on the **Present In Source** checkbox, which will enable to field to be used within the template. If you need to re-order any of the fields then select the field and then click on the **Up** or **Down** buttons to rearrange them.

Once you have all of the fields selected and you have them in the right order then click on the **Generate Sample File** button.

www.dynamicsaxcompanions.com
Dynamics AX Companions
- 320 -
www.blindsquirrelpublishing.com
© 2015 Blind Squirrel Publishing, LLC, All Rights Reserved
BLIND SQUIRREL
PUBLISHING

Step By Step Walkthrough

Creating a Journal Names Import Entity

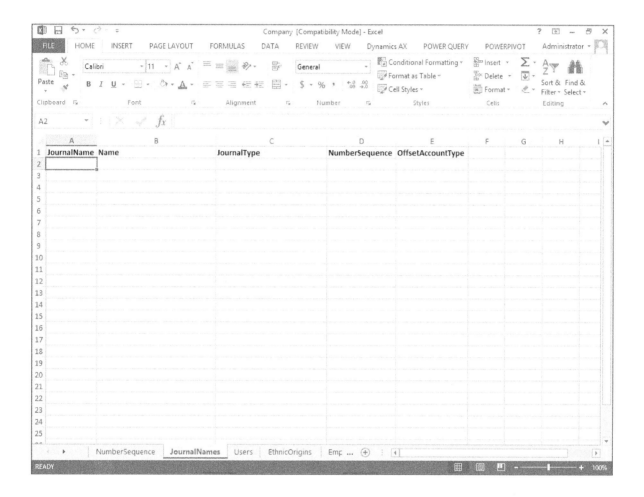

This will create another Excel Workbook for you just like before and the first sheet will already be set up with the fields that you need for the **Journal Names** import.

Open up the **MasterData** template that you created in the previous step and add a new Worksheet to the workbook by clicking on the **+** button and rename it to **JournalNames.**

Now return to the workbook that was automatically generated by the wizard and select the auto-generated columns and copy them (**CTRL+C**) and paste (**CTRL+V**) them into the **JournalNames** worksheet within the **MasterData** workbook. You may also want to format the columns to make it look tidy.

When you have done that, close out of the **MasterData** workbook.

Step By Step Walkthrough

Creating a Journal Names Import Entity

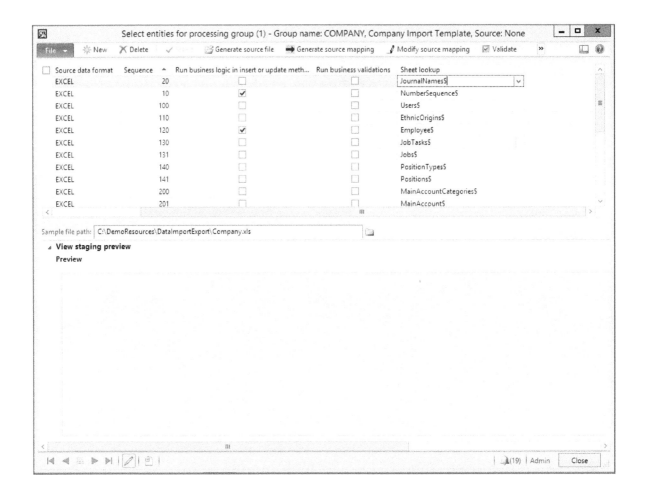

When you return back to the wizard, just click on the **Finish** button to exit from the form which will return you to the **Processing** Groups maintenance form. Click on the **Folder** icon to the right of the **Sample File Path** field.

When the file explorer opens navigate to where you saved your **MasterData** worksheet that you just created, and then click on the **Open** button.

Click on the **Sheet Lookup** dropdown list and select the **JournalNames$** record.

Finish off the process by clicking on the **Generate Source Mapping** button within the menu bar. If everything is linked up correctly and you have all of the key fields within your map, then you will get a quick message saying that the entity mapping was completed and you can click on the **Close** button.

www.dynamicsaxcompanions.com
Dynamics AX Companions
- 322 -
www.blindsquirrelpublishing.com
© 2015 Blind Squirrel Publishing, LLC , All Rights Reserved
BLIND SQUIRREL
PUBLISHING

Example Data

Creating a Journal Names Import Entity

Now that you have the worksheet created you can start populating the worksheet with your own set of **Journal Names**. Here is an example of how the data should look.

JournalName	CustPay
Name	Customer Payment
JournalType	Customer Payment
NumberSequence	CustPay_01
OffsetAccountType	Ledger

Sample Data

Creating a Journal Names Import Entity

If you are looking for some sample **Journal Name** data to load then here is a snapshot of the data that we use in the sample template.

JournalName	Name	JournalType	NumberSequence	OffsetAccountType
CustPay	Customer Payment	Customer Payment	CustPay_01	Ledger
Allocation	Ledger allocations	Allocation	Alloc_01	Ledger
APInvApp	AP Invoice Approval	Approval	APInvApp01	Ledger
APInvoice	AP Invoice	Vendor invoice recording	APInv_01	Ledger
APInvReg	AP Invoice Register	Invoice register	APInvReg01	Ledger
ARCnsmp	AR Consumption journal	Daily	ExpJrn_01	Ledger
Broker	Broker Liability	Vendor invoice recording	BroClm_01	Ledger
Budget	Budget Appropriation	Budget	Budget_01	Ledger
CheckRev	Check Reversal	Bank check reversal	Bank_01	Ledger
DeductJrnl	Deduction journal	Daily	DedJrn_01	Ledger
DepRev	Deposit Reversal	Bank deposit slip cancellation	Bank_02	Ledger
FABudget	FA Budget	Fixed asset budget	FABud_01	Ledger
FACur	Fixed Asset Entries - Current	Post fixed assets	FACur_01	Ledger
FAOper	Fixed Asset Entries - Operations	Post fixed assets	FAOper_01	Ledger
FATax	Fixed Asset Entries - Tax	Post fixed assets	FATax_01	Ledger
GenJrn	General Journal	Daily	GenJrn_01	Ledger
IntJrn	Intercompany Journal	Daily	IntJrn_01	Ledger
LGJrn	Letter of guarantee journal	Daily	LOG_01	Ledger
Payroll	Payroll Journal	Payroll disbursement	Payroll_01	Bank
PerJrn	Periodic Journal	Periodic	PerJrn_01	Ledger
PrjJrn	Project Journal	Project - expenses	PrjJrn_01	Ledger
RebAccrual	Rebate accrual journal	Daily	RebAcc_01	Ledger
Royalty	Royalty accruals	Daily	Royalty_01	Ledger
ServExp	Services Expenses	Project - expenses	SrvJrn_01	Ledger
TrvExp	Expense Journal	Daily	ExpJrn_01	Ledger
VendPay	Vendor Payment	Vendor disbursement	VendPay_01	Bank
WriteOff	Write-off Journal	Daily	WriteOff01	Ledger

Summary

Wow! Now you have all (or at least most) of the key entities configured so that you can import in all of the data from one single Excel spreadsheet. This may seem like a lot of work to get this configured, but once you have this template then loading in all of the base information into Dynamics AX takes a matter of minutes rather than hours, or even days.

Now we can move onto the next step which is loading the data into Dynamics AX.

IMPORTING IN A BASE COMPANY TEMPLATE

Now that we have the template configured, lets populate it with our company data and import it into Dynamics AX. This is where all of the preparation that you have done will really pay off.

daxc   www.dynamicsaxcompanions.com
Dynamics AX Companions

- 329 -

www.blindsquirrelpublishing.com
© 2015 Blind Squirrel Publishing, LLC , All Rights Reserved

BLIND SQUIRREL
PUBLISHING

Populating The Excel Template With Data

Before we can start the import process we need to first populate the excel template with all of our data. Since this is in Excel though this is a pretty simple process because we just have to cut and paste the data in.

daxc

www.dynamicsaxcompanions.com
Dynamics AX Companions

- 331 -

www.blindsquirrelpublishing.com
© 2015 Blind Squirrel Publishing, LLC, All Rights Reserved

BLIND SQUIRREL
PUBLISHING

Step By Step Walkthrough

Populating The Excel Template With Data

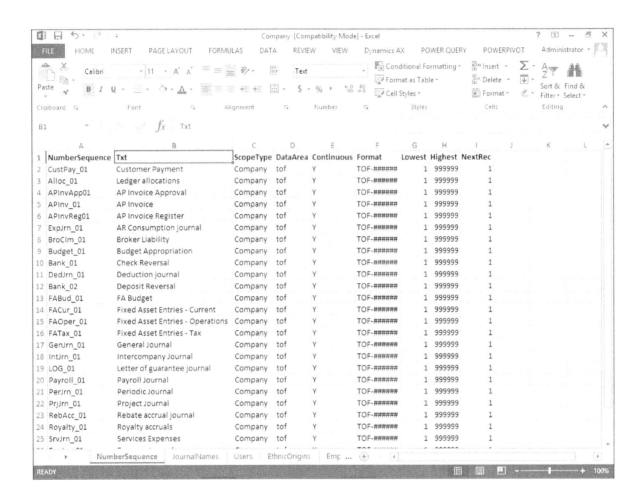

Start off by loading in all of the **Number Sequences** into the master data template. Here is an example of what it should look like.

daxc   www.dynamicsaxcompanions.com
Dynamics AX Companions

- 332 -

www.blindsquirrelpublishing.com
© 2015 Blind Squirrel Publishing, LLC, All Rights Reserved

BLIND SQUIRREL
PUBLISHING

Step By Step Walkthrough

Populating The Excel Template With Data

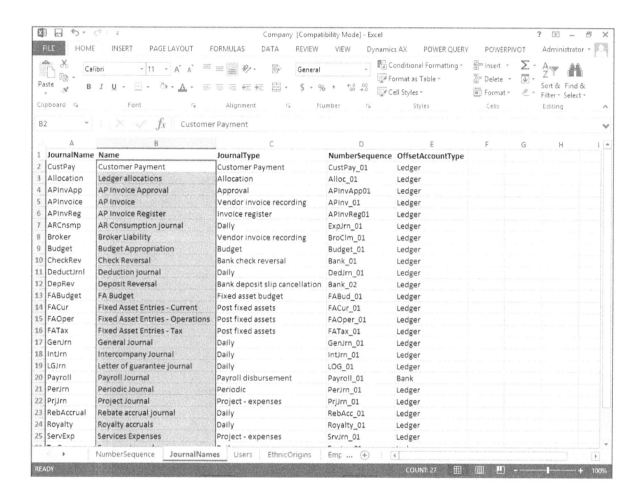

Then load in all of the **Journal Names** into the master data template. Here is an example of what it should look like.

www.dynamicsaxcompanions.com
Dynamics AX Companions
- 333 -
www.blindsquirrelpublishing.com
© 2015 Blind Squirrel Publishing, LLC, All Rights Reserved
BLIND SQUIRREL
PUBLISHING

BARE BONES CONFIGURATION GUIDE
CONFIGURING A COMPANY IMPORT TEMPLATE USING DYNAMICS AX 2012

IMPORTING IN A BASE COMPANY TEMPLATE

Step By Step Walkthrough

Populating The Excel Template With Data

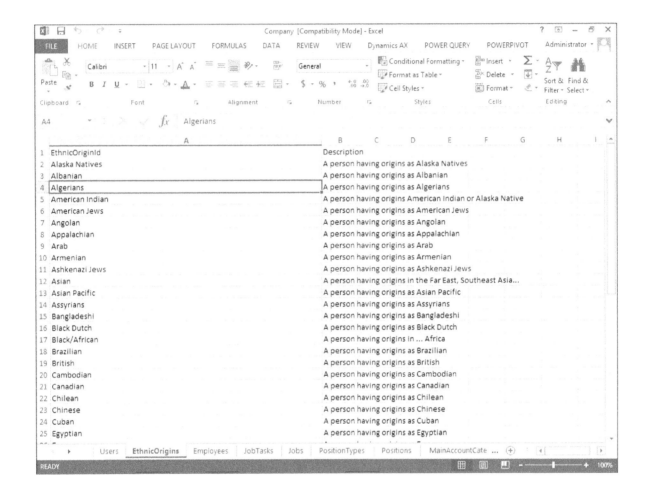

If you want to add more **Ethnic Origins** into the master data template then it would look like this.

www.dynamicsaxcompanions.com
Dynamics AX Companions

- 334 -

www.blindsquirrelpublishing.com
© 2015 Blind Squirrel Publishing, LLC, All Rights Reserved

BLIND SQUIRREL
PUBLISHING

Step By Step Walkthrough

Populating The Excel Template With Data

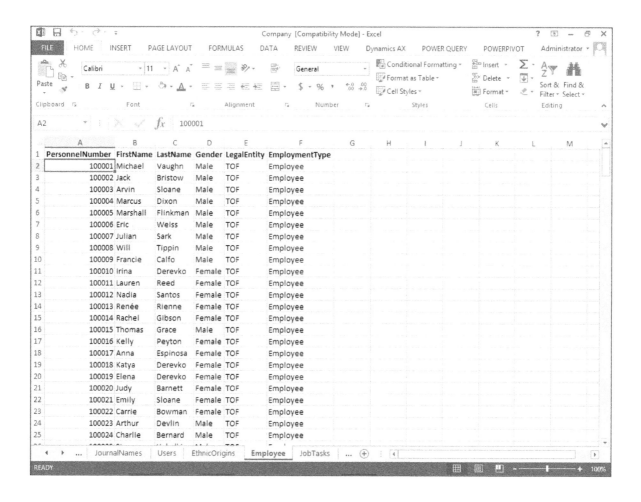

Now load in all of the **Employees** into the master data template. Here is an example of what it should look like.

Step By Step Walkthrough

Populating The Excel Template With Data

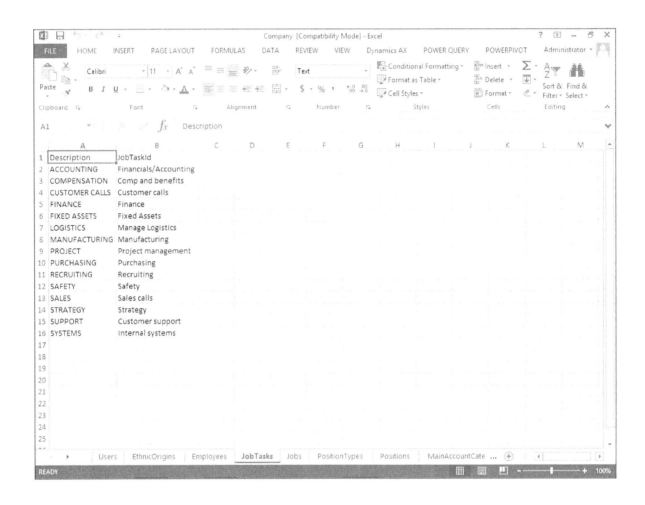

Now start loading in all of the job data into the master template. Start off with the **Job Tasks**.
Here is an example of what it should look like.

daxc
www.dynamicsaxcompanions.com
Dynamics AX Companions

- 336 -

www.blindsquirrelpublishing.com
© 2015 Blind Squirrel Publishing, LLC, All Rights Reserved

BLIND SQUIRREL
PUBLISHING

Step By Step Walkthrough

Populating The Excel Template With Data

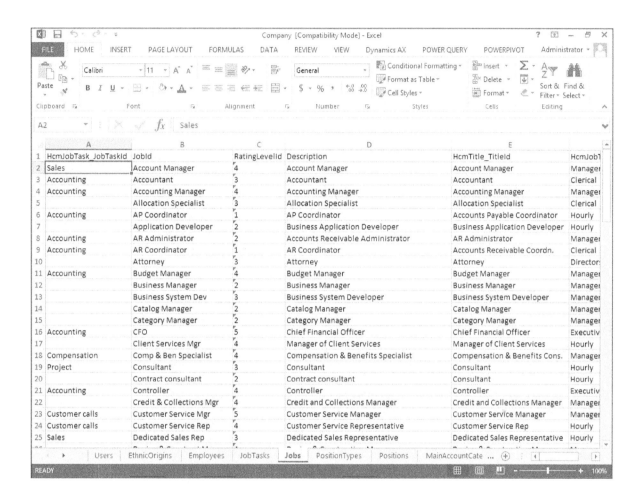

Then paste in all of the **Jobs** into the master data template. Here is an example of what it should look like.

Step By Step Walkthrough

Populating The Excel Template With Data

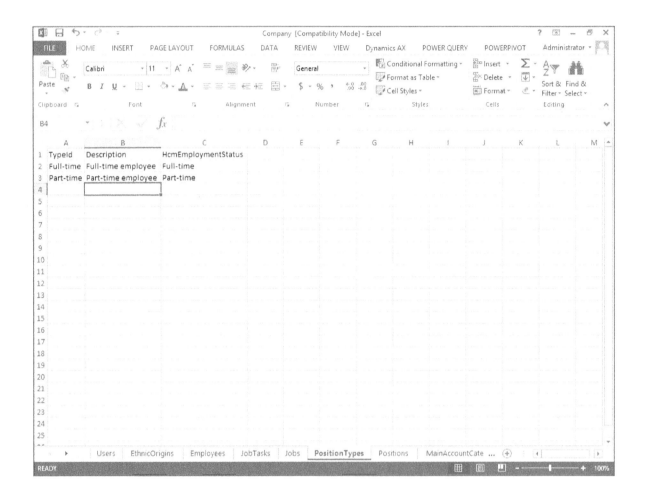

Now paste in all of the **Position Types** into the master data template. Here is an example of what it should look like.

Step By Step Walkthrough

Populating The Excel Template With Data

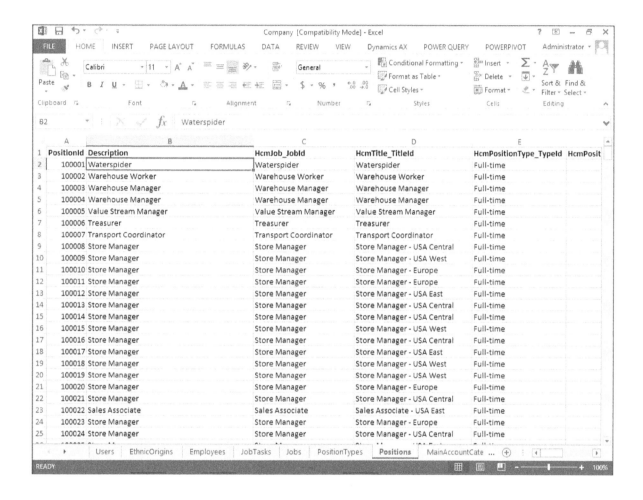

You can then load in in all of the **Positions** into the template. Here is an example of what it should look like.

www.dynamicsaxcompanions.com
Dynamics AX Companions

- 339 -

www.blindsquirrelpublishing.com
© 2015 Blind Squirrel Publishing, LLC, All Rights Reserved

BLIND SQUIRREL
PUBLISHING

Step By Step Walkthrough

Populating The Excel Template With Data

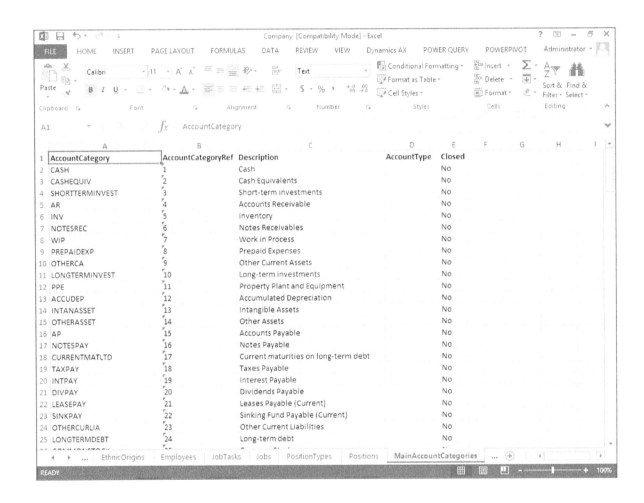

Now paste in all of the additional **Account Categories** into the master data template. Here is an example of what it should look like.

daxc   www.dynamicsaxcompanions.com
Dynamics AX Companions

- 340 -

www.blindsquirrelpublishing.com
© 2015 Blind Squirrel Publishing, LLC, All Rights Reserved

BLIND SQUIRREL
PUBLISHING

Step By Step Walkthrough

Populating The Excel Template With Data

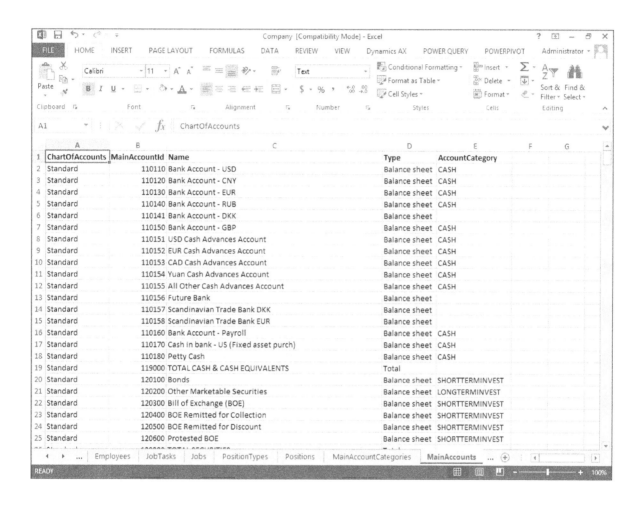

This will then lead into the loading of all of the **Main Accounts**. Here is an example of what it should look like.

Step By Step Walkthrough

Populating The Excel Template With Data

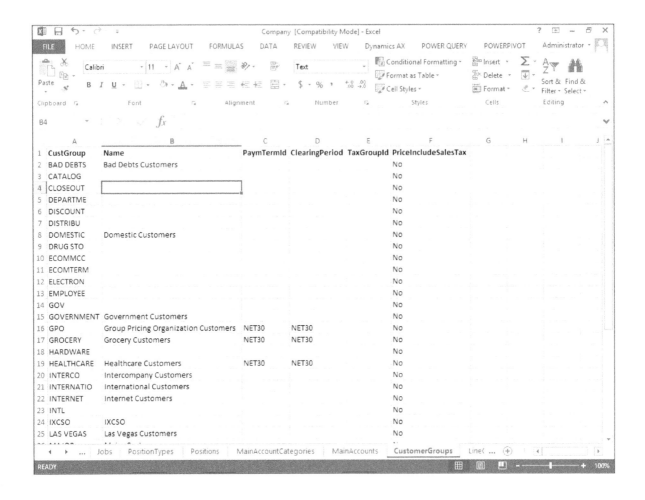

Now paste in all of the **Customer Groups** into the master data template. Here is an example of what it should look like.

Step By Step Walkthrough

Populating The Excel Template With Data

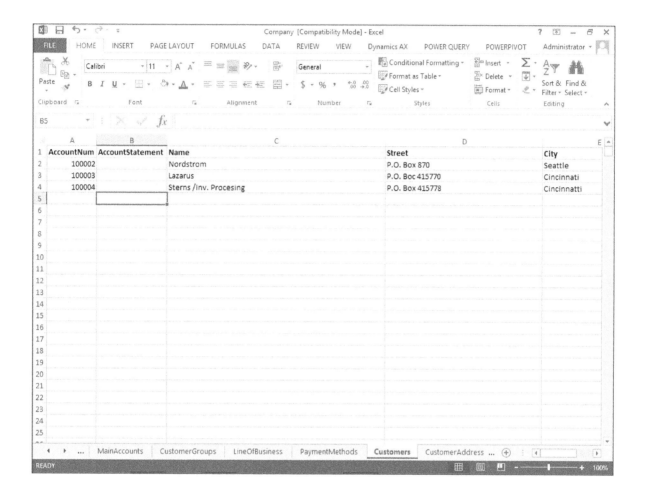

Now paste in all of the **Customer** into the master data template. Here is an example of what it should look like.

Step By Step Walkthrough

Populating The Excel Template With Data

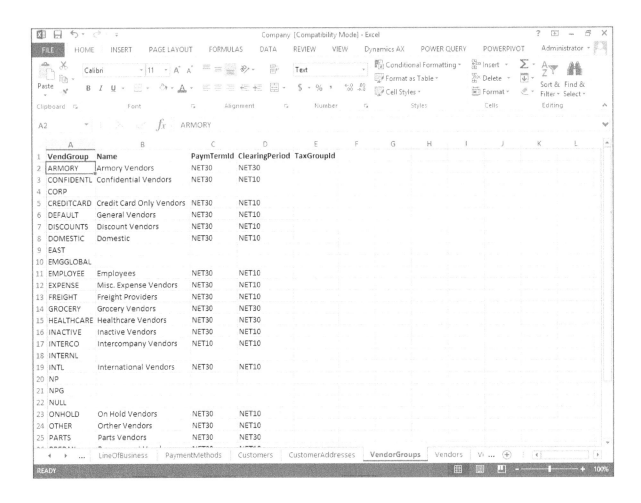

Now we will start working on the Vendors. Start off by pasting in all of the **Vendor Groups** into the master data template. Here is an example of what it should look like.

daxc   www.dynamicsaxcompanions.com
Dynamics AX Companions

- 344 -

www.blindsquirrelpublishing.com
© 2015 Blind Squirrel Publishing, LLC, All Rights Reserved

BLIND SQUIRREL
PUBLISHING

Step By Step Walkthrough

Populating The Excel Template With Data

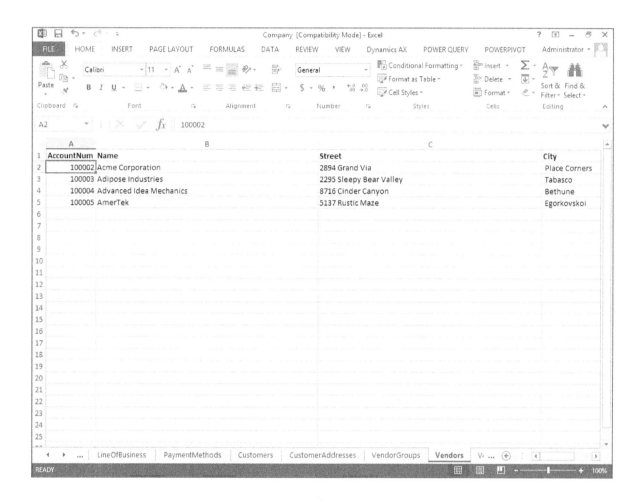

Now paste in all of the **Vendors** into the master data template. Here is an example of what it should look like.

dauc www.dynamicsaxcompanions.com
Dynamics AX Companions

- 345 -

www.blindsquirrelpublishing.com
© 2015 Blind Squirrel Publishing, LLC , All Rights Reserved

BLIND SQUIRREL
PUBLISHING

Step By Step Walkthrough

Populating The Excel Template With Data

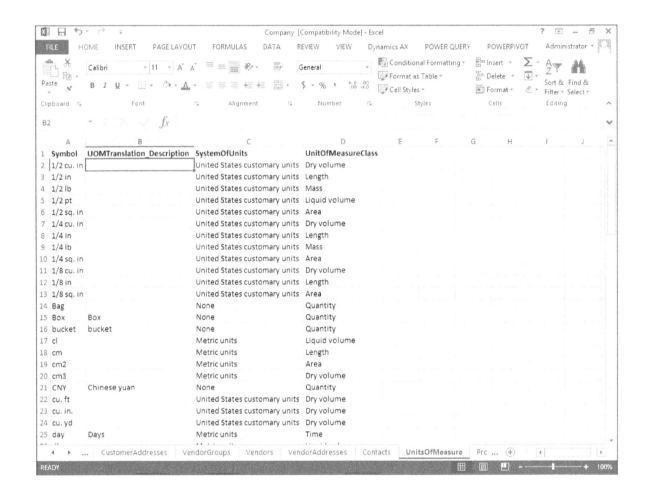

To add any additional **Units Of Measure** paste them into the master data template. Here is an example of what it should look like.

Step By Step Walkthrough

Populating The Excel Template With Data

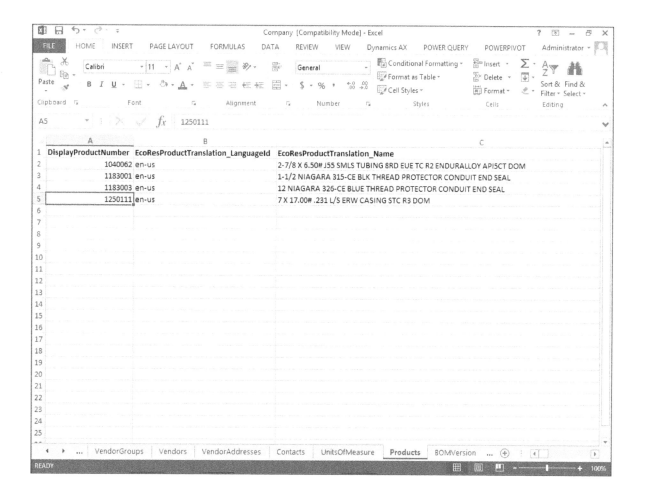

Now paste in all of the **Products** into the master data template. Here is an example of what it should look like.

Step By Step Walkthrough

Populating The Excel Template With Data

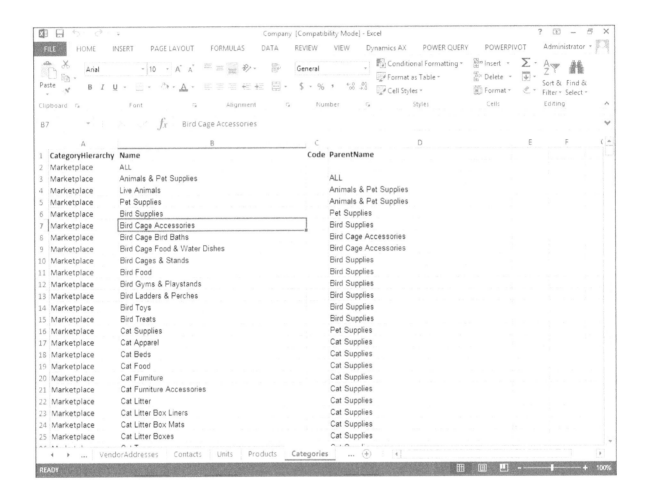

Now paste in all of the **Categories** into the master data template. Here is an example of what it should look like.

www.dynamicsaxcompanions.com
Dynamics AX Companions

- 348 -

www.blindsquirrelpublishing.com
© 2015 Blind Squirrel Publishing, LLC, All Rights Reserved

BLIND SQUIRREL
PUBLISHING

Step By Step Walkthrough

Populating The Excel Template With Data

To configure the BOM's start by pasting in all of the **BOM Version** into the master data template. Here is an example of what it should look like.

Step By Step Walkthrough

Populating The Excel Template With Data

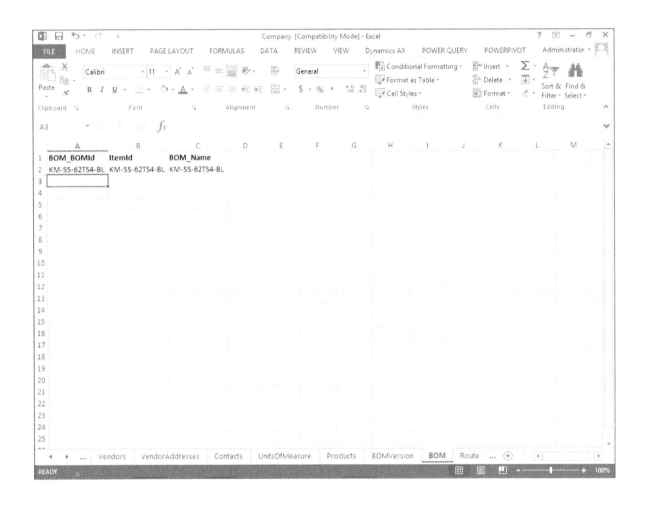

Then paste in all of the **BOMs** into the master data template. Here is an example of what it should look like.

Step By Step Walkthrough

Populating The Excel Template With Data

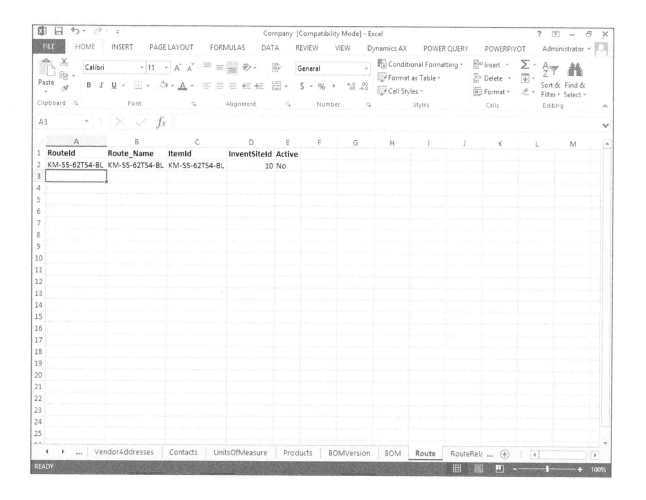

To configure the Route's start by pasting in all of the **Routes** into the master data template. Here is an example of what it should look like.

Step By Step Walkthrough

Populating The Excel Template With Data

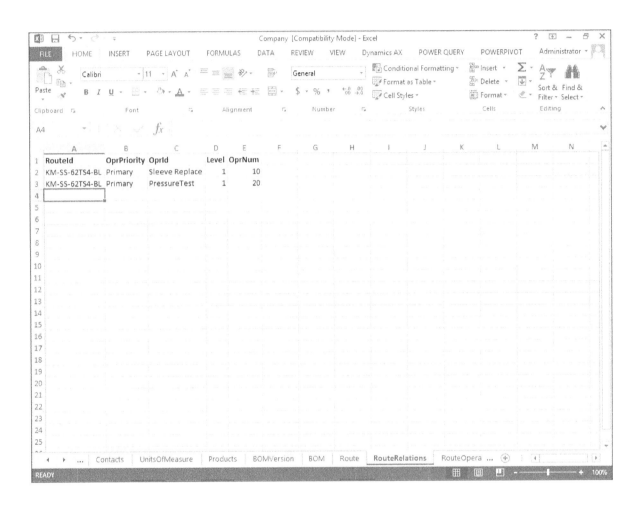

Then paste in all of the **Route Relations** into the master data template. Here is an example of what it should look like.

daxc   www.dynamicsaxcompanions.com
Dynamics AX Companions
- 352 -
www.blindsquirrelpublishing.com
© 2015 Blind Squirrel Publishing, LLC, All Rights Reserved

BLIND SQUIRREL
PUBLISHING

Step By Step Walkthrough

Populating The Excel Template With Data

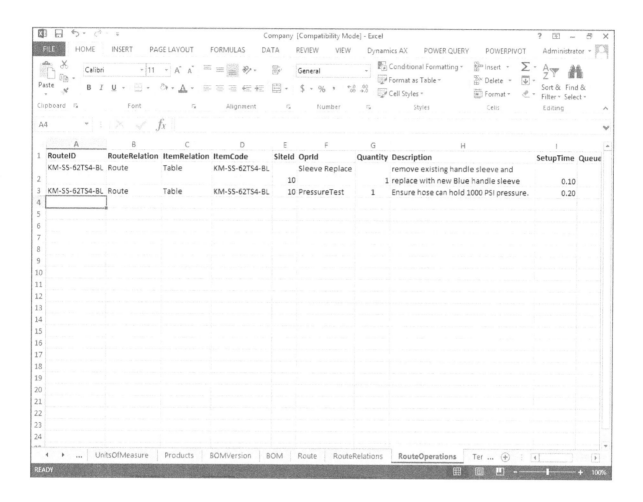

And then paste in all of the **Route Operations** into the master data template. Here is an example of what it should look like.

www.dynamicsaxcompanions.com
Dynamics AX Companions

- 353 -

www.blindsquirrelpublishing.com
© 2015 Blind Squirrel Publishing, LLC , All Rights Reserved

BLIND SQUIRREL
PUBLISHING

Step By Step Walkthrough

Populating The Excel Template With Data

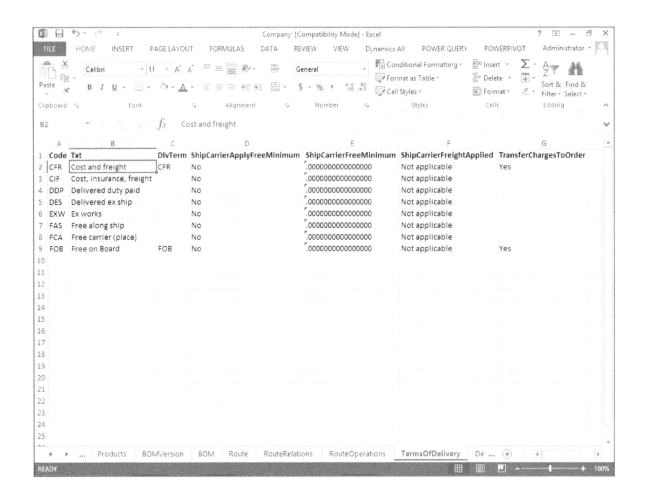

In order to import the sales orders paste in all of the **Terms of Delivery** that you will be using into the master data template. Here is an example of what it should look like.

Step By Step Walkthrough

Populating The Excel Template With Data

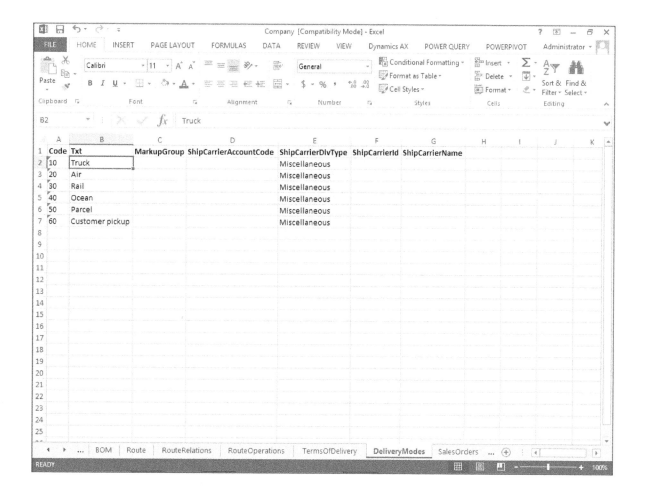

And also paste in all of the **Delivery Modes** that you will be using into the master data template. Here is an example of what it should look like.

Configuration A Chart Of Accounts Record

If you are wanting to import all of the data into a new blank instance of Dynamics AX then there is a little bit of pre-setup that you will need to do because we haven't worked out how to do this through the Data Import Export Framework.

Don't worry – it's not a lot – all we need to do is create a place holder for the Chart Of Accounts that we will be loading..

 www.dynamicsaxcompanions.com
Dynamics AX Companions

- 357 -

www.blindsquirrelpublishing.com
© 2015 Blind Squirrel Publishing, LLC, All Rights Reserved

BLIND SQUIRREL
PUBLISHING

Step By Step Walkthrough

Configuration A Chart Of Accounts Record

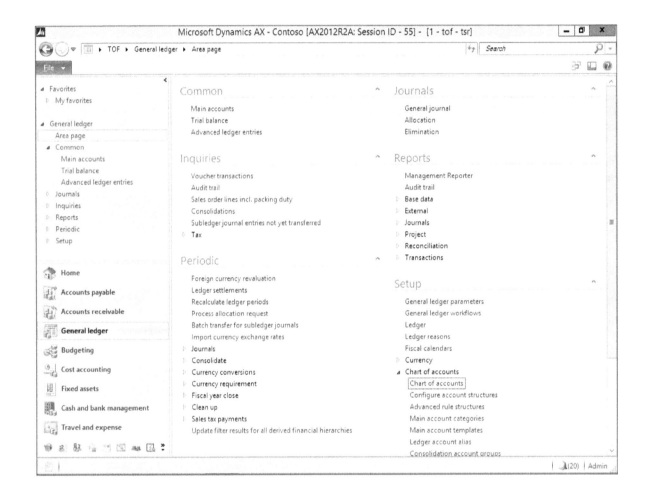

Start off by clicking on the **Chart Of Accounts** menu item within the **Chart Of Accounts** folder of the **Setup** group within the **General Ledger** area page.

daxc
www.dynamicsaxcompanions.com
Dynamics AX Companions

- 358 -

www.blindsquirrelpublishing.com
© 2015 Blind Squirrel Publishing, LLC, All Rights Reserved

BLIND SQUIRREL
PUBLISHING

Step By Step Walkthrough

Configuration A Chart Of Accounts Record

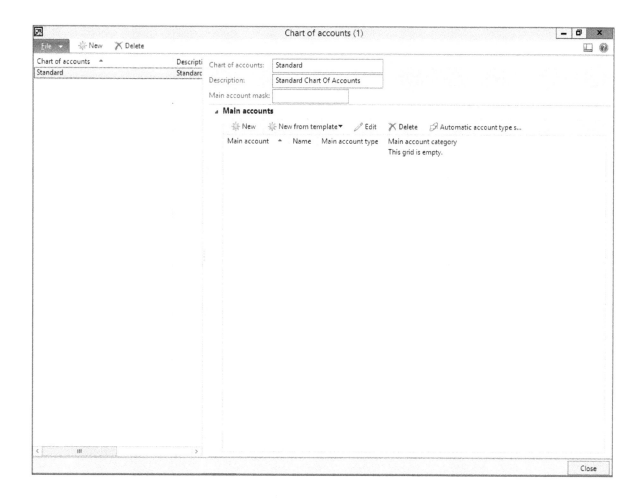

When the **Chart of Accounts** maintenance form is displayed, click on the **New** button in the menu bar to create a new record, set the **Chart Of Accounts** code to **Standard**, and the **Description** to **Standard Chart Of Accounts**.

After you have done that, click on the **Close** button to exit out of the form.

daxc   www.dynamicsaxcompanions.com
Dynamics AX Companions
- 359 -
www.blindsquirrelpublishing.com
© 2015 Blind Squirrel Publishing, LLC, All Rights Reserved
BLIND SQUIRREL
PUBLISHING

Importing The Base Company Data Into Staging

Now that we have the data within the template we can start the process of loading all of the data in. This is a two-step process where the data is moved to a staging location and then it is processed and moved into the main tables. Let's start off the process by importing the data into the staging tables.

www.dynamicsaxcompanions.com
Dynamics AX Companions

- 361 -

www.blindsquirrelpublishing.com
© 2015 Blind Squirrel Publishing, LLC, All Rights Reserved

BLIND SQUIRREL
PUBLISHING

Step By Step Walkthrough

Importing The Base Company Data Into Staging

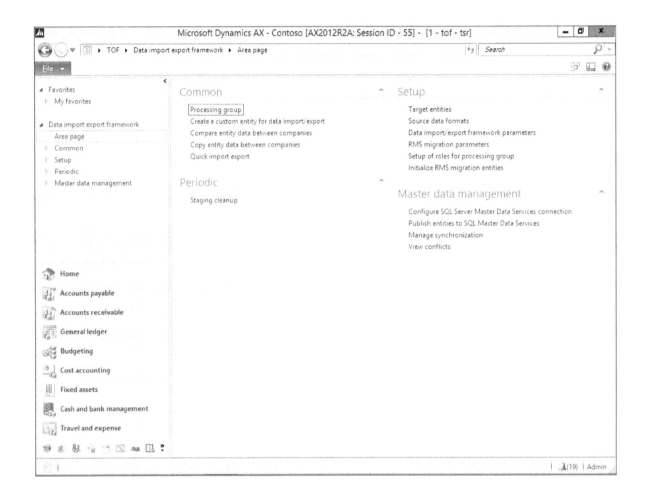

To do this, click on the **Processing Group** menu item within the **Common** group of the **Data Import Export Framework** area page.

Step By Step Walkthrough

Importing The Base Company Data Into Staging

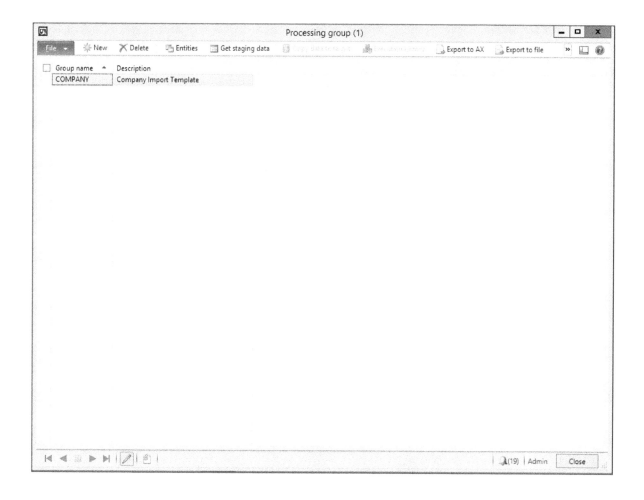

When the **Processing Group** list page is displayed, click on the **MasterData** processing group and then click on the **Get Staging Data** button in the menu bar.

daxc
www.dynamicsaxcompanions.com
Dynamics AX Companions

- 363 -

www.blindsquirrelpublishing.com
© 2015 Blind Squirrel Publishing, LLC , All Rights Reserved

BLIND SQUIRREL
PUBLISHING

Step By Step Walkthrough

Importing The Base Company Data Into Staging

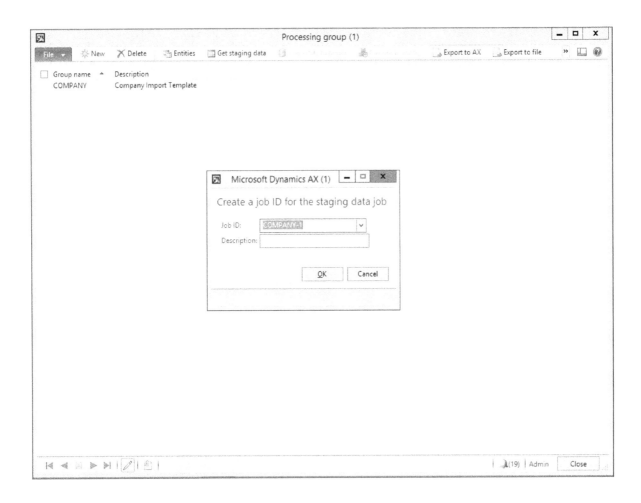

This will open up a dialog for the new import.

Step By Step Walkthrough

Importing The Base Company Data Into Staging

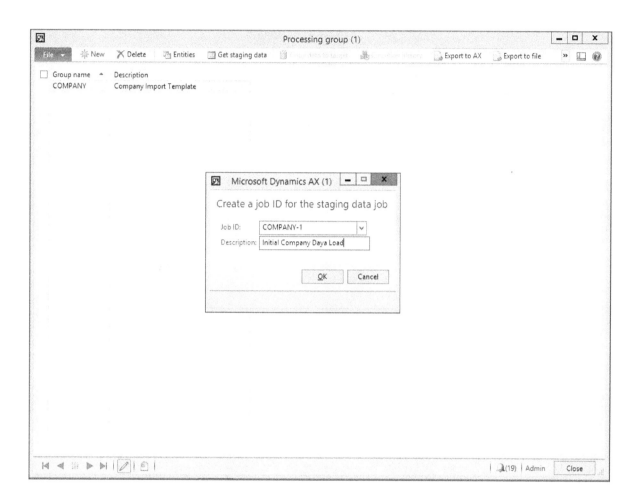

If you want you can give the import job a **Description** – i.e. **Initial Company Data Load** so that you can identify it later on and then click on the **OK** button.

daxc
www.dynamicsaxcompanions.com
Dynamics AX Companions

- 365 -

www.blindsquirrelpublishing.com
© 2015 Blind Squirrel Publishing, LLC, All Rights Reserved

BLIND SQUIRREL
PUBLISHING

Step By Step Walkthrough

Importing The Base Company Data Into Staging

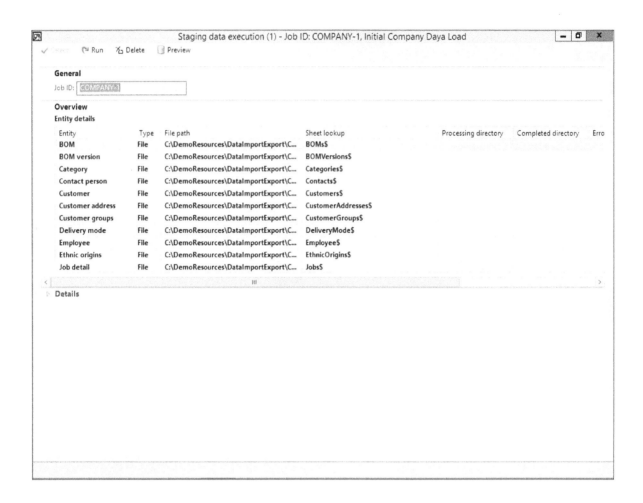

This will take you to the **Staging Execution** form.

daxc   www.dynamicsaxcompanions.com
Dynamics AX Companions

- 366 -

www.blindsquirrelpublishing.com
© 2015 Blind Squirrel Publishing, LLC, All Rights Reserved

BLIND SQUIRREL
PUBLISHING

Step By Step Walkthrough

Importing The Base Company Data Into Staging

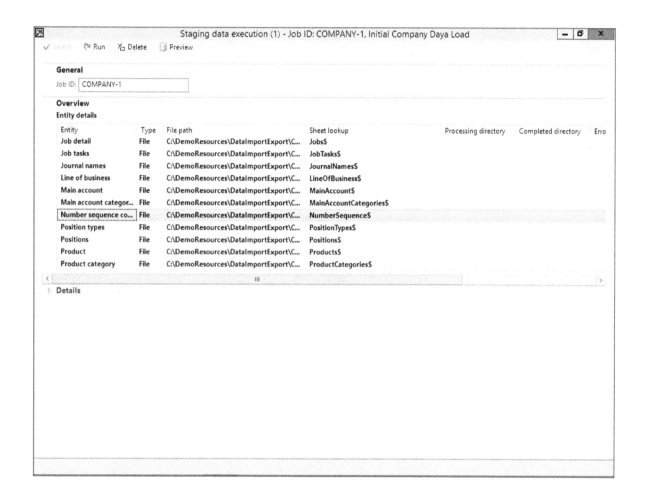

If you want to test the load then you can select any of the Entities – like the **Number Sequences** and then click on the **Preview** button in the menu bar.

Step By Step Walkthrough

Importing The Base Company Data Into Staging

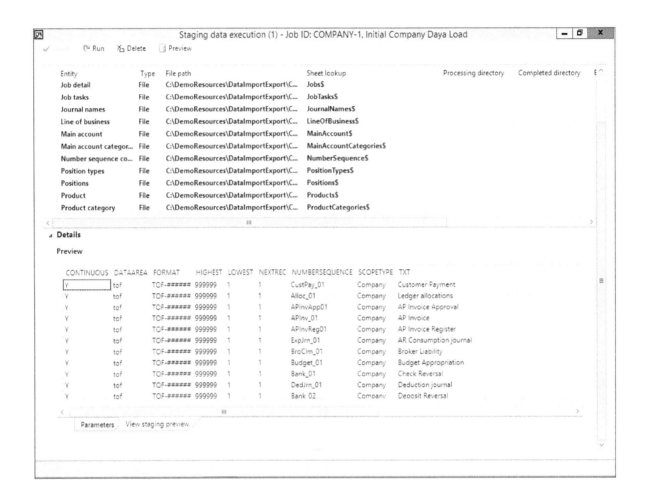

If you expand the **Details** footer tab and then select the **View Staging Preview** then you should see all of the data that you have loaded into the template.

Step By Step Walkthrough

Importing The Base Company Data Into Staging

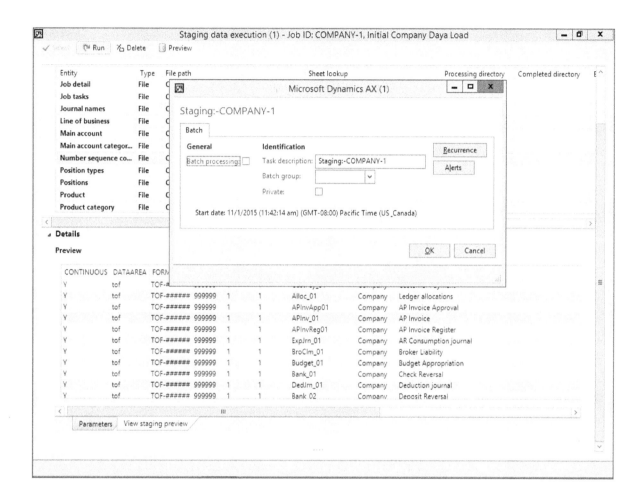

To start the import into the staging tables, click on the **Run** button in the menu bar. This will open up a processing dialog box and all you need to do is click on the **OK** button.

Step By Step Walkthrough

Importing The Base Company Data Into Staging

If everything is configured correctly then you will get an **InfoLog** that tells you how many records were moved into the staging location and you can just click on the **Clsoe** button to exit out.

daxc   www.dynamicsaxcompanions.com
Dynamics AX Companions

- 370 -

www.blindsquirrelpublishing.com
© 2015 Blind Squirrel Publishing, LLC , All Rights Reserved

BLIND SQUIRREL
PUBLISHING

Copying the Staging Data Into The Main Tables

Now that we have all of the data in the staging tables it's time to start the real process, which is to move all of the data into Dynamics AX.

daxc
www.dynamicsaxcompanions.com
Dynamics AX Companions

- 371 -

www.blindsquirrelpublishing.com
© 2015 Blind Squirrel Publishing, LLC, All Rights Reserved

BLIND SQUIRREL
PUBLISHING

Step By Step Walkthrough

Copying the Staging Data Into The Main Tables

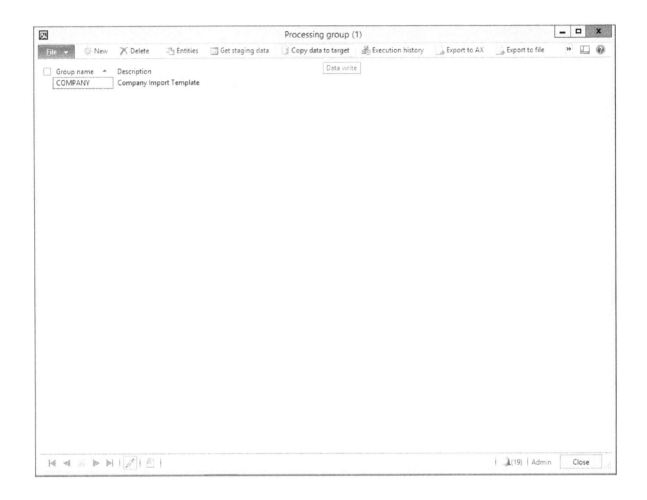

To do this, return to the **Processing Group** list page is displayed, click on the **MasterData** processing group and then click on the **Copy Data To Target** button in the menu bar – which is now enabled.

Step By Step Walkthrough

Copying the Staging Data Into The Main Tables

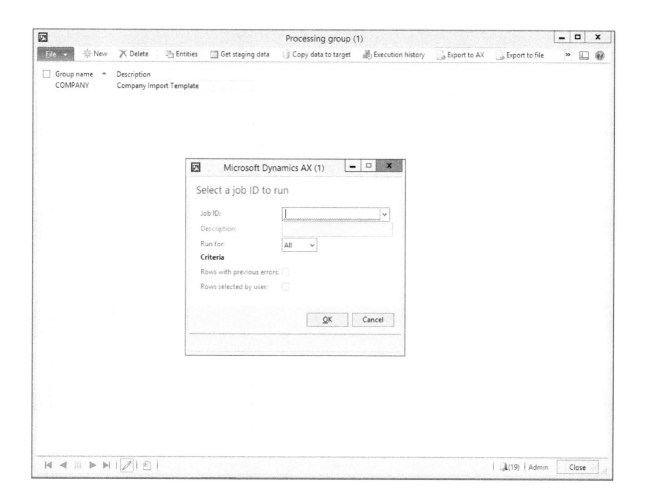

This will open up a dialog box asking you which import job do you want to update to the real tables.

Step By Step Walkthrough

Copying the Staging Data Into The Main Tables

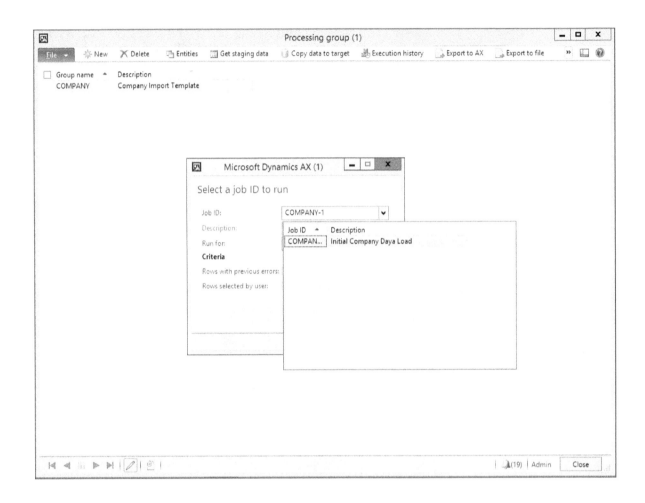

Click on the **Job ID** dropdown box and you will be able to see the job that you just processed and moved into the staging tables.

daxc
www.dynamicsaxcompanions.com
Dynamics AX Companions

- 374 -

www.blindsquirrelpublishing.com
© 2015 Blind Squirrel Publishing, LLC , All Rights Reserved

BLIND SQUIRREL
PUBLISHING

Step By Step Walkthrough

Copying the Staging Data Into The Main Tables

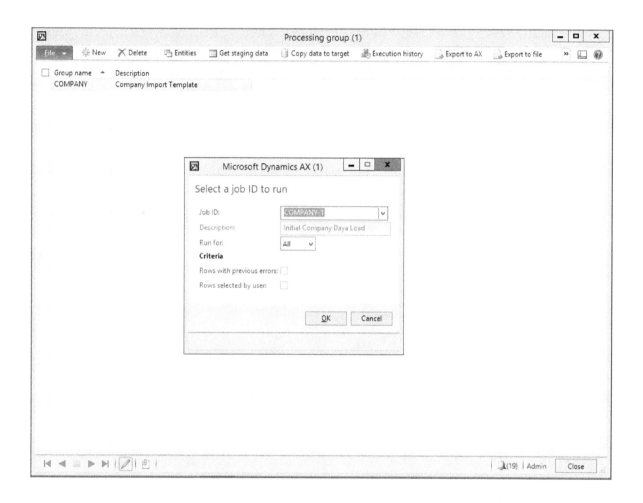

After you have selected the job, click on the **OK** button to continue on.

Step By Step Walkthrough

Copying the Staging Data Into The Main Tables

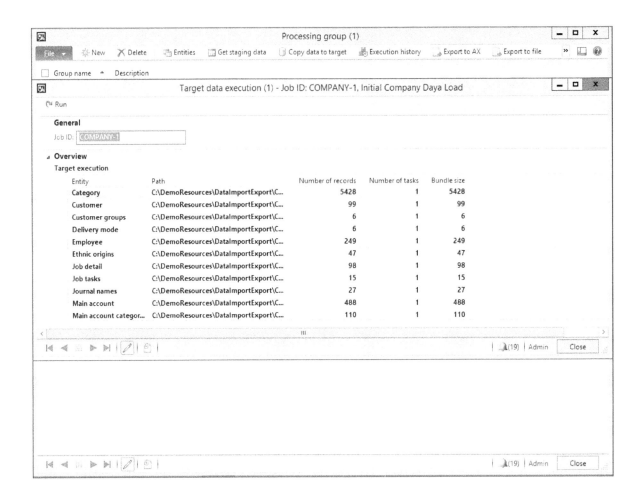

This will take you to the **Target Data Execution** form where you will see all of the data that is within the staging tables for the job. All you need to do is click on the **Run** button in the menu bar.

daxc

www.dynamicsaxcompanions.com
Dynamics AX Companions

- 376 -

www.blindsquirrelpublishing.com
© 2015 Blind Squirrel Publishing, LLC, All Rights Reserved

BLIND SQUIRREL
PUBLISHING

Step By Step Walkthrough

Copying the Staging Data Into The Main Tables

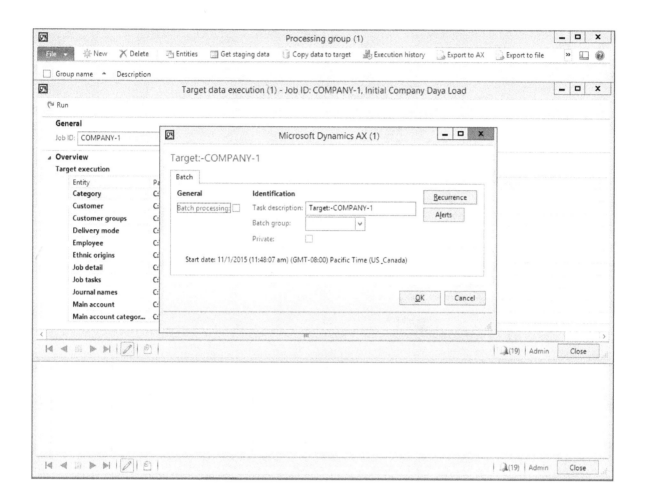

This will open up another dialog box for the execution of the job. Just click on the **OK** button.

daxc   www.dynamicsaxcompanions.com
Dynamics AX Companions

- 377 -

www.blindsquirrelpublishing.com
© 2015 Blind Squirrel Publishing, LLC, All Rights Reserved

BLIND SQUIRREL
PUBLISHING

Step By Step Walkthrough

Copying the Staging Data Into The Main Tables

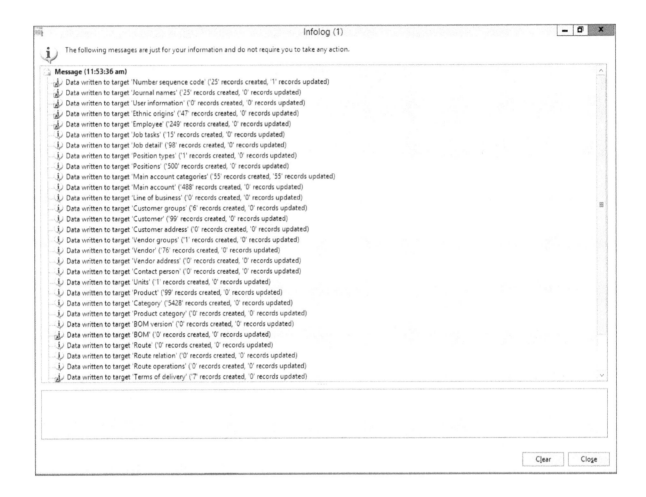

This will take a little bit longer to run than the job that put the data into the staging location, but after it is done you will get a message showing you all of the records that were moved over into Dynamics AX.

BAM!

At this point all you need to do is click on the **Close** button to exit the form.

Reviewing the Data

Now that you have all of the data loaded in, you can take a look at it. After all of this work its time to bask in the glory of all your data.

daxc
www.dynamicsaxcompanions.com
Dynamics AX Companions

- 379 -

www.blindsquirrelpublishing.com
© 2015 Blind Squirrel Publishing, LLC, All Rights Reserved

BLIND SQUIRREL
PUBLISHING

Step By Step Walkthrough

Reviewing the Data

If you open up the **Chart Of Accounts** then you will see that all of the main accounts that you loaded in are there for you to start using.

dαℵc
www.dynamicsaxcompanions.com
Dynamics AX Companions

- 380 -

www.blindsquirrelpublishing.com
© 2015 Blind Squirrel Publishing, LLC, All Rights Reserved

BLIND SQUIRREL
PUBLISHING

Step By Step Walkthrough

Reviewing the Data

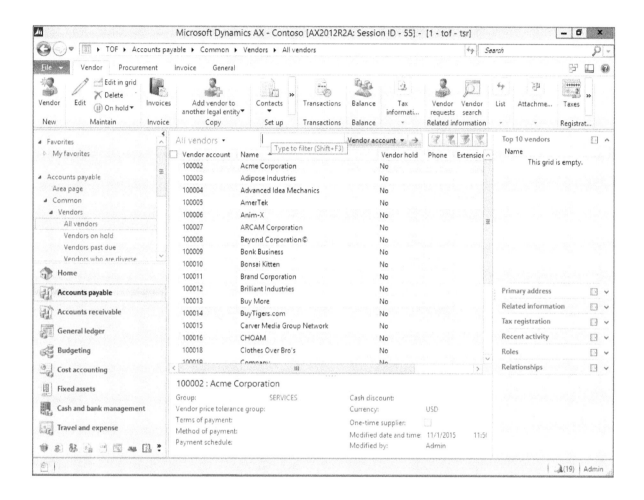

If you open up the **Vendors** then you will see all of your vendors are ready for you to receive invoices against.

daxc
www.dynamicsaxcompanions.com
Dynamics AX Companions

- 381 -

www.blindsquirrelpublishing.com
© 2015 Blind Squirrel Publishing, LLC, All Rights Reserved

BLIND SQUIRREL
PUBLISHING

Step By Step Walkthrough

Reviewing the Data

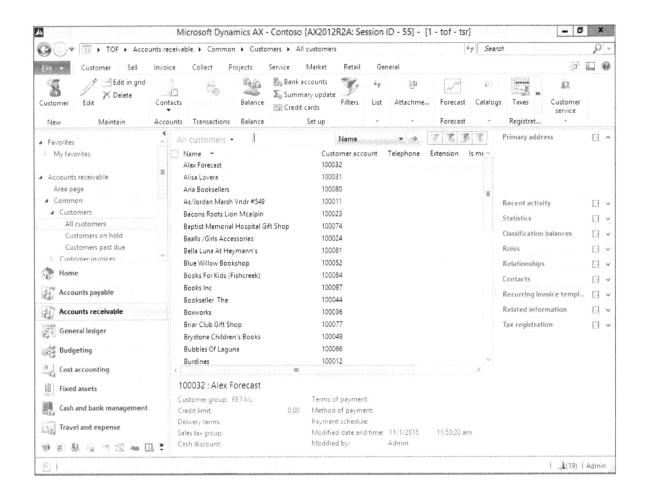

If you look at all of the **Customers** then you will see that all of them are ready for you to place orders for.

daxc www.dynamicsaxcompanions.com
Dynamics AX Companions

- 382 -

www.blindsquirrelpublishing.com
© 2015 Blind Squirrel Publishing, LLC , All Rights Reserved

BLIND SQUIRREL
PUBLISHING

Step By Step Walkthrough

Reviewing the Data

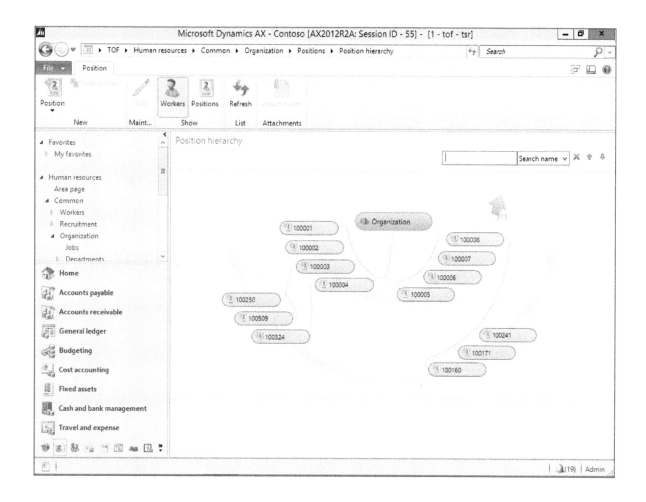

And what's even better is all of your position hierarchies are loaded in with jobs associated with them so you can start managing all of the employees.

Summary

Once you have configured all of the import templates, loading in of the data is really a non-event. If you find that there is data that you missed then don't worry, you can just update the spreadsheet and then re-run the import. The **Data Import Export Framework** is smart enough to realize that you have already added the data if there are duplicates and will just update the records for you.

daxc
www.dynamicsaxcompanions.com
Dynamics AX Companions

- 385 -

www.blindsquirrelpublishing.com
© 2015 Blind Squirrel Publishing, LLC, All Rights Reserved

BLIND SQUIRREL
PUBLISHING

CONCLUSION

The **Data Import Export Framework** is the best thing since sliced bread when it comes to loading your data into Dynamics AX. It is pre-configured with almost all of the data entities that you may need to start off the company setup.

Of course there is a little more work that you need to do before you can go live with the data, but that is really just tying up the loose ends of the data that you loaded, and also connecting a few of the dots that were missed. But this is definitely a jump start that will save you a lot of up front setup.

Also we have only scratched the surface on the entities that are available within the **Data Import Export Framework**. At the time of writing this guide there are over 180 standard entities delivered with Dynamics AX, and they start growing over time. You can extend out this import template for example to include **Purchase Orders** just by adding the new entities and updating the spreadsheet.

Also we did not choose to add all of the available fields into the templates that we created, but that doesn't mean that you can't. If you browse through the available fields then you will probably find more that are specific to your organization, and you can include those in the import as well.

Hopefully this guide has given you all an idea of how the **Data Import Export Framework** works, and will save you all a lot of time in data entry and custom import scripts.

www.dynamicsaxcompanions.com
Dynamics AX Companions

- 387 -

www.blindsquirrelpublishing.com
© 2015 Blind Squirrel Publishing, LLC , All Rights Reserved

BLIND SQUIRREL
PUBLISHING

About The Author

Murray Fife is an Author of over 20 books on Microsoft Dynamics AX including the Bare Bones Configuration Guide series of over 15 books which step the user through the setup of initial Dynamics AX instance, then through the Financial modules and then through the configuration of the more specialized modules like production, service management, and project accounting. You can find all of his books on Amazon (www.amazon.com/author/murrayfife) and also even more on the BSP (www.blindsquirrelpublishing.com) site.

Murray is also the curator of the Dynamics AX Companions (www.dynamicsaxcompanions.com) site which he built from the ground up as a resource for all of the Dynamics AX community where you can find walkthroughs and blueprints that he created since first being introduced to the Dynamics AX product.

Throughout his 25+ years of experience in the software industry he has worked in many different roles during his career, including as a developer, an implementation consultant, a trainer and a demo guy within the partner channel which gives him a great understanding of the requirements for both customers and partner's perspective.

He is also a great supporter of the Dynamics AX community and has hosted scores webinars for the AX User Group (www.axug.com) and MS Dynamics World (www.msdynamicsworld.com), and has spoken at Microsoft Convergence and AXUG Summit conferences more times than he can count.

For more information on Murray, here is his contact information:

Email: murrayfife@dynamicsaxcompanions.com
Twitter: @murrayfife

Facebook: facebook.com/murraycfife
Google: google.com/+murrayfife
LinkedIn: linkedin.com/in/murrayfife

Blog: atinkerersnotebook.com
Docs: docs.com/mufife

Amazon: amazon.com/author/murrayfife

 www.dynamicsaxcompanions.com
Dynamics AX Companions

- 389 -

www.blindsquirrelpublishing.com
© 2015 Blind Squirrel Publishing, LLC , All Rights Reserved

 BLIND SQUIRREL
PUBLISHING

Need More Help With Dynamics AX

The Bare Bones Configuration Guides for Dynamics AX was developed to show you how to set up a company from the ground up and configure all of the common modules that most people would need, and a few that you might want to use.

It aims to demystify the setup process and prove that Dynamics AX is only as hard to configure as you make it, and if you are a mid-range customer that even you can get a company configured and working without turning on every bell and whistle and without breaking the bank.

There are 15 volumes in the current series and although each of these guides have been designed to stand by themselves as reference material for each of the modules within Dynamics AX, if they are taken as a whole series they are also a great training system that will allow even a novice on Dynamics AX work through the step by step instructions and build up a new company from scratch and learn a lot of the ins and outs of the system right away. The current guides are:

1. Configuring a Base Dynamics AX 2012 System
2. Configuring an Organization Within Dynamics AX 2012
3. Configuring The General Ledger Within Dynamics AX 2012
4. Configuring Cash And Bank Management Within Dynamics AX 2012
5. Configuring Accounts Receivable Within Dynamics AX 2012
6. Configuring Accounts Payable Within Dynamics AX 2012
7. Configuring Product Information Management Within Dynamics AX 2012
8. Configuring Inventory Management Within Dynamics AX 2012
9. Configuring Procurement & Sourcing Within Dynamics AX 2012
10. Configuring Sales Order Management Within Dynamics AX 2012
11. Configuring Human Resources Within Dynamics AX 2012
12. Configuring Project Management & Accounting Within Dynamics AX 2012
13. Configuring Production Control Within Dynamics AX 2012
14. Configuring Sales & Marketing Within Dynamics AX 2012
15. Configuring Service Management Within Dynamics AX 2012

If you are interested in finding out more about the series and also view all of the details including topics covered within the module then browse to the Bare Bones Configuration Guide landing page on the Dynamics AX Companions website. You will find all of the details, and also downloadable resources that help you with the setup of Dynamics AX. If you decipher the code in the signature at the bottom of this email then you can get 20% off the books. Here is the full link:

http://www.dynamicsaxcompanions.com/barebonesconfig

 www.dynamicsaxcompanions.com
Dynamics AX Companions
- 391 -
www.blindsquirrelpublishing.com
© 2015 Blind Squirrel Publishing, LLC , All Rights Reserved
 BLIND SQUIRREL PUBLISHING

Usage Agreement

Murray Fife (the Author) agrees to grant, and the user of the eBook agrees to accept, a nonexclusive license to use the eBook under the terms and conditions of this eBook License Agreement ("Agreement"). Your use of the eBook constitutes your agreement to the terms and conditions set forth in this Agreement. This Agreement, or any part thereof, cannot be changed, waived, or discharged other than by a statement in writing signed by you and Murray Fife. Please read the entire Agreement carefully.

1. **EBook Usage.** The eBook may be used by one user on any device. The user of the eBook shall be subject to all of the terms of this Agreement, whether or not the user was the purchaser.

2. **Printing.** You may occasionally print a few pages of the eBook's text (but not entire sections), which may include sending the printed pages to a third party in the normal course of your business, but you must warn the recipient in writing that copyright law prohibits the recipient from redistributing the eBook content to anyone else. Other than the above, you may not print pages and/or distribute eBook content to others.

3. **Copyright, Use and Resale Prohibitions.** The Author retains all rights not expressly granted to you in this Agreement. The software, content, and related documentation in the eBook are protected by copyright laws and international copyright treaties, as well as other intellectual property laws and treaties. Nothing in this Agreement constitutes a waiver of the author's rights. The Author will not be responsible for performance problems due to circumstances beyond its reasonable control. Other than as stated in this Agreement, you may not copy, print, modify, remove, delete, augment, add to, publish, transmit, sell, resell, license, create derivative works from, or in any way exploit any of the eBook's content, in whole or in part, in print or electronic form, and you may not aid or permit others to do so. The unauthorized use or distribution of copyrighted or other proprietary content is illegal and could subject the purchaser to substantial damages. Purchaser will be liable for any damage resulting from any violation of this Agreement.

4. **No Transfer.** This license is not transferable by the eBook purchaser unless such transfer is approved in advance by the Author.

5. **Disclaimer.** The eBook, or any support given by the Author are in no way substitutes for assistance from legal, tax, accounting, or other qualified professionals. If legal advice or other expert assistance is required, the services of a competent professional person should be sought.

6. **Limitation of Liability.** The eBook is provided "as is" and the Author does not make any warranty or representation, either express or implied, to the eBook, including its quality, accuracy, performance, merchantability, or fitness for a particular purpose. You assume the entire risk as to the results and performance of the eBook. The Author does not warrant, guarantee, or make any representations regarding the use of, or the results obtained with, the eBook in terms of accuracy, correctness or reliability. In no event will the Author be liable for indirect, special, incidental, or consequential damages arising out of delays, errors, omissions, inaccuracies, or the use or inability to use the eBook, or for interruption of the eBook, from whatever cause. This will apply even if the Author has been advised that the possibility of such damage exists. Specifically, the Author is not responsible for any costs, including those incurred as a result of lost profits or revenue, loss of data, the cost of recovering such programs or data, the cost of any substitute program, claims by third parties, or similar costs. Except for the Author's indemnification obligations in Section 7.2, in no case will the Author's liability exceed the amount of license fees paid.

7. **Hold Harmless / Indemnification.**
7.1 You agree to defend, indemnify and hold the Author and any third party provider harmless from and against all third party claims and damages (including reasonable attorneys' fees) regarding your use of the eBook, unless the claims or damages are due to the Author's or any third party provider's gross negligence or willful misconduct or arise out of an allegation for which the Author is obligated to indemnify you.
7.2. The Author shall defend, indemnify and hold you harmless at the Author's expense in any suit, claim or proceeding brought against you alleging that your use of the eBook delivered to you hereunder directly infringes a United States patent, copyright, trademark, trade secret, or other third party proprietary right, provided the Author is (i) promptly notified, (ii) given the assistance required at the Author's expense, and (iii) permitted to retain legal counsel of the Author's choice and to direct the defense. The Author also agrees to pay any damages and costs awarded against you by final judgment of a court of last resort in any such suit or any agreed settlement amount on account of any such alleged infringement, but the Author will have no liability for settlements or costs incurred without its consent. Should your use of any such eBook be enjoined, or in the event that the Author desires to minimize its liability hereunder, the Author will, at its option and expense, (i) substitute a fully equivalent non-infringing eBook for the infringing item; (ii) modify the infringing item so that it no longer infringes but remains substantially equivalent; or (iii) obtain for you the right to continue use of such item. If none of the foregoing is feasible, the Author will terminate your access to the eBook and refund to you the applicable fees paid by you for the infringing item(s). THE FOREGOING STATES THE ENTIRE LIABILITY OF THE AUTHOR AND YOUR SOLE REMEDY FOR INFRINGEMENT OR FOR ANY BREACH OF WARRANTY OF NON-INFRINGEMENT, EXPRESS OR IMPLIED. THIS INDEMNITY WILL NOT APPLY TO ANY ALLEGED INFRINGEMENT BASED UPON A COMBINATION OF OTHER SOFTWARE OR INFORMATION WITH THE EBOOK WHERE THE EBOOK WOULD NOT HAVE OTHERWISE INFRINGED ON ITS OWN.

www.dynamicsaxcompanions.com
Dynamics AX Companions
- 393 -
www.blindsquirrelpublishing.com
© 2015 Blind Squirrel Publishing, LLC , All Rights Reserved

BLIND SQUIRREL
PUBLISHING